NEP-2020 Philosophy: Indian Philosophical Thoughts and Contribution of Thinkers to the field of Education

Edited by

Dr. Muttu Vemula

ISBN 979-8-89673-028-6

Contents

Foreword

Prof.Ramesh. Ghanta
Former Professor
School of Education and Training
Moulana Azad National Urdu University (MAANU) Hyderabad

I am delighted that Mizoram University; Aizawl organized several webinars across different disciplines inviting eminent scholars from our country and other countries. In this process School of Education, MZU organized a Three-day National Seminar on "NEP-2020 Philosophy: Indian Philosophical Thoughts and Contribution of Thinkers to the Field of Education inviting scholarly papers from different universities in the country. After thorough deliberations, the papers were revised and edited to bring them out in the form of a book for wider dissemination.

India's National Education Policy 2020 (NEP-2020) marks a significant milestone in the nation's educational journey. This ambitious policy seeks to transform the education system, making it more equitable, inclusive, and aligned with the country's cultural and philosophical heritage. At the heart of NEP-2020 lies a deep-rooted connection to Indian philosophical thought.

This book, NEP-2020 Philosophy: Indian Philosophical Thoughts and Contribution of Thinkers to the Field of Education, offers a valuable exploration of the philosophical foundations that underpin the policy. It delves into the rich tapestry of Indian philosophical traditions, tracing the contributions of renowned thinkers whose ideas have shaped the nation's intellectual and educational landscape for centuries.

By examining the philosophical underpinnings of NEP-2020, this book provides a deeper understanding of the policy's goals and aspirations. It highlights the importance of incorporating Indian philosophical wisdom into the educational curriculum, fostering a sense of cultural identity, and promoting holistic development.

I commend the authors for their insightful exploration of this vital topic. This book is a valuable resource for educators, policymakers, and anyone interested in the philosophical underpinnings of India's educational system. It offers a thought-provoking and enlightening perspective on the future of education in India.

I take this opportunity to Congratulate Dr. Muttu Vemula and his colleagues for their efforts to edit seminar papers and facilitate the faculty and students in understanding the NEP-2020 philosophy for effective implementation.

Preface

A New Dawn for Indian Education: The Philosophical Foundations of NEP 2020

The National Education Policy (NEP) 2020 represents a significant milestone in the history of Indian education. This landmark policy, formulated after extensive consultations and deliberations, envisions a transformative shift in the country's educational landscape.

The present volume, *NEP-2020 Philosophy: Indian Philosophical Thoughts and Contribution of Thinkers to the Field of Education*, delves into the philosophical underpinnings of this transformative policy. It draws inspiration from the rich tapestry of Indian philosophical thought, exploring the contributions of eminent thinkers to the field of education.

This book is a compilation of the insightful papers presented at the National Seminar organized by the Department of Education, Mizoram University, Aizawl. The seminar provided a platform for scholars, researchers, and educators to engage in a critical examination of NEP 2020, its philosophical foundations, and its implications for the future of Indian education.

The contributions in this volume offer a diverse range of perspectives on the policy's philosophical underpinnings. They delve into the historical context of Indian education, analyze the key principles and objectives of NEP 2020, and explore the contributions of various philosophical traditions to the shaping of this policy.

We hope that this book will serve as a valuable resource for researchers, policymakers, educators, and students alike. It is our belief that by understanding the philosophical foundations of NEP 2020, we can better appreciate its significance and work towards its successful implementation

Acknowledgement

First of all, I am indebted to the GOD ALMIGHTY for giving me an opportunity to excel in my efforts to complete this seminar on time.

I'm Dr. Muttu Vemula, convenor of ICSSIR sponsored Three Days' National Seminar on "NEP-2020 Philosophy: Indian Thinkers and Philosophers contributions to the field of Education on behalf of Department of Education, Mizoram University and sponsored organization ICSSR. New Delhi and on my own. behalf extend a hearty gratitude & thanks to

Dr. Hari Babu Kambhampati, Hon'ble Governor of Mizoram inaugurated and addressed the National Seminar on "NEP-2020 Philosophy: Indian Philosophical Thoughts and Contribution of Thinkers to the Field of Education" at the Department of Education, Mizoram University sponsored by the Indian Council of Social Science Research (ICSSR) under Azadi Ka Amrit Mahotsav.

Dr. R Lalthangliana Hon'ble Minister of Higher& Technical Education, Mizoram.

Prof. Prabakar Rath Hon'ble Vice Chancellor. Mizoram University for his encouragement and cooperation to organize the seminar.

Prof. Lalnundanga, Registrar, Mizoram University, for his encouragement and cooperation.

Prof. Ramesh Ghanta, Kakatiya University for his impressive and motivational Valedictory address.

Prof. Lokanath Mishra, Head, Department of Education, Mizoram University The inaugural program commenced with a welcome address.

Prof. Lalhmasai Chuaungo, Dean, Department of Education for excellent Introduction about the department of Education and the seminar.

Prof. K.C Sahoo Department of Education, Visva-Bharati Santiniketan for valedictory address.

My heartfelt gratitude to all the Resources Persons for their acceptance, to their cooperation and support.

My heartfelt gratitude to all the faculty members of the Department of Education to their cooperation and support.

My science thanks to the Indian Council of Social Science Research (ICSSR), New Delhi, India for sponsored grant under Azadi Ka Amrit Mahotsav.

Last but not the least Dr. Arthi Mishra, co-coordinator and 1 express gratitude to all the moderators of the seminar. All the participants, paper presenters, Students, scholars and my friends and well-wishers for their moral support making the seminar a grand success.

Dr Muttu Vemula

Speech Delivered by
Dr. Haribabu Kambhampati

Hon'ble Governor of Mizoram
NPE 2020 Philosophy for Higher Education

Dear Vice-Chancellor, learned professors, teaching and non-teaching faculty members, and participants welcome to one and all. I am happy to note that the Department of Education, Mizoram University is organizing the conference with ICSSR collaboration on the most pertinent theme "NEP-2020 Philosophy. Yes, it's high time that every citizen, especially those concerned with the field of Education, must have a proper understanding of the Philosophy of NEP-2020. The conference theme attracted my attention as it focuses on "Indian Philosophical thoughts, and contributions of thinkers to the field of Education". It's one of the central points of the philosophy of NEP-2020.

On this occasion, I would like to talk about the National Education Policy 2020 Philosophy for Higher Education, which is a document that lays out the vision and direction for higher education in India now onwards for several years to come in this 21st century.

The NPE 2020 Philosophy for Higher Education level is built on three key principles – access, equity, and quality. These principles are critical for ensuring that every student has an equal opportunity to pursue higher education, regardless of their social or economic background.

One of the key features of the NPE 2020 Philosophy is the emphasis on multidisciplinary education. This means that students will be encouraged to pursue a wide range of courses across different disciplines, including science, humanities, and social sciences. This will help students develop a holistic understanding of the world around them and prepare them for the complex challenges of the 21st century.

Another important aspect of the NPE 2020 Philosophy for Higher Education level is the emphasis on research and innovation. The policy recognizes that research is critical for driving economic growth and development, and therefore, it seeks to create a culture of research and innovation in Indian universities. This will help India become a knowledge-based economy and

The NPE 2020 is a comprehensive policy that aims to transform the entire education system in our country. It covers all aspects of education, from early childhood care and education to higher education. The policy has been developed after extensive consultations with educationists, experts, and stakeholders, and it reflects the aspirations and needs of the people of our country.

One of the key aspects of the NPE 2020 is its focus on transforming the higher education system in our country. The policy recognizes that higher education is crucial for the development of our country and that it plays a vital role in creating a knowledge-based society. The policy aims to make higher education accessible, inclusive, and equitable for all, and to transform higher education institutions into vibrant centers of learning and research.

The philosophy of the NPE 2020 related to higher education is based on three key principles: autonomy, accountability, and academic freedom. These principles are essential for creating a world-class higher education system that can compete with the best in the world.

Autonomy refers to the freedom of higher education institutions to decide their own academic programs, admission criteria, and evaluation systems. This autonomy will enable institutions to innovate and adapt to the changing needs of society and the economy. The policy recognizes that different institutions have different strengths and needs, and autonomy will enable them to develop their unique identities and niches.

Accountability refers to the responsibility of higher education. It is important at all levels of Education with special reference to Teacher Education. As I note most of you are from Higher education and especially from Teacher Education, I am sure you will discuss and come out with a clear understanding of the Philosophy of NEP-2020 which our teachers, students, and all citizens concerned to know and appreciate for bright future of our education system.

Thank you all, looking forward to the deliberations and recommendations of this conference, which I am sure will go far in the successful implementation of NEP-2020 in its true spirit.

JAI BHARATH

Indian Thinkers and Philosophers and Their Contributions to Education Aligned with NEP 2020

Dr Muttu Vemula

Introduction

The National Education Policy (NEP) 2020 is a comprehensive framework that aims to transform India's education system. It draws inspiration from India's rich philosophical heritage, seeking to integrate ancient wisdom with modern pedagogical practices. This paper explores the contributions of several key Indian thinkers and philosophers whose ideas have significantly influenced the development of NEP 2020.

1. Swami Vivekananda (1863-1902)

- **Philosophy of Education:** Vivekananda's philosophy of education emphasized character building, practical knowledge, and service to humanity. He advocated for a holistic education that would develop not only the intellect but also the soul and the body.
- **Educational Implications for NEP 2020:**
  - **Character Development:** NEP 2020 emphasizes the importance of values education, moral development, and ethical behavior, aligning with Vivekananda's vision of a well-rounded individual.
  - **Practical Knowledge:** The policy promotes vocational education and skill development, reflecting Vivekananda's emphasis on practical learning and self-reliance.

- **Service to Humanity:** NEP 2020 encourages students to engage in social service and community development, echoing Vivekananda's call for selfless service.

2. Mahatma Gandhi (1869-1948)

- **Philosophy of Education:** Gandhi's philosophy of education was rooted in the principles of non-violence, truth, and self-sufficiency. He advocated for basic education, craft-based learning, and the promotion of rural development.
- **Educational Implications for NEP 2020:**

  - **Basic Education:** NEP 2020 focuses on foundational literacy and numeracy, aligning with Gandhi's emphasis on basic education for all.
  - **Experiential Learning:** The policy promotes experiential learning, including hands-on activities and project-based learning, which is consistent with Gandhi's emphasis on learning by doing.
  - **Rural Development:** NEP 2020 aims to strengthen rural education and vocational training, reflecting Gandhi's vision of empowering rural communities.

3. Jiddu Krishnamurti (1895-1986)

- **Philosophy of Education:** Krishnamurti emphasized the importance of individual freedom, critical thinking, and self-discovery. He believed that education should foster creativity, compassion, and a deep understanding of oneself and the world.
- **Educational Implications for NEP 2020:**

  - **Critical Thinking:** NEP 2020 promotes critical thinking and problem-solving skills, aligning with Krishnamurti's emphasis on independent thought.
  - **Experiential Learning:** The policy advocates for experiential learning, which is consistent with Krishnamurti's emphasis on learning through direct experience.

- **Holistic Development:** NEP 2020 aims to develop well-rounded individuals, emphasizing physical, mental, and emotional well-being, which is in line with Krishnamurti's holistic approach to education.

4. Rabindranath Tagore (1861-1941)

- **Philosophy of Education:** Tagore believed in the importance of creativity, imagination, and the development of the whole person. He emphasized the role of nature, art, and music in education.
- **Educational Implications for NEP 2020:**

  - **Creative Expression:** NEP 2020 promotes the arts and humanities, encouraging students to express themselves creatively.
  - **Nature-Based Learning:** The policy emphasizes the importance of environmental education and outdoor learning, aligning with Tagore's love for nature.
  - **Holistic Development:** NEP 2020 aims to develop well-rounded individuals, emphasizing physical, mental, and emotional well-being, which is in line with Tagore's holistic approach to education.

5. Aurobindo Ghosh (1872-1950)

- **Philosophy of Education:** Aurobindo's philosophy of education emphasized the integral development of the individual, encompassing physical, mental, and spiritual growth. He advocated for a system of education that would prepare individuals for a higher consciousness.
- **Educational Implications for NEP 2020:**

  - **Holistic Development:** NEP 2020 aims to develop well-rounded individuals, emphasizing physical, mental, and emotional well-being, which is in line with Aurobindo's holistic approach to education.

- o **Spiritual Development:** The policy recognizes the importance of values education and character development, which are central to Aurobindo's philosophy

1. GANDHIAN PHILOSOPHY OF EDUCATION AND NEP-2020

Introduction

The National Education Policy (NEP) 2020 is a transformative reform initiative to overhaul the Indian education system to meet 21st-century needs while staying rooted in India's cultural ethos. This review explores the philosophical alignment between NEP 2020 and Mahatma Gandhi's educational ideals, particularly his Nai Talim (Basic Education) concept. By examining the NEP's principles and reforms in light of Gandhian thought, this paper highlights their synergies in promoting holistic, inclusive, and value-based education

Mahatma Gandhi envisioned an education system that harmonized the development of the head, heart, and hands, emphasizing self-reliance, moral values, and practical skills. His *Nai Talim* philosophy integrates productive labor with academics, aiming for a self-sustaining and equitable society. Similarly, NEP 2020 envisions a learner-centric education system, fostering creativity, critical thinking, and ethical behavior. This paper investigates how NEP 2020 embodies Gandhian ideals, contributing to a more sustainable and just society.

Gandhian Philosophy of Education: A Brief Overview

1. **Nai Talim (Basic Education)**: Introduced in 1937, it focused on integrating manual labor into education, emphasizing the dignity of labor and self-sufficiency.
2. **Moral and Ethical Development**: Gandhi emphasized value-based education to nurture individuals with strong ethical principles.
3. **Rural Development**: Education was seen as a tool for rural upliftment, fostering self-reliant communities.

4. **Holistic Learning**: Gandhi advocated experiential and activity-based learning, encouraging the development of body, mind, and spirit.

NEP 2020: Core Philosophy

1. **Holistic and Multidisciplinary Learning**: NEP promotes flexible curricula integrating arts, sciences, and vocational education, echoing Gandhi's call for well-rounded development.
2. **Skill-Based Education**: Vocational training is prioritized to bridge the gap between education and employability, resonating with Gandhian ideals of self-reliance.
3. **Value-Based Education**: NEP aims to instill ethics, constitutional values, and a sense of service, aligning with Gandhian principles.
4. **Focus on Equity and Inclusion**: Special provisions for marginalized communities in NEP reflect Gandhi's vision of social justice and upliftment of the underprivileged.

Synergies Between NEP 2020 and Gandhian Philosophy

1. **Integration of Work and Knowledge**: NEP's emphasis on experiential learning and vocational training mirrors Gandhi's *Nai Talim*.
2. **Localized Content and Pedagogy**: Gandhi's focus on education rooted in local culture aligns with NEP's call for regionally relevant content and use of mother tongues.
3. **Ethical Foundations**: Both philosophies prioritize character building over rote learning.
4. **Community-Centric Learning**: NEP's commitment to community participation resonates with Gandhi's belief in education as a means of societal transformation.

Challenges in Implementation

While the NEP echoes Gandhian ideals, challenges remain:

1. **Infrastructure Gaps**: Rural schools often lack the facilities to implement vocational training effectively.

2. **Teacher Training**: Educators need orientation to adopt experiential and value-based pedagogies.

3. **Resistance to Change**: Transitioning from traditional rote-based systems to experiential learning can face resistance.

Conclusion

NEP 2020 revitalizes Indian education by integrating modern needs with age-old wisdom. Its alignment with Gandhian ideals, particularly in fostering holistic, value-driven, and skill-based education, demonstrates its potential to build a self-reliant and equitable society. Successful implementation, however, requires overcoming systemic challenges and ensuring sustained commitment to its foundational principles.

2. RABINDRANATH TAGORE'S IDEALS: NEP-2020

Education is the cornerstone of human development, fostering creativity, critical thinking, and holistic growth. Rabindranath Tagore, a Nobel laureate and visionary, proposed an education system that emphasized freedom, creativity, and connection with nature. The National Education Policy (NEP) 2020 seeks to reform the Indian education system, emphasizing flexibility, experiential learning, and cultural rootedness. This topic explores the alignment between NEP 2020 and Tagore's educational philosophy, highlighting their shared vision of holistic and inclusive education.

1. Tagore's Educational Philosophy

Rabindranath Tagore envisioned education as a means to nurture the individual's creative and spiritual potential. His key principles include:

1. **Education in Harmony with Nature**: Tagore believed that learning should be conducted in a natural environment, fostering a sense of wonder and respect for the world.

2. **Freedom and Creativity**: He advocated for an education system that promotes free thinking, curiosity, and artistic expression.

3. **Holistic Development**: Education should encompass physical, intellectual, emotional, and spiritual growth.

4. **Global Humanism with Local Roots**: While celebrating universal values, Tagore emphasized the importance of local culture, traditions, and languages.

5. **Experiential and Activity-Based Learning**: He believed in learning by doing, making education an engaging and practical experience.

2. NEP 2020: A Transformative Vision

The National Education Policy 2020 introduces significant reforms to the Indian education system, aligning with global standards while celebrating India's heritage. Its core principles include:

1. **Holistic and Multidisciplinary Education**: NEP promotes well-rounded development, integrating arts, sciences, and vocational skills.

2. **Experiential Learning**: It emphasizes hands-on learning, critical thinking, and problem-solving skills.

3. **Flexibility and Creativity**: The policy encourages flexible learning pathways and innovation.

4. **Cultural and Linguistic Diversity**: NEP supports mother tongue instruction and preservation of India's diverse cultural heritage.

5. **Equity and Inclusion**: Special provisions are made for marginalized communities to ensure universal access to quality education.

3. Philosophical Synergy Between NEP 2020 and Tagore's Ideals

1. **Learning in Harmony with Nature**: NEP's emphasis on environmental awareness and outdoor education reflects Tagore's advocacy for nature-based learning.

2. **Freedom and Individual Growth**: Both emphasize flexibility in learning, allowing students to explore their interests and cultivate creativity.

3. **Holistic Development**: NEP's multidisciplinary approach aligns with Tagore's vision of integrating intellectual, physical, and emotional growth.

4. **Promotion of Local Languages and Culture**: Tagore's insistence on mother-tongue instruction resonates with NEP's focus on regional languages and cultural preservation.

5. **Global Citizenship with Indian Roots**: Like Tagore, NEP envisions education fostering global competencies while staying rooted in Indian traditions.

4. Implementation Challenges and Opportunities

- **Challenges**:

  - Transitioning from rote-based education to flexible, experiential models requires systemic reforms and teacher training.
  - Infrastructure constraints in rural and underprivileged areas may hinder implementation.
  - Resistance to adopting regional languages in education could pose barriers.

- **Opportunities**:

  - NEP 2020's focus on creativity and holistic learning can rejuvenate education, making it more engaging and meaningful.
  - By incorporating Tagore's ideals, NEP can inspire a generation of learners who are rooted in culture, connected to nature, and equipped for global challenges.

5. Conclusion

The NEP 2020 and Rabindranath Tagore's educational philosophy share a profound synergy, rooted in fostering holistic development, cultural pride, and creative freedom. By embracing Tagore's ideals of education in harmony with nature, freedom of expression, and experiential learning, NEP 2020 paves the way for a transformative education system that nurtures well-rounded, compassionate, and innovative individuals. Together, these philosophies create a vision for education that prepares learners for the challenges of the modern world while staying true to India's cultural and philosophical heritage.

This harmonious integration offers an educational blueprint that balances tradition with innovation, equipping students to thrive in a globalized yet culturally diverse world.

3. NEP 2020 PHILOSOPHY AND JIDDU KRISHNAMURTI'S IDEALS

The National Education Policy (NEP) 2020 envisions a transformative approach to education that emphasizes holistic, value-based, and learner-centric pedagogy. Jiddu Krishnamurti, an eminent philosopher and educationist, also advocated an educational philosophy focusing on self-awareness, creativity, and the integration of intellect and emotions. This paper explores the philosophical alignment between NEP 2020 and Krishnamurti's ideals, highlighting their shared vision for fostering critical thinking, emotional well-being, and individuality in education.

Introduction

Jiddu Krishnamurti's educational philosophy emphasized self-discovery, freedom from conditioning, and the cultivation of a harmonious individual capable of navigating the complexities of life. The NEP 2020, similarly, reimagines the Indian education system to balance academic excellence with personal growth and ethical values. This paper examines the convergence of NEP 2020's principles with Krishnamurti's vision, presenting a synergistic model for education in the 21st century.

1. Jiddu Krishnamurti's Philosophy of Education

Key tenets of Krishnamurti's educational thought include:

- **Self-Awareness**: Education should foster inner awareness and understanding of one's thoughts and emotions.
- **Freedom and Inquiry**: He advocated for an environment free of dogma, encouraging critical thinking and inquiry.

- **Holistic Development**: Emphasizing the integration of intellectual, emotional, and physical growth.
- **Ethical Living**: He believed education should nurture sensitivity, compassion, and moral responsibility.
- **Learning Beyond Academics**: Krishnamurti stressed the importance of understanding relationships, society, and the environment, preparing individuals for life rather than just careers.

2. NEP 2020: A Transformational Framework

The NEP 2020 aligns with Krishnamurti's ideals in the following ways:

- **Holistic and Multidisciplinary Approach**: NEP emphasizes balanced development of cognitive, emotional, and physical faculties, akin to Krishnamurti's holistic vision.
- **Critical Thinking and Inquiry-Based Learning**: Encourages creativity and problem-solving over rote memorization.
- **Ethics and Values**: Instills moral values and emotional intelligence to nurture compassionate individuals.
- **Flexibility and Individual Growth**: Promotes personalized education pathways, respecting each learner's unique potential.
- **Sustainability and Global Citizenship**: Emphasizes ecological consciousness and global responsibility, reflecting Krishnamurti's call for harmony with nature.

3. Philosophical Synergy Between NEP 2020 and Krishnamurti's Ideals

1. **Freedom in Learning**: Krishnamurti's belief in freedom from fear and authority in education resonates with NEP's learner-centric and flexible curriculum.
2. **Emphasis on Self-Discovery**: NEP's focus on experiential learning parallels Krishnamurti's emphasis on inner exploration and real-world engagement.
3. **Value-Driven Education**: Both frameworks advocate for nurturing ethical awareness, emotional intelligence, and social responsibility.

4. **Non-Competitive Learning Environment**: Krishnamurti's disdain for excessive competition aligns with NEP's efforts to create inclusive and non-stressful learning spaces.
5. **Focus on Sustainability**: The NEP's integration of environmental awareness echoes Krishnamurti's concern for ecological harmony.

4. Challenges in Implementation

While NEP 2020 embodies many of Krishnamurti's ideals, practical challenges include:

- **Teacher Training**: Educators need to embrace the role of facilitators rather than authoritarian figures, a shift requiring significant training.
- **Infrastructure**: Schools, especially in rural areas, may lack resources to implement experiential and holistic learning methods.
- **Resistance to Change**: Overcoming entrenched traditional practices in education remains a significant hurdle.

5. Conclusion

The alignment between NEP 2020 and Jiddu Krishnamurti's educational philosophy presents an opportunity to reshape education into a transformative force for individual and societal growth. By fostering critical thinking, ethical living, and emotional well-being, NEP 2020 resonates deeply with Krishnamurti's vision of an education that transcends mere academics. With effective implementation, this synergy can create a system that prepares learners not only for careers but also for life as conscious, compassionate, and responsible global citizens.

4. NEP 2020 PHILOSOPHY AND AUROBINDO GHOSH'S IDEALS: ABSTRACT

The National Education Policy (NEP) 2020 is a transformative document envisioning a holistic, inclusive, and value-based education system for India. It aims to equip learners with global competencies while retaining cultural roots. Sri Aurobindo, a philosopher and educationist, advocated for an education system that emphasized integral development—physical, emotional, intellectual, and spiritual. This paper explores the philosophical alignment between NEP 2020 and Aurobindo Ghosh's educational ideals, focusing on their shared vision for nurturing individuals as complete beings.

Introduction

Sri Aurobindo envisioned education as a means of self-discovery and self-realization, striving to integrate spiritual growth with intellectual and physical development. NEP 2020 aligns closely with these ideals, emphasizing value-based education, holistic development, and experiential learning. This paper investigates how NEP 2020 embodies Aurobindo's vision and its implications for shaping India's future.

Aurobindo Ghosh's Philosophy of Education

Sri Aurobindo articulated a comprehensive philosophy of education focused on the following principles:

1. **Integral Education**: Emphasizing the harmonious development of the five aspects of a human being: physical, emotional, intellectual, psychic, and spiritual.
2. **Self-Realization**: Education as a means to achieve one's highest potential and divine purpose.
3. **Value-Based Learning**: Instilling moral and ethical values for inner and outer harmony.
4. **Experiential Learning**: Encouraging practical knowledge and self-directed exploration over rote memorization.
5. **Global Perspective with Indian Roots**: While being open to global knowledge, education should preserve Indian cultural and spiritual heritage.

NEP 2020: Philosophical Tenets

NEP 2020 sets out to reform India's education system with principles that echo Aurobindo's ideals:

1. **Holistic and Multidisciplinary Education**: A focus on developing the intellectual, emotional, and practical skills of learners.
2. **Ethics and Human Values**: Promoting values such as empathy, respect, and service.
3. **Experiential and Flexible Learning**: Fostering critical thinking and creativity through hands-on and learner-centric approaches.
4. **Cultural Preservation**: Encouraging education in local languages and integrating traditional knowledge.
5. **Lifelong Learning**: Education is seen as a continuous journey of growth and transformation.

Synergies Between NEP 2020 and Aurobindo's Ideals

1. **Integral Development**: NEP's holistic learning directly reflects Aurobindo's concept of integral education.
2. **Spiritual and Ethical Foundation**: The NEP's emphasis on values and constitutional ethics aligns with Aurobindo's vision of education fostering inner growth and higher consciousness.
3. **Learner-Centric Approach**: NEP promotes flexibility and experiential learning, akin to Aurobindo's advocacy for self-directed education.
4. **Preservation of Indian Heritage**: Both stress the importance of drawing strength from India's cultural and spiritual traditions.
5. **Focus on the Individual and Society**: NEP and Aurobindo's ideas see education as a means to not only develop the individual but also contribute to societal transformation.

Challenges and Implementation

1. **Infrastructure and Resources**: Realizing holistic and integral education requires substantial investment in resources and teacher training.
2. **Teacher Preparedness**: Educators need orientation in value-based and multidisciplinary pedagogies.
3. **Integration of Spiritual Learning**: Balancing spirituality with secular education could face ideological resistance.

Conclusion

NEP 2020 and Sri Aurobindo's ideals share a profound synergy, emphasizing the need for education that nurtures the complete individual—physically, mentally, emotionally, and spiritually. By incorporating Aurobindo's vision, NEP 2020 has the potential to revolutionize Indian education, fostering not just employable individuals but enlightened, ethical, and globally responsible citizens.

The alignment of these philosophies offers a pathway for India to achieve a harmonious blend of modernity and tradition in its educational framework, contributing to a more equitable and spiritually conscious society.

5. NEP 2020 PHILOSOPHY AND VIVEKANANDA'S IDEALS: A SYNERGISTIC VISION FOR EDUCATION

Abstract

The National Education Policy (NEP) 2020 is a milestone in India's educational reform, emphasizing holistic development, inclusivity, and value-based learning. These principles resonate deeply with the educational philosophy of Swami Vivekananda, who envisioned education as the manifestation of the perfection already present in individuals. This paper explores the alignment between the NEP 2020 and Vivekananda's ideals, underscoring their shared commitment to intellectual growth, moral development, and national rejuvenation.

Introduction

Swami Vivekananda, a key figure in India's spiritual and educational renaissance, championed the idea of education as a tool for individual and societal transformation. His philosophy emphasizes the integration of academic knowledge with ethical and spiritual growth. NEP 2020, with its learner-centric and inclusive approach, mirrors these values. This review highlights the philosophical synergy between Vivekananda's ideals and NEP 2020, illustrating how the latter embodies his vision for a balanced and empowering education system.

Vivekananda's Philosophy of Education

1. **Holistic Development**: Vivekananda believed in the harmonious development of the body, mind, and soul.
2. **Self-Realization**: He defined education as the process of discovering and manifesting the divine potential within every individual.
3. **Character Building**: Education, according to Vivekananda, should focus on building character, courage, and resilience.
4. **Practical Knowledge**: He advocated for education that equips individuals with practical skills to navigate life successfully.
5. **National Integration and Service**: Vivekananda emphasized the role of education in fostering patriotism, unity, and service to humanity.

NEP 2020 Philosophy

1. **Holistic and Multidisciplinary Approach**: NEP emphasizes an integrated learning approach that nurtures cognitive, emotional, and social skills.
2. **Value-Based Education**: The policy promotes ethics, empathy, and constitutional values as integral to learning.
3. **Inclusivity and Accessibility**: Special provisions ensure equitable education opportunities for all, especially marginalized groups.
4. **Skill Development**: Focus on vocational training and lifelong learning aligns with the needs of a globalized and dynamic world.
5. **Rooted in Indian Culture**: NEP encourages education that respects India's heritage while embracing modern advancements.

Philosophical Synergies Between NEP 2020 and Vivekananda's Ideals

1. **Holistic Learning**: Both emphasize nurturing the complete individual—intellectually, emotionally, physically, and spiritually.
2. **Character and Ethics**: NEP's emphasis on value-based education echoes Vivekananda's belief in character as the cornerstone of education.

3. **Practical and Vocational Skills**: NEP's focus on skill development aligns with Vivekananda's advocacy for practical and relevant knowledge.
4. **Nation-Building**: The policy's aim to develop responsible citizens reflects Vivekananda's vision of education as a tool for national progress.
5. **Empowerment Through Knowledge**: NEP's learner-centered approach resonates with Vivekananda's call to awaken the inner strength and potential of every individual.

Challenges in Realizing this Synergy

1. **Implementation Barriers**: Effective integration of values and practical skills requires robust teacher training and infrastructure.
2. **Balancing Tradition and Modernity**: Aligning Vivekananda's spiritual ideals with modern technological advancements needs careful planning.
3. **Social Inequities**: Bridging the gap between policy vision and ground realities in marginalized communities remains a challenge.

Conclusion

NEP 2020 and Swami Vivekananda's educational philosophy converge on key ideals, including holistic development, value-based education, and societal upliftment. Together, they offer a framework for a transformative education system that empowers individuals to excel while contributing to national progress. By effectively implementing NEP 2020 in line with Vivekananda's vision, India can foster a generation of individuals who are intellectually capable, morally upright, and socially responsible.

6. NEP 2020 AND THE ANCIENT INDIAN EDUCATION SYSTEM

Introduction

The National Education Policy (NEP) 2020 marks a significant step toward redefining education in India, with its emphasis on integrating modern advancements with traditional values. The policy draws inspiration from India's ancient education system, which was rooted in holistic development, ethical values, and practical learning. This article explores the parallels between NEP 2020 and the ancient Indian education system, examining how the policy reinterprets timeless principles for the contemporary world.

India's ancient education system, epitomized by institutions like Takshashila, Nalanda, and Gurukuls, emphasized the all-round development of individuals. It fostered knowledge in diverse fields such as philosophy, sciences, arts, and practical skills, underpinned by a strong foundation of ethics and discipline. NEP 2020, introduced to address the challenges of the 21st century, aligns closely with the ethos of ancient education by emphasizing holistic, inclusive, and value-based learning.

The Ancient Indian Education System

1. **Holistic Learning**: Ancient Indian education integrated knowledge of various disciplines, including mathematics, astronomy, medicine, arts, and spirituality.
2. **Gurukul System**: Education was imparted by Gurus in a close-knit, student-centered environment, focusing on individual growth.
3. **Value-Based Education**: Emphasis was placed on developing character, discipline, and social responsibility.
4. **Practical Knowledge**: Education aimed to equip individuals with life skills and vocational expertise for societal contribution.
5. **Inclusivity**: Despite variations in accessibility over time, ancient systems were designed to nurture individual talents and align education with the natural abilities of students.

NEP 2020: A Modern Reflection of Ancient Principles

1. **Holistic Development**: NEP 2020 introduces multidisciplinary learning, encouraging students to explore diverse fields, mirroring the breadth of ancient education.

2. **Skill-Based Learning**: The policy emphasizes vocational training and life skills, akin to the practical focus of ancient systems.
3. **Teacher-Student Relationship**: NEP stresses the role of teachers as mentors, echoing the Guru-Shishya (teacher-student) tradition.
4. **Use of Mother Tongue**: The policy promotes education in regional languages at the foundational level, aligning with the ancient practice of teaching in the student's mother tongue.
5. **Ethics and Values**: By embedding moral and constitutional values in the curriculum, NEP resonates with the value-based education of the past.

Parallels Between Ancient Education and NEP 2020

Aspect	Ancient System	NEP 2020
Curriculum	Multidisciplinary, including science, arts, and spirituality	Multidisciplinary with flexibility in subject combinations
Teaching Approach	Experiential and personalized in Gurukuls	Focus on experiential and interactive learning
Language	Education in Sanskrit and local languages	Promotion of mother tongue in early education
Ethical Emphasis	Strong focus on moral and ethical training	Inclusion of ethics, human values, and life skills
Practical Orientation	Training in practical and vocational skills	Integration of vocational training in schools

Challenges in Reviving Ancient Principles

1. **Scalability**: The Gurukul model focused on small groups, whereas modern education must cater to large populations.
2. **Modern Needs**: While inspired by ancient practices, education must address contemporary challenges like technology integration and globalization.
3. **Infrastructure and Resources**: Effective implementation of NEP's holistic and value-based approach requires significant investments in infrastructure and teacher training.

Conclusion

NEP 2020 successfully bridges the wisdom of the ancient Indian education system with the demands of the modern world. By fostering holistic development, inclusivity, and ethical grounding, the policy lays a strong foundation for an empowered and enlightened citizenry. Drawing from India's rich educational heritage, NEP 2020 offers a vision of education that is both rooted in tradition and forward-looking, creating a harmonious blend of past.

References

1. Ministry of Education, Government of India. (2020). *National Education Policy 2020*. Retrieved from Official NEP 2020 Document.

2. Vivekananda, S. (1963). *The Complete Works of Swami Vivekananda* (Vol. 1-8). Advaita Ashrama.

3. Singh, R. (2019). *Vivekananda's Philosophy of Education: Relevance in Contemporary Times*. International Journal of Indian Culture and Business Management, 19(2), 143-156.

4. Nanda, S. K. (2021). *NEP 2020 and Its Philosophical Roots in Vivekananda's Thought*. Journal of Indian Education, 47(3), 34-45.

5. Tilak, J. B. G. (2021). *Educational Reforms and India's Future: NEP 2020*. Indian Journal of Education, 35(1), 10-20.

6. Ministry of Education, Government of India. (2020). *National Education Policy 2020*. Retrieved from https://www.education.gov.in/nep2020/.

7. Sri Aurobindo. (1920). *A System of National Education*. Pondicherry: Sri Aurobindo Ashram.

8. Chaudhuri, H. (1972). *The Philosophy of Sri Aurobindo: Indian and Western Perspectives*. New York: Philosophical Library.

9. Kapur, M. (2021). *NEP 2020 and Integral Education: A Comparative Analysis*. International Journal of Educational Research, 48(3), 245-258.

10. Tilak, J. B. G. (2021). *Educational Reforms and Indian Philosophy*. Economic and Political Weekly, 46(2), 23-28

11. Krishnamurti, J. (1953). *Education and the Significance of Life*. HarperCollins Publishers.

12. Rajagopal, K. (2001). *Jiddu Krishnamurti and Education: A Critical Study*. New Delhi: Sterling Publishers.

13. Pathak, A. (2013). *Education for Freedom: Jiddu Krishnamurti's Perspective*. Contemporary Education Dialogue, 10(2), 273-288.

14. Singh, M. (2021). *Reimagining Education: NEP 2020 in the Light of Krishnamurti's Philosophy*. Indian Journal of Education and Development, 47(3), 59-74

15. Gandhi, M. K. (1937). *The Wardha Scheme of Education*. Ahmedabad: Navajivan Trust.

16. Kumar, K. (2005). *Educational Reforms and Gandhian Philosophy*. Economic and Political Weekly, 40(2), 141-146. Tilak, J. B. G. (2021). *NEP 2020 and Its Implications*. Indian Journal of Educational Planning and Administration, 35(1), 1-20.

NEP 2020: Towards Concretizing and Uplifting the Educational Landscape of India

Sayed Iram Tabish*
Prof. Syed Zahoor Ahmad Geelani*

syediramtabish254@gmail.com
zahoorgeelani@cukashmir.ac.in
*School of Education, Central University of Kashmir, Ganderbal J&K, India

ABSTRACT: *NEP 2020 is a holistic and comprehensive approach towards an effective and accurate model of education. It essentially has made an entire structural change in the existing educational skeleton promoting an equitable, inclusive, and skill education. The world is transforming very rapidly and the technology is driving the method of operation of almost everything. Therefore, it has become important to update and be in conjunction with these changes. The purpose of education is to be a person with skill and expertise. NEP 2020 encompasses all the parameters that includes the skill development, personality development and the quality education. It focuses on the robust learning by promoting the digital learning. One of the key aspects of it is the grooming and development of cognitive skills, creative and critical thinking and the problem-solving approach. The key recommendations of NEP 2020 is improving the Gross Enrollment Ratio to a substantial level. Earlier, the socially and economically disadvantaged/ backward societies as well as female and the transgender class have faced an indignant and unjust school drop-out ratios. The major hurdle regarding the dropping out of school is that the schools are located in the remote places, early marriages, non-availability of toilets, and financial constraints. The recent policy on education ensures the minimum drop out ratios by providing the infrastructure, security and the hostel stay facilities etc. Also, there is a great focus on the logical and computational learning and discarding the notion of rote learning and learning for the sake of qualifying exams only. NEP 2020 has a special attention on the inclusion of ideals and ethos that is related to our identity and culture. It asserts that there should be a special importance for imbibing* *the respect for the basic constitutional values and the respect for the elders. In the document, there is a great emphasis on the teacher whose role and responsibility is central to the whole picture. In fact, they have used the word empowered teacher who is critical to bringing a plausible change in the society. The empowered teacher must possess core skills that include digital skills, emotionally intelligence, and life skills. It is important that an individual is well acquainted with the life skills because it prepares him/her to handle various challenges and difficult situations effectively and efficiently.*

1.0 INTRODUCTION

Since Independence, India has brought a complete and concrete first Education Policy known as National Education Policy 2020. The National Education policy was drafted by its chairperson Mr. Krishnaswamy Kasturirangan. It consists of four parts and twenty-seven chapters. The policy broadly eyes on achieving inclusivity, national integration, national development, cultural preservation, social justice, quality education etc. It also discusses the recruitment process of teachers and concretizing the educational setup and establishment which will set up the base for a robust teaching learning process. It further describes the nurturing and identifying the unique potential in the students. It has a great focus on the practical understanding, creativity and critical understanding and the other life skills. The main objective is the complete overhaul of the educational system, and reshaping it to fulfill the demands and challenges of the upcoming times. Besides the numerous nuances that it underpins, it completely stands out to the spirit of inclusivity and coherence of the education. It is believed that the policy will be a beacon of hope and may bring a huge change on the absurd and primitive lines of gender inequality and many other facets. The policy aims to annihilate the gender hegemony and the factors that deter the women and the other marginalized sections towards the studies. The policy promises for the quality education, equitable and just society.

One of the key concerns that the policy focused on is to improve the education in the secondary school and attain the hundred percent education by 2020. In the past years, there has been a considerable decrease in the female education and the girl drop out ratio provides a serious setback to the overall development of the country. MHRD published a data in the year 2018 which shows that around 30 % women don't continue their studies due to their involvement in the domestic activities, 4% leave their studies due to the non-availability of the school in their vicinity and 14% discontinue the studies because of the early marriage. However, a small segment doesn't continue their studies because of the other reasons which include the lack of toilet facilities, and non-availability of the female teachers and the financial constraints.

Another key feature includes the integration of seemingly unrelated and diverse set of skills. It also intends to inculcate the values and constitutional ethos, gender sensitivity and respect for senior citizens.

1.1 IDEAS AND INNOVATIONS IN NEP 2020

1. The foreign universities will be facilitated to function in India and the vice versa.
2. The classroom will be studded with the new technologies and smart digital access will promote better learning experiences.
3. There will be the curriculum freedom and the flexibility of the curriculum will generate the interest in students.
4. The faculty will enjoy the incentives which will be fixed based on their performance of research and academics.
5. All the promotions of higher education faculty will be based on the research contributions.
6. Sustainable improvement of GER by 2030.
7. More focus on learning of skills than mere acquiring the knowledge of the subject.
8. Strengthening of the vocational subjects to at minimum the 50% of the population.
9. Promoting and encouraging the students to take the online courses like SWAYAM, etc.

10. Including the research projects and training to the students at undergraduate level.

11. Strict and consistent monitoring of the quality of education.

12. Increasing employability by introducing the knowledge of ICT, Nano-technology at the undergraduate level.

13. Creation of smart labs, virtual labs to promote the digital competence.

14. Comprehensive evaluation mechanism for the promotion of fair education.

15. Focus on effective and efficient learning by the induction of the qualified and competent recruitment.

16. To be in conjunction with the technological advancements, the focus is high on the digital tools and content.

1.2 IMPLICATIONS OF NATIONAL EDUCATION POLICY 2020 ON HIGHER EDUCATION SYSTEM OF INDIA

1. It is believed that the education system will get transformed under the potent leadership by inducting the qualified and apt people in the system who are at the positions of the vice chancellor or director etc. Earlier there was no cap at such levels. In the current education system, there is no requirement for the person holding such positions to have reputed publications, patent, innovations, discoveries and sophisticated policy making. This has serious repercussions which has eventually degraded our education sector. The right policy by the right people can bring gamut of changes in the system which will flourish the idea of the research and innovation in the higher education system.

2. The replacement of the single discipline course to a multi discipline course will promote the interface studies which are very crucial viz a viz career and discoveries. Also, the rigid structure of the courses laid by the inefficient bureaucrats have deeply anguished the education system. There is a need to introduce the novel courses

which will promote the excellence and bring a transformation in the system paying way to the innovation.

3. The education sector so far has succumbed to the misuse of power which has ultimately reduced the quality of education. NEP 2020 ascertains that the Board of Governors who are committed to right planning and concrete policy making are mandatory to every Institution. They will be responsible for maintaining the quality and outcomes of the institutions.

1.3 HOW WILL NEP 2020 BENEFIT STUDENTS?

1. It is a flexible and student centric model. The approach to teaching curriculum will favor students and give them the choice to pursue the courses of their interest. This will bring the clarity in the student so that they can make the right carrier choice.

2. The new policy is based on the skills and caters the competence of the students based on the real knowledge which is based on sheer understanding rather than memory. This will encourage the confidence building and promote the problem-solving skills in the students.

3. The key purpose of the new education policy is to seek the solutions through innovation and research. The cornerstone of this education policy is interpretation of the knowledge through a systematic analysis.
   The policy has shifted the motto of learning from mere information to research and innovation.

4. To bring an all-round development in the students and to promote science and technology, reconciliation of STEM with humanities and arts and design is endowed in the NEP 2020. This is known as STEAM. It inculcates the experimental learning which will pave the way for an overall transformation.

5. It stresses to bring social justice and promotes the merit-based appointments in the colleges and universities.

6. It promotes the use of ICT and other online platforms of learning, AI, AR and VR etc. The pandemic has thrown serious challenges which has put has put cap on physical meetings. Therefore, it has become important to think of an alternate option which involves the use of digital technology.

7. Robust assessment, quality assure mechanism and accreditation to promote quality education and research in the higher education.

8. Boosting GER by giving free and quality education.

1.4 CONCLUSION

The policy aims to bring the two-fold change: the operational mechanism of education and its substance. It will give flexibility and the liberty to students to pursue as per the personal aspirations and admirations. With this, "Education for All" can be realized. With a flexibility that the policy underpins, it will give an opportunity for the complete overhaul and revival of the spirit of true education in the lower primary and middle classes. The changes in the lower level will be a watershed in the overall education system. The nation can witness the scientists, reformers, leaders, and potent professionals in various sectors which will truly boom the development. The new education policy has great focus on the digital technology which can help the education system not suffer in case of any colossal emergency.

References

1. Kumar, A. (2022). Digital Education: Vision, Perspectives and Problems in Changing Paradigms of NEP-2020.

2. Gupta, B. L., & Choubey, A. K. (2021). Higher education institutions–some guidelines for obtaining and sustaining autonomy in the context of NEP 2020. *International Journal of All Research Education and Scientific Methods (IJARESM)*, *9*(1).

3. Kumar, A. (2021). New education policy (NEP) 2020: A roadmap for India 2.0. *University of South Florida M3 Center Publishing*, *3*(2021), 36

4. Kalyani, P. (2020). An empirical study on NEP 2020 [National Education Policy] with special reference to the future of Indian education system and its effects on the Stakeholders. *Journal of Management Engineering and Information Technology, 7*(5), 1-17.

5. Smitha, S. (2020). National Education Policy (Nep) 2020-Opportunities and Challenges in Teacher Education. *International Journal of Management (IJM), 11*(11).

Education in Ancient India

Dr. SAILAJA C.S

Assistant Professor of Botany, Government Degree College, Kuppam, Chittoor (Dt), AndhraPradesh-517425.

Email: sailajarajaram2009@gmail.com

ABSTRACT: *Education is a purposeful endeavor aimed at transmitting knowledge and cultivating skills and character traits like understanding, rationality, kindness, and honesty. Critical thinking is pivotal in differentiating education from indoctrination, and opinions vary on whether it should foster student improvement or maintain a value-neutral stance. Pedagogy, supported by diverse philosophies and theories, underpins teaching methods, while education reform endeavors seek to enhance its quality and relevance for modern society. The right to education is recognized by some governments and the United Nations. Historically, education focused on instilling ethical values and occurred in various settings. Today, education is an ongoing process extending beyond formal schooling, encompassing learning from diverse sources, and striving for contemporary goals like liberating learners and developing vital skills. Education is classified into formal, non-formal, and informal types, each offering distinct approaches and methods. Ancient India's education system, blending formal and informal elements, emphasized self-education and mental growth.*

Key Words: *Education, Formal, Non-formal, Informal, Primary Education, Right to Education,*

2.0 INTRODUCTION

Education in its broadest, general sense is the means through which the aims and habits of a group of people lives on from one generation to the next. Generally, it occurs through any experience that has a formative effect on the way one thinks, feels, or acts. In its narrow, technical sense, education is the formal process by which society deliberately transmits its accumulated knowledge, skills, customs and values from one generation to another. In ancient India, both formal and informal ways of education system existed. Indigenous education was imparted at home, in temples, pathshalas, tols, chatuspadis and gurukuls. There were people in homes, villages and temples who guided young children in imbibing pious ways of life. In a gurukul, students had to memorize lessons that were taught orally. After completing their education, the students paid guru dakshina according to their means. The students led simple and highly disciplined lives in gurukul. The examination was oral one. The student was required to give oral answers in a congregation of scholars. If he satisfied them, he was given a degree. The main objective of education was to equip the students with a good quality of education. The education mostly focused on the enrichment of culture, character, and personality, development, and cultivation of noble ideals. The objective was gaining the mental, physical, and intellectual personality of students, to make the students future-ready and survive in any situation.

During the ancient period, the state government and the people did not interfere in designing curriculum, payments of fees, regulation of teaching hours. There was a strong bonding between teacher and student. Every student was allotted with one teacher and more emphasis was given to the student-teacher relationship, each student used to meet teachers personally to learn and gain instructions from them. During ancient times, royal families, as well as kings of states, used to donate their wealth to improve the education system and quality. The syllabus was designed in accordance with the demands of that era. At that time students used to leave their houses and went to live with their gurus until their education was completed. During the early Vedic period, women's education was also given more emphasis. The education focuses on the physical and mental development of students. The course duration was about 10–12 years, as there were no books so students used to memorize all things, memory played a crucial role during learning. The education was imparted in forests away from cities and peoples to give students a pleasant and silent environment of study.

2.1 METHODOLOGY

The main purpose of this paper is to convey what all the things need to adopt in our current education system from ancient and medieval times and also some new trends associated with it. The paper is mainly focused on ancient system, including sub-sections such as Importance of society in ancient educational system, Curriculum, Skill Development, Values, Beliefs and Habits, Methods of learning, Meanings used in those days, advantages, and disadvantages of the education system, Result and Discussion.

2.2 IMPORTANCE OF SOCIETY IN ANCIENT EDUCATIONAL SYSTEM

In those days the society played an important role in educational system like giving places for educational buildings, lands for construction of universities, temples, gurukulas, etc., for teaching purposes. At that time knowledge was considered as sacred one and no fee was collected from the students. Contributions towards education were considered the highest form of donation. All members of the society contributed in some form or the other. Financial support came from rich merchants, wealthy parents and society. This form of free education was also prevalent in other ancient universities like Valabhi, Vikramshila and Jagaddala. At the same time in the south of India, agraharas served as centers of learning and teaching. South Indian kingdoms also had other cultural institutions known as Ghatika and Brahmapuri. A Ghatika was a Centre of learning including religion and was small in size. An agrahara was a bigger institution, a whole settlement of learned Brahmins, with its own powers of government and was maintained by generous donations from the society. Temples, Mathas, Jain Basadis and Buddhist Viharas also existed as other sources of learning during this period. Many travelers from various regions having different climates and cultures began to visit parts of India from early times. The Indian education system continued in the form of ashrams, in temples and as indigenous schools. During the medieval period, maktabas and madrassas became part of the education system. During the pre-colonial period, indigenous education flourished in India. This was an extension of the formal system that had taken roots earlier. This system was mostly religious and spiritual form of education. Tols in Bengal, pathshalas in western India, chatuspadis in Bihar, and similar schools existed in other parts of India. Local resources via donations supported education. References in texts and memoirs inform that villagers also supported education in southern India. As we understand, the ancient education system of India focused on the holistic development of the students, both inner and outer self, thus preparing them for as free and not centralized. Its foundations were laid in the rich cultural traditions. India thereby helping in the development of the physical, intellectual, spiritual and artistic aspects of life holistically. Our present-day education system has a lot to learn from the ancient education system of India. Therefore, the stress is being laid on connecting learning to the world outside the school. Today educationists recognize the role and importance of multilingual and multicultural education, thereby connecting the multicultural education, thereby connecting the ancient and the traditional knowledge with contemporary learning.

2.3 SYLLABUS

Curriculum plays an essential role in the education system. It was dynamic and not static; it was made up of different stages. The fundamental goal of building a good curriculum was to develop students physically and mentally. The education was totally through orals and debates, and the exams were conducted every year. The education system of the ancient period focused on subjects like warfare, military, politics, religion.

2.4 SKILL DEVELOPMENT

Technological improvement has boosted the economic growth in India. Science and technology have an important role in the economic development of India. Compared to other developed countries, India has more youth manpower. Proper education will play a significant role in making youth future-ready and increasing economic growth by providing skilled persons which will also boost industrial development. In the modern era of education, every institution or university is adapting new teaching methods using their teaching methodologies. Indian education is the biggest and well-known education systems in the world. During ancient education, there were 5 big well-known universities like Takshashila, Nalanda, Vallabhi, etc., which focus on the all-round development of students and those in the medieval period there exists 2 institutions madrasah and maqtabs which mostly focus on building student religious and leaders of the future. In modern education, there are well known autonomous institutes like IITs and IIMs which are famous all around the world.

2.5 VALUES, BELIEFS AND HABITS

During ancient education, students live away from their parents, their education comprises of subjects like physical education, mental education, politics, economics, etc. They were shaped in a way that they can live in any condition considering how difficult the situation will be. Medieval education also followed the same protocol as ancient education in spite that their education mostly focuses on religion. In today's modern era of big institutes like the Indian Institute of Technology (IITs) and Indian Institute of Management (IIMs), everything is changed like the living standard of students, curriculum, all-round development. The principle objective of the student has been to just achieve its goal and be successful. Only the big institutes like IITs, IIMs, and some other private and aided universities have adopted modern methods of learning. There is a difference in curriculum, teaching methods, and living standards of students in every institute. The syllabus of the current education system is not industry-oriented and also not according to new upcoming trends. The main objective of education is mostly theoretical and not practically implemented. So during ancient education there was value-added education which brings beliefs in the student community and learn good habits which is useful for their future generation.

2.6 METHODS OF LEARNING

- Students had to memorize lessons that were taught orally
- The examination was oral one.
- The student was required to give oral answers in a congregation of scholars.

WORDS USED IN THOSE DAYS

WORDS	MEANINGS
Purushartahs	Human goal, an object of desire
Artha	For economic security
Kama	Sensuous aesthetic satisfaction
Chatuspadis	A resting place with four pillars around
Moksha	Spiritual welfare
Dharma	Moral and social order
Upanayana	The formal admission ceremony
Ashrama	Home where he would receive education
Dvijya	Twin born
Parisads	An assembly
Arthasahtra	Political science or statecraft
Vedas	Knowledge, collection of poems or hymns
Puranas	Sanskrit sacred writings on Hindu mythology and folklore of varying date and origin.
Yoga	To yoke or to unify or integration of personality, and is the method of achieving union

2.7 UNIVERSITIES IN ANCIENT INDIA

- Taxila
- Mithila
- Nalanda
- Vallabi
- Vikramasila
- Jagaddala
- Odantapuri

- Nadia
- Madura
- Kanchi
- Benares

2.8 ADVANTAGES OF THE EDUCATION SYSTEM

Students were taught to appreciate the balance between human beings and nature. Teaching and learning followed the tenets of Vedas and Upanishads fulfilling duties towards self, family and society, thus encompassing all aspects of life. Education system focused both on learning and physical development.

2.9 DISADVANTAGES OF THE EDUCATION SYSTEM

The ancient education system was lacking in the technological sector hence they knew very little about the technology we have today. The ancient education system was confined to education locally hence knowing everything about every place possible on earth was a bit difficult at that time.

2.10 RESULT AND DISCUSSION

Education is the process of receiving or giving systematic instruction, especially at a school or university. Formal education takes place in education and training institutions, is usually structured by curricular aims and objectives, and learning is typically guided by a teacher. In most regions, formal education is compulsory up to a certain age and commonly divided into educational stages such as kindergarten, primary school and secondary school. Non formal education occurs as addition or alternative to formal education. Informal education refers to a lifelong learning process, whereby each individual acquires attitudes, values, skills, and knowledge from the educational influences and resources in his or her own environment and from daily experience. Primary Education is compulsory to all the citizens of India. A right to education has been recognized by some governments and the United Nations. During the ancient period, the state government and the people did not interfere in designing curriculum, payments of fees, regulation of teaching hours. There was a strong bonding between teacher and student. Every student was allotted with one teacher and more emphasis was given to the student-teacher relationship, each student used to meet teachers personally to learn and gain instructions from them. At that time students used to leave their houses and went to live with their gurus until their education was completed. During the early Vedic period, women's education was also given more emphasis. The education focuses on the physical and mental development of students. The course duration was about 10–12 years, as there were no books so students used to memorize all things, memory played a crucial role during learning. The education was imparted in forests away from cities and peoples to give students a pleasant and silent environment of study. This type of education system is needed in present days because of pollution, radiation, high technological gadgets the present generation is not concentrating on studies. Finally, this leads to the lack of development of the country in all the aspects.

Reference

1. https://files.eric.ed.gov>fulltext
2. https://www.researchgate.net>publication>356536063
3. https://brill.com>view>tittle:
4. https://www.slideshare.net deepakrenuse>education.

NEP 2020: A Comparative Analysis of National Educational Policies of Higher Education

Jumri Riba[1]
Ph.D. Scholar, Department of Education, Mizoram University
Email- jumriba1244@gmail.com
&
Dr.Vemula Muttu[2]
Asst. Professor, Department of Education, Mizoram University
Email- drmuttuedu@gmail.com

ABSTRACTS: *The education system in India has been changing to date. The Government of India created the National Policy on Education (NPE) to advance and oversee education in India. The policy encompasses both rural and urban India's primary and secondary education as well as higher education. Since India's independence, three prime ministers—Prime Minister Indira Gandhi in 1968, Prime Minister Rajiv Gandhi in 1986, and Prime Minister Narendra Modi in 2020—have essentially introduced three education plans. The current study is descriptive in nature and analyses pertinent National Education Policies texts. The proposals for national education policies for higher education are discussed in the current study. And contrast the three decisions the Indian government took. The national education policy of India with regard to higher education has faced numerous difficulties. The Indian educational system is prepared to satisfy the needs of the current generation with the adoption of the new NEP 2020. The present administration has created the New Education Policy of 2020 in order to give the younger generation a high-quality education that also equips them with technological know-how and employability. However, uniform and open implementation at all levels is the key to its success.*

3.0 INTRODUCTION

The first national education strategy was unveiled by Prime Minister Indira Gandhi's administration in 1968. It advocated for radical reform and equitable educational opportunities in order to promote national integration and better cultural and economic growth. According to the directive, all children up to the age of 14 had to finish the mandatory education required by the Indian Constitution, and teachers had to receive specific education and licensing. The policy outlined the trilingual formula to be used in secondary education, teaching in English, the official language of the state where the school was headquartered, and Hindi. It also called for a focus on studying regional languages. To close the intellectual divide between the masses and the intelligentsia, language education was considered crucial. The policy called for the consistent promotion of Hindi use and learning in order to promote Hindi as a common language for all Indians, despite the fact that the decision to select Hindi as the national language had proven to be contentious. The ancient Sanskrit language, which was regarded as an essential component of India's culture and legacy, was also supported by the strategy.

A 6 percent increase in education funding was recommended in the NPE in 1986. A new national education policy was introduced by the Rajiv Gandhi administration. The main points of this policy were as follows: To achieve such social integration, policies have called for expanding scholarships, and adult education, hiring more teachers from the SCs, encouraging poor families to send their children to school regularly, developing new institutions, and providing financial aid to those who qualify. The Indira Gandhi National Open University, established in 1985, expanded the open university system and endorsed the NPE's call for a child-centered approach to primary education. The policy also called for the establishment of a rural university model based on Mahatma Gandhi's teachings to support grassroots economic and social development in rural India. 6% of GDP was allocated to education in the 1986 education policy.

Several public consultations were held when the Department of Human Resources Development published a draught of the Education Policy 2019 in 2019. The concept of NEP emphasizes decreasing curriculum content to improve critical thinking, experiential learning, and more all-encompassing discussion- and analysis-based learning. In order to optimize learning for pupils based on children's cognitive growth, it also discusses changing the curriculum and pedagogical framework from a 10+2 system to a 5+3+3+4 system design. To make a number of reforms to the current Indian educational system, the Cabinet adopted a new National Education Policy on July 29, 2020. India's national education policy is always evolving in an effort to create the best policy, yet there are certain difficulties, benefits, and restrictions. The primary goal of this essay is to conduct a comparative analysis of the three government policies of India.

3.1 REVIEW OF LITERATURE

Pallathadka, et al. (2020) conducted a paper on "Journey through the Indias National Education Policy Previous and the Present". In this special research contribution, an outlook on the importance and necessity of educational policy is given. It also focuses on three major national education policies introduced by the Government of India in the previous year 1968, 1986 and 2020. This article compares the goals and other important factors of the three national education policies that have been successful in bringing about changes in the Indian education sector from time to time.

Shubhada & Niranth (2021). The research entitled "New Education Policy 2020: A Comparative Analysis with the Existing National Education Policy 1986" was undertaken. The article compares the 1986 New Education Policy and the 2020 New Education Policy, highlighting the key differences between both. Additionally, an effort was made to pinpoint the problems with the policies that were already in place that gave rise to NDP 2020. There was also a quick overview of NDP 2020's highlights. The information was gathered from a variety of websites run by the government as well as journals, reports, and print media. This article only uses secondary data for its research. Despite the fact that NEP 2020 has new goals that must be met by 2035, attempts have been made to draw attention to its advantages and shortcomings. The answer depends on how well GDP 2020 is achieving its goals because it is one of the most promising plans ever adopted.

3.2 OBJECTIVES

1. To study the relevant documents of NEP 1968, NEP 1986, & NEP 2020 on higher education
2. To examine and appraise the policies of the Government of India NEP 1968, NEP 1986, & NEP 2020 on higher education
3. To make a comparative analysis of NEP 1968, NEP 1986, & NEP 2020 of higher education

3.3 METHODOLOGY

Research Methodology: The methodology chosen for this study aims to extract the government policy on higher education from the official state documents at different times in India. Education policy is like an effective tool that the state uses to control and manage the entire academic scenario in terms of the well-being and development of its population. The present study deals with the public higher education policy at different times in India.

Nature of the Study: The present study has a descriptive character and analyzes the university-relevant documents from NEP 1968, NEP 1986 & NEP 2020. The data obtained from the content-related investigation are qualitatively examined and interpreted with regard to the objective of the investigation.

Source of Data: The information (data) has been derived by in-depth content analysis of policy documents of NEP 1968, NEP 1986, & NEP 2020.

Method of Data Collection: The research technique used in data collection is content analysis. The data were openly examined without predefined hypotheses when studying the NEP 1968, NEP 1986 and NEP 2020 documents. It has been observed that certain preference terms appear repeatedly in these three documents, while some observations are unique to particular documents.

Analysis of Data: Firstly, documents from NEP 1968, NEP 1986 and NEP 2020 were analyzed in the context of their contemporary socio-political and cultural context to outline the government's higher education policy. Secondly, the document of NEP 1968, NEP 1986 and NEP 2020 was compared based on emerged and identified categories through inductive analysis. The categories that emerged from document analysis and compared between the NEP 1968, NEP 1986 and NEP 2020 documents are as follows

- Focus of policies
- Control and management of higher education
- Finance & Higher education
- Medium of instruction in Higher education
- Research in higher education
- Women in higher education
- Stakeholders in the policy-making process

Objective 1 To study the relevant documents of NEP 1968, NEP 1986, & NEP 2020 on higher education

3.4 MAJOR RECOMMENDATIONS OF NEP 1968 ON HIGHER EDUCATION

- The number of full-time students accepted into a university or college
- Establishing new universities only after making sufficient financial arrangements.
- Focus on post-graduate programs and enhancements to training and research infrastructure
- Improvement of advanced study centers, such as "clusters of centers"
- Appropriate lab, library, staff, and other facilities for students.

3.5 MAJOR RECOMMENDATIONS OF NEP 1986 ON HIGHER EDUCATION

- The development of numerous autonomous colleges;
- The selective establishment of autonomous sections inside institutions.

- To better fulfil the demands of specialization, college courses and programs will be changed.
- The emphasis will be on linguistic proficiency and course selection.
- Councils of Higher Education will be used for state-level planning and coordination.
- The Councils and UGC will monitor standards.
- Admission will be governed by capacity.
- The use of technology devices and audio-visual aids to enhance traditional teaching techniques.
- To ensure high-quality research, the UGC will take the necessary actions to improve support services in institutions.
- In order to improve coordination and consistency in policy, a national organization that encompasses higher education in general and sprawls over the agricultural, medical, technical, legal, and other professional domains, in particular, will be established.

3.6 MAJOR RECOMMENDATIONS OF NEP 2020 ON HIGHER EDUCATION

- Promotion of vocational education in the educational system at the secondary and tertiary levels • Holistic and Multidisciplinary Education with Multiple Entry/Exit Options
- Establishment of an Academic Bank of Credit;
- NTA to administer the Common Entrance Examination for Admission to Higher Education
- Multidisciplinary Education and Research Universities (MERUs),
- The establishment of the National Research Foundation (NRF),
- "Light but Tight" regulation,
- Higher Education Commission of India (HECI), a solitary, all-encompassing umbrella organization for the promotion of the higher education sector.
- Higher Education Grants Council (HEGC)
- National Higher Education Regulatory Council (NHERC), National Accreditation Council (NAC),

- Widening access to open and distance education to boost the Gross Enrolment Ratio (GER).
- The system of higher education will include professional education as well as the internationalization of education.
- Multi-disciplinary institutions

Objective 2. To examine and appraise the policies of the Government of India NEP 1968, NEP 1986, & NEP 2020 on higher education.

3.7 POLICIES OF THE GOVERNMENT OF INDIA

1. **Focus of policies:** Radical reorganization and the promotion of equitable educational opportunities for all were the two principal focuses of NEP 1968. number of full-time applicants that a college or institution will accept. universities should only be founded after receiving enough financing. focus on graduate programs, as well as improvements to training and research facilities. Enhancing Centers for Advanced Studies as groupings of institutions. own lab, library, personnel, and other resources for students. NEP 1986 focuses on the creation of numerous autonomous colleges. the selective establishment of independent departments within universities. Moreover, emphasize your course combination and language proficiency. The UGC works with these councils to jointly manage the standards. The UGC has taken the necessary steps to enhance the support provided at the institutions in order to guarantee the caliber of research. establishment of properly governed national research entities within the university system. A national organization founded for improved policy coordination and coherence that covers higher education in general and in the sectors of agriculture, medicine, technology, law, and other professions in particular. The NEP 2020 placed a strong emphasis on presenting vocational training within the university system and raising the CEFR in higher education to 50%. Interdisciplinary and holistic training with many entry and exit options. establishment of the National Research Foundation

(NRF) and multidisciplinary education and research universities (MERUs). The Indian Higher Education Commission (HECI), which serves as a single umbrella organization for the promotion of higher education but excludes medical and legal education, has independent bodies for setting standards, including the General Education Council, the Council for Higher Education Scholarships (HEGC), the National Accreditation Council (NAC), and the National Higher Education Regulatory Council (NHERC). The importance of vocational training in the higher education system.

2. **Control and management of higher education**: NEP 1986 recommended planning and coordination at the state level through higher education councils. The UGC and the university councils were jointly developing methods to monitor the standards. And in order to ensure high-quality research, UGC was commissioned to take an appropriate step, which was a good initiative. In 2020, NEP recommended NTA offer a common entrance exam for admission to higher education institutions. The Academic Bank of Credits is a virtual or digital warehouse that holds information about credits earned by individual students throughout their learning journey. National Research Foundation (NRF) to take care of all disciplines to strengthen India's research and innovation. Light but strict regulation to ensure integrity, transparency, and resources. The only umbrella organization supporting the higher education industry is the Higher Education Commission of India (HECI). Grants for higher education are facilitated by the Higher Education Grants Council (HEGC). National Higher Education Regulatory Council (NHERC) and National Accreditation Council (NAC) were created for regulation and accreditation, respectively.

3. **Finance & Higher education:** The NEP of 1968 calls for raising education spending to 6% of the national income. There are differences between the state governments' scholarship systems and educational levels. The government has regularly pledged to boost

spending for education so that it reaches at least 6% of national revenue ever since the proposals of the Education Commission (1966–1966) and the National Policy on Education in 1968 and 1986.

4. **Medium of instruction in Higher education:** The Kothari Commission maintained the use of English as a library language at the university level, and a reasonable level of English is expected of students for a master's degree. In large universities, English should be used as the language of instruction since the faculty and students in such institutions are related to the whole of India. However, regional languages were used for basic education and some Hindi-speaking states in northern India emphasized the use of Hindi and the central government made efforts to produce and translate books in Hindi. The NPE 1986 has also focused on the production of study and reference materials in Modern Indic languages and the translation of textbooks and other reference books from English into Modern Indic languages. States differed significantly in language policies and hence the use of English in Indian higher education has likely increased, especially in all central universities and specialized research institutions sponsored by the central government, IITs, IIMs, and in the private higher education sector. English has consistently remained the predominant language of instruction in India.

5. **Research in higher education:** The Kothari Commission claimed that enrollment would increase at the postgraduate level, but deterred entry of unworthy candidates by imposing strict regulations and rigorous admission tests. Most of the postgraduate study and research work should be centralized in universities and university centers where 3-4 excellent affiliated colleges cooperatively develop good programs under the direction of the university. The commission gave high priority to postgraduate studies and research in higher education, emphasizing that they

have a seed value and can improve the entire education system. It also pointed out inadequate facilities for the scholarship recipients and strongly advocated scholarships for the students at this stage. The 1986 National Education Policy (NPE) and 1992 Action Program placed great emphasis on research and considered it an essential part of higher education institutions. It also emphasized the maintenance of a research database to avoid wasting time and money on repetition and improves efficiency in research coordination and planning by keeping scientists informed of work in different institutions. It also highlighted the formation of a research committee in the State Council for Higher Education that, in collaboration with university departments and various other external bodies, would help government agencies and industries to identify issues of concern to different sectors and regions

Objective 3. To make comparative analysis of NEP 1968, NEP 1986, & NEP 2020 of higher education

3.8 COMPARISON BETWEEN NEP 1968, NEP 1986 & NEP 2020

Entrance Exam: No such guideline has been established for the implementation of admission to higher education. And NEP 1986 recommends that colleges and universities conduct an entrance exam to gain admission into their respective colleges and universities. According to the New Education Policy 2020, the National Testing Agency (NTA) conducts an aptitude test at least twice a year.

Credit System: NEP 1968 has no such credit system policy. In 2015-16, UGC introduced the Choice Based Credit System (CBCS). It aims to make the student centered rather than system-centered or teacher-centered. NEP 2020 introduced multiple entry and exit options for incomplete courses. Credits will be transferred through the Academic Bank of Credits.

Graduation:

NEP 1968	For Graduation 1 option was given	3 years Graduation
NEP 1986	For Graduation, 4 options were given	1-year Diploma
		2-year Diploma
		3- year Graduation
		4- year Graduation with research
NEP 2020	For Graduation, 4 options were given	1-year diploma
		2- year Advanced Diploma
		3- year Graduation
		4- year Graduation with research

Post-Graduation

NEP 1968	After Graduation	2 years for a Master's degree
NEP 1986	After graduation	2 years for a Master's degree
NEP 2020	After graduation	Master's degree of 1 year
		2 years with research options are given

Master of Philosophy (M.Phil.): No such policy for M.Phil. during NEP 1968. M.Phil. started in 1971 in India. After NEP 1986 First M.Phil. then a doctorate possible. NEP 2020 discontinued. M.Phil. can be promoted after the Master.

Foreign University: NEP 1968 and 1986 did not have such a policy. The top Indian universities are encouraged to open campuses abroad, and the top 100 foreign institutions are encouraged to establish themselves in India, according to the new education strategy. In 2030 every district will have at least one large multidisciplinary institution nearby.

Affiliation: The majority of colleges have connections to public universities. All colleges fall into one of three categories: autonomous degree-granting colleges, teaching universities, or research universities.

Controlling Authority: Under NEP 1968 and NEP 1986, UGC and AICTE were in charge of higher education. The Higher Education Council of India (HECI) would be in charge of overseeing higher education, according to New Education Policy 2020.

Research Fund: The University Grants Commission (UGC) provided funding for the study, according to the NEP from 1986. The National Research Foundation (NRF) provides funding for research initiatives under the current policy.

3.9 CONCLUSION: Indeed, the recommendations made by the National Education Policy are progressive. The national education policy of India with regard to higher education has faced numerous difficulties. With the implementation of the new NEP 2020, the emphasis is on cutting back on curriculum content to improve foundational learning, critical thinking, and more holistic experiential, discussion-based, and analysis-based learning, ensuring that the Indian education system is prepared to meet the needs of the current generation. The NEP will be a key factor in determining the future of the nation because it intends to reduce the stress of tuition and in-class testing on students. The present administration has created the New Education Policy of 2020 in order to give the younger generation a high-quality education that also equips them with technological know-how and employability. However, the uniformity and openness of its application throughout all higher education levels in India is what makes it successful.

References

1. Akhtar, S. (2021). New Education Policy 2020 of India: A Theoretical Analysis. *International Journal of Business and Management Research*, *9*(3), 302-306.
2. Aalam, C. S., & Selvan, S. A. Education Policies in India since Independence: A.
3. Kaur, H., & Manekeyeva, R. (2022). Scientific research congress-xiii.
4. The Ministry of Education Government of India. (1968). national policy on education.
5. https://www.education.gov.in/sites/upload_files/mhrd/files/document-reports/NPE-1968.pdf

6.   The Ministry of Education Government of India. (1986, July 20). National policy on education.

7.   https://www.education.gov.in/sites/upload_files/mhrd/files/upload_document/npe.pdf

8.   Ministry of Human Resource Development Government of India. (2020, July 29). National Education Policy 2020

9.   https://www.education.gov.in/sites/upload_files/mhrd/files/NEP_Final_English_0.pdf

10. Pallathadka, H. A. R. I. K. U. M. A. R., Manoharmayum, D. D., Pallathadka, L. K., & Makki, V. R. R. (2021). Journey through India's National Education Policy–Previous and the Present. *Journal of Contemporary Issues in Business and Government*, *27*(03), 272-279.

NEP 2020: Vision on Technological Education

Ignes R Lalmuanpuii* & Nitu Kaur**
*Research Scholar, School of Education, Mizoram University
**Assistant Professor, School of Education, Mizoram University

ABSTRACT: *The present research article focuses on the review of National Education Policy (NEP) 2020 and its vision on technological education. Technological Education is very promising in 21st century and has a potential to have a huge impact upon the National Education. Human are destined to grow overtime and not remain in a same place forever and in the same way our educational systems need to be changed and reviewed overtime for the development and to deliver learning in a simpler way. Involving and adopting technology in our learning system will affect the educational sub-systems especially students and teachers as they are not well equipped with the adoption of the latest digital learning. The NEP 2020 is speaking on the inclusion of technology in both school education and higher education. At school level digital literacy, coding, and computational thinking is a must inclusion and concerted curricular and pedagogical initiatives, including the introduction of contemporary subjects such as artificial intelligence, design thinking is thought to be introduced. Activities involving coding will be introduced in Middle Stage compulsorily as stated in NEP, 2020. However, this technological embedment may take some time as the reality of digital divide is not new in Indian context. Also, the socioeconomic class differences are not to be ignored. The new road to technology needs to be paved with precautionary ground work so that the hurdles can be transformed into assets. It is expected that this new technology driven learning system will add value to the learning systems, will help people to grow and adapt to receive new knowledge systems and yield successful outcome for the coming generations.*

4.0 INTRODUCTION

The National Education Policy (NEP) 2020 marks a significant milestone in the transformation of India's educational landscape, with a visionary focus on technological education. In the 21st century, technological education has emerged as a powerful catalyst for change, poised to reshape the way we teach and learn. The NEP 2020 recognizes the need for dynamic evolution in our educational systems to keep pace with the ever-growing demands of the modern world. This research article delves into the NEP 2020's vision for technological education and its potential to revolutionize the national education framework.

In an era marked by rapid advancements in technology, stagnation in educational methods is no longer an option. The integration of technology into education holds the promise of not only enhancing learning outcomes but also democratizing access to quality education. However, this transition to a technology-driven education ecosystem is not without its challenges, particularly concerning digital literacy, equitable access, and socioeconomic disparities.

This article explores the multifaceted approach taken by the NEP 2020 in addressing these challenges. It outlines the imperative of digital literacy, coding skills, and computational thinking in school education. The policy emphasizes the introduction of contemporary subjects such as artificial intelligence and design thinking, reflecting a forward-looking perspective that prepares students for the digital age.

Yet, the road to technological integration in education is not a straightforward one, especially in a diverse and resource-constrained context like India. The digital divide and disparities across socioeconomic classes cannot be ignored, and the NEP 2020 acknowledges these hurdles. It underscores the need for meticulous groundwork to transform these challenges into opportunities and assets.

Ultimately, the NEP 2020's vision for technological education is aimed at adding value to the learning experience, facilitating adaptability to new knowledge systems, and fostering success for future generations. This research article will delve deeper into the specific provisions and strategies outlined in the policy, shedding light on how they align with the global shift towards technology-driven education.

4.1 TECHNOLOGICAL EDUCATION IN NEP 2020

National Education Policy (NEP) 2020 aimed to transform the education system with a better and advance method of learning by the introduction of technology which can reach out to a more remote and distant geographical regions. In this way a uniform learning styles can be delivered to all the students at the same time that can cover the syllabus at a more rapid rate. At first, both the students and teachers will struggle for a while but they can adjust and adapt overtime as we all have to go through tough times to overcome difficulties. Moreover, everything has its pros and cons and these components too have flaws and threats that can negatively impact the lives of younger people although it contains a huge benefit for the society's well-being. Therefore, the paper studies and reviews the vision of NEP 2020 basically on the adoption of technological education.

4.2 CRITICAL ANALYSIS OF SOME STUDIES ON NEP 2020

Kumar (2020) has pointed out that NEP 2020 aimed to provide instructional technology at all level of education in order to improve teaching and learning. The new NEP 2020 aimed to transform the teacher-centred learning to a more student-centred which will enhance the knowledge of the students at a more advance and a rapid rate. Students can learn whenever they liked by looking back to a pre recoded lessons and parents too can understand and help their children with the new learning method. The implementation of digitalization in the learning systems will be a great improvement but there also exist some obstacles on the way. However, a successful implementation of technology in the educational levels requires a stable internet connection, an expert instructor, infrastructure etc. Geographical differences may hamper the deliverance of learning and lack of computer literacy among the teacher and students can be a big hurdle in executing the roadmap to technology driven pedagogy. Also, the lower socioeconomic classes will face lots of difficulty when it comes to digitalization. So, the government have to look after and provide the necessary requirement for the successful implementation of technology in our learning systems.

Venkateshwarlu (2020) said that adopting digital learning will face many hurdles at some schools and in rural regions as most schools do not have an adequate set-up to support these tools and also due to its un-affordability for all schools to use, particularly government schools need to improve digital infrastructure.

Kalyani (2020) finds that majority of people support the new system of NEP 2020 and accept the fact that change and upgradation of leaning styles is necessary for improving. However, it is doubted that many of the stakeholder will find it difficult to adapt and struggle for a while to accept the introduction of technology as traditional methods had been used for a while. The implementation and success of NEP strategy will soon be seen and shaping the future of the coming generation.

Muralidharan, Shanmugan and Klochkov (2021) reflect on the quality of digitalization and stated that the implementation requires a proper time and financial support to be useful and such needs of sources are not adequately met. Social and cultural rigidities, socially disadvantage groups and economically weaker sections will find it difficult to deliver the new system and it can be taken care of only if those needs are satisfied.

Soy (2021) pointed out that the vision of NEP 2020 is to prepare the youth to be able to involve in building up the society into an all-round socio-economic development at the national and international level. In order to achieve this, Government should look into the care of ICT activities to attained quality education. Teaches are required to receive adequate training to be able to make themselves fit for quality online content creators to produce a learner –oriented learning. Blended approach will be adopted to substitute the traditional type of examination for different subjects.

Kasinathan (2021) stated that NEP 2020 stresses on the use of technology for teachers' development and that teacher itself should become skilled expert in digital to overcome many harmful things that technology have brought. WhatsApp is the most common social-media platform used by teachers during Covid-19 pandemic although it is not safe as there are certain risks when it comes to privacy. Artificial intelligence (AI)-based assessments will have a negative impact upon the learners as it can fail to encourage their conceptual understanding. Besides this, coding will be introduced at middle section which can make young children face the addiction and abuse of internet and technology at a very young age. So, NEP should also emphasize on the awareness of digital adoption and prevention on the misuse of technology among the students so that they will be safe from various threads of cyber-crimes and the negative impact of digitalization.

Arora (2021) evaluates the traditional methods of teaching as well as multimedia teaching and stated that traditional methods of teaching such as talk and chalk do not bring out the best in learners as there is no appropriate interaction between the students and teachers due to lack of proper feedback and response from the learners. Traditional method is just a one-way teaching where students listen and teachers talk without having a proper communication. Sharing of ideas will make both the students and teachers more creative. The use of technology makes learning more interesting and has a large impact upon the students and thus gained better understanding of the conceptual learning.

Rashmi (2021) examined the innovative new classroom and stated that our classroom needs to aligned with the latest technological developments to make the students technologically efficient. Coding which is the latest innovation in our educational system will break the old patter of one-way learning. It will help to grow the child's curiosity and give them the ability to observe and analyse everything around them. NEP, 2020 aimed to teach coding to school students from as early as class 6th onwards. This is a new concept which needs to be popularized as most teachers are unaware of it so teacher should get trained and so they can teach students.

Mondal (2021) investigated the initiatives taken by government of Seven Sister States (Arunachal Pradesh, Assam, Meghalaya, Manipur, Mizoram, Nagaland and Tripura) for digitizing education with reference to the Government of India (GoI) and found that digitalization of education is not so easy to achieve in India. These states struggle to afford quality network connections for education mainly due to India's extreme poverty. Students from disadvantage groups and weaker sections of the society could not afford digital education even during lockdowns when teaching was carried on through online mode at schools, colleges and universities. So, is suggest Government to make digital learning free or as much cheaper as possible to make those students easily accessible to online learning.

Gautam & Jadaun (2021) analyzed the role of technology in imparting meaningful education and found that the digital divide in the country is the main barrier to inequality of learning resources. Modern technology eliminates the barrier of time and place but in a developing country like India, particularly in rural area face major challenges of poor access to electricity, smartphones, computers and the internet. There is a huge lack of the required infrastructure that can provide uninterrupted connections and devices to teach students digitally. It suggests Government to take necessary steps to narrowed down this digital divide at a rapid rate.

Sharma (2022) stated that NEP 2020 focuses on a learner-oriented approach by improving and changing the assessment systems, adopting relevant digital infrastructure and curriculum at the secondary and at the higher level. Students will learn better if they are required to solve their problems by reading and searching their answers by their own before classes and giving them feedback to strengthen their mind through flipped classroom and blended learning. E merging technologies like 3D, simulation, robotics, artificial intelligence (AI) are also included in the new systems. However, several problems regarding technology such as poor connections, lack of information, poverty, reluctant to change attitude will always remain obstacle for the poor and rural regions. But this can be conquered and adapt gradually over time.

Sheergugri and Raj (2022) stated that NEP 2020 also aimed to minimized dropout rates and to maximized GER at higher level by establishing private sectors and autonomous institutions and help students with scholarships. Minimizing digital divide among users will enhance the benefit of digitalization in education and this can be achieved through making affordable computing devices easily available to them. Teachers should go through necessary training to handle online environment effectively. So, a relevant well-designed curriculum and education policy is required to achieve good quality education at all levels of education in our country.

Sharma, Devi, Raj and Kumar (2022) determined the students' perceptions on the application of blended learning (BLA) an approach towards NEP 2020 and found that students at higher level support the use of blended learning as an alternate method to traditional learning and also suggest to emphasize the use of blended learning approach at the university level towards achieving the aim of NEP.

Agarwal (2022) found that allocating more funds, training teachers to be specialized and to develop effective e-content and a relevant awareness campaign regarding technology are the key components toward successful implementation of digital learning laid down in NEP 2020.

Terang (2022) analyse the importance a flexibility of NEP 2020 and stated that the flexibility NEP is vital for the holistic development of the learner which helps them to pursue education as per their needs and interest. The pattern of new board examination also reduces stress among students and learning by mother tongue helps to develop their communication skills. Students from weaker sections and those who face challenges during their learning benefitted the most from Multiple Entry and Exit system as they can continue their learning as per their pace and convenience.

Khatak, Wadhwa and Kumar (2022) analyze the opinion of students and teachers about new education policy in light of NEP 2020 and stated that jumping directly to decisions and implement new policy in days or years is not a good idea. It takes long time to establish particular trend in cultural traditional India. Digitalizing education will be a major problem because it hinders the financially weaker students to enter the college as responded by more than sixty percent of the participants suggests the government to come up with some regulations on the same. So, in order to avoid any further chaos Government should look into the provision of basic infrastructure in developing countries like India and furnished those digital tools before implementing any policy as education is a pivotal milestone that shapes the future of youth and any country's economic growth.

4.3 AN OVERVIEW OF THE REVIEWED STUDIES

A successful implementation of technology in education requires a lot of efforts and resources. A stable internet connection is necessary to deliver education, only a well-trained instructor can hand on knowledge to learner, infrastructure and equipment is needed to settle digital learning at various levels of education. Geographical differences are a one big thing that hampers smooth deliverance of learning as most schools in rural areas find it hard to acquire technological tools where government schools particularly find it hard to afford such requirement. Moreover, in a place where traditional learning is popular, most stakeholders struggle to utilize these tools because they find it uneasy to use it. This situation can be overcome by giving them more time to adapt themselves and by providing them with adequate financial support in order to make it function. Government should also consider the care of ICT activities to attained quality education so that the society can develop itself to the national and international level in terms of socio-economic development. Minimizing digital divide will enhance the benefit of digitalization in education and this can be achieved through making affordable computing devices easily available to the users. Implementing digital learning needs a careful consideration and a thorough investigation before adopting a new policy as it requires a lot of efforts and financial support to carried out successfully.

4.4 HOW MUCH TECHNOLOGY READY ARE WE?

Based on the reviewed studies it is very evident that technological embedment in Indian scenario is not an easy task. Financial challenge is the major obstacle for people in countries like India. Most people in rural regions struggles to afford tools of digital learning even during pandemic times where institutions were shut down and only online mode is the key to continue learning. However, learning system needs to evolve if we want to upgrade our lifestyles.

The traditional method is mainly teacher-centered where the teacher talks and students listen without knowing the student's response and feedback. Teaching is mainly carried out on lecture notes and textbook based on theoretical with no practical aspects at all. This made the learning memorizing things without knowing exactly what the lessons wants to teach. However, the adoption of technology in learning makes the students more lively and keep them interest while learning their lessons. Flipped classroom where students solve and find their own answers using various technologies helps them to be an independent learner. Teaching through virtual reality helps the learner to become active and interest and they can retain their memory for a long time. Teaching through 3D printing technology, Cloud Computing and audio-visual learning tools helps them to gain better conceptual learning as per their pace and convenience.

Technological advances will deliver lots of positive vibes and development to the education-sub-systems and also brought revolutionary changes due to its countless importance for raising the standard of human lives. At first, the implementation and adoption will cost lots of efforts and finances but its importance and usefulness will last for a lifetime due to its inclusive and diverse traits.

However, it should be kept in mind that early exposure to technological devices and internet has many negative effects upon the lives of youngster. Abusing these technological devices can destroy the entire lives of children who are the foundation-to-be at an early age, if necessary, awareness and proper utilization of social media platforms are not given to them. Cyber-crimes, theft issues on documentation, unsafe privacy, distraction by the website, lack of seriousness in learners due to exposure to digital devices, etc. all can destroy the bright future of children if not given necessary precautions. So, the government should raise concerned regarding the adoption of technology in learning systems in order to construct a sound political, economic and society.

Digital learning will bring a lot of advantages to the learning system by making the students learn whatever and whenever they want through recorded lessons. Smart classroom is now widely used in different parts of India particularly at higher level which makes the students help to grasp the concept more rapidly and easily and students can focus more on digital learning than the traditional method of learning. However, everything has its pros and cons and this type of learning too had some disadvantages among the learner particularly among the young ones. Children at lower level tends to have less self-control when it comes to technology which can lead them to misuse of the tools rather than utilizing it for the better. Young children are more prone to addiction of technology if not giving them proper awareness and parents should look after them with proper care in order to avoid the victim of cyber threads.

4.5 CONCLUSION

Education system in India needs to catch up with the latest technological advancement in order to achieve quality learning at all levels of education. Digital learning will make the students to observe and analysed the things more curiously. India, being a developing country finds it hard to cope with the new learning system due to its poverty. Majority of people in India belongs to weaker and disadvantaged section of the society where these people struggle to afford connections and devices to support their learning. Moreover, introducing the new policy of technology needs a careful consideration and investigation to make it successfully worked. Adopting the new system to change our learning styles overnight will not always be the best idea as education is the key factor that shape the future of students and affect the societal and economic growth for every country. The new system should be able to produce students to be technologically efficient making them to become socially and emotionally competent to bear a meaningful life. Thus, financial support, a trained and qualified teacher, and by making digital learning more cheaper or free to students will be the best way to achieve the goals of policy.

References

1. Agarwal, K. (2022). Digitalized Education and NEP 2020: Reinventing the Classroom.

2. Arora, M. N. (2021). (INNOVATIVE CLASSROOM PRACTICES. *TWENTYFIRST CENTURY PUBLICATIONS PATIALA*, 56.

3. Gautam & Jadaun, (2021). ROLE OF TECHNOLOGY IN IMPARTING MEANINGFUL EDUCATION. Meaningful Education Edition-1 (pp 95-99).

4. Kalyani, P. (2020). An empirical study on NEP 2020 [National Education Policy] with special reference to the future of Indian education system and its effects on the Stakeholders. *Journal of Management Engineering and Information Technology*, *7*(5), 1-17.

5. Kasinathan, G. (2021) National Education Policy 2020–Imagining Digital Technologies as a Resource to Achieve Educational Aims. *Voices of Teachers and Teacher Educators*, 20.

6. Khatak, S., Wadhwa, N., & Kumar, R. (2022). NEP, 2020- A Review cum Survey Based Analysis of Myths and Reality of Education in India. *Int. J. Adv. Manage., Technol. Eng. Sci*, *12*(1), 12-22.

7. Kumar, A. (2022). Digital Education: Vision, Perspectives and Problems in Changing Paradigms of NEP-2020. *UGC Care List Group-1 Journal under Arts and Humanities Category* ,19 .111-117

8. Mondal (2021). Dgitalization Of Education in Seven Sister States. Meaningful Education Edition-1 (pp 81-88).

9. Muralidharan, K., Shanmugan, K., & Klochkov, Y. (2022). The New Education Policy 2020, Digitalization and Quality of Life in India: Some Reflections. *Education Sciences*, *12*(2), 75.

10. Rashmi, S. (2021). NEW WORLD: NEW CLASSROOM. Meaningful Education Edition-1 (pp 56-60).

11. Sharma. (2022). Integration of Technology: A Key Factor of NEP. *Journal of Emerging Technologies and Innovation Research*.

12. Sharma, M., Devi, M., Raj, T., & Kumar, S. (2022). A Study on Students' Perceptions on Application of Blended Learning (BLA) an Approach Towards NEP. *International Journal of Health Sciences, 6*, 1580-1589.

13. Sheergugri, A., & Raj, M. (2022). National Education Policy 2020 and Online and Digital Education - A Brief Review. *International Journal of Advanced Research in Science, Communication and Technology.*

14. Soy, S. (2021). A Revolutionary Step Towards Digital IndiaVision of NEP 2020. *Journal of Emerging Technologies and Innovation Research.*

15. Terang, A. (2022). FLEXIBILITY IN NEW EDUCATION POLICY (NEP) 2020 AND ITS SIGNIFICANCE FOR LEARNER. *Towards Excellence, 14*(3)

16. Venkateshwarlu, B. (2021). A critical study of NEP 2020: issues, approaches, challenges, opportunities and criticism. *International Journal of Multidisciplinary Educational Research, 2 (5)*, 2277-7881.

A Comparative Analysis of National Education Policies of India With Reference to Teacher Education

VELMALA SANTHOSH KUMAR

M.Ed

University of Hyderabad, Hyderabad.

Velmala.santhosh2@gmail.com

Mobile.No-9493532915

NIBEDITA AGRAWALLA

Field Assistant (IoE project)

Department of management studies

University of Hyderabad, Hyderabad.

nehaagrawalla200@gmail.com

Mobile.No-8249297849

ABSTRACT: *Indeed, National Education Policies aims to bring revolutionary and innovative transformation in Indian education System. The policies would bring a sea change in planning, implementation, governance and accreditation of educational courses and systems in India. The policy envisions that the well-qualified, skilled, quality and competent teachers are the essential and inseparable components of the process of imparting Outcome based as well as skills based. The first NPE 1968 programme had intended for a national school system, which meant that all pupils would have access to instruction of equivalent quality up to a certain degree, regardless of creed, sex or caste. The NPE, 1986 demands a significant increase in both the working conditions and the standard of teacher education. The Policy also highlights the responsibility of the instructors to the students, their parents, the community, and their own field. The National Education Policy-2020 seeks to cultivate students who will help shape the country's future. The centre of the significant changes to the educational system must be the teacher. Because they* *actually mould our next generation of citizens, the new education strategy must assist in re-establishing teachers as the most revered and significant members of our society at all levels. The study aims to compare the status of teacher education in India with reference to several national policies. The study used documentary analysis method by using secondary data which was collected from policy documents, journals, etc. This paper concentrates on highlighting the policies and with its comparison with the existing policy, merits, implications, and improvements.*

Key words*: Teacher Education, recommendations, commissions, National education policies, comparison.*

5.0 INTRODUCTION

Three separate education policies, the National Policy of Education (NPE) 1968, National Policy of Education 1986, and the latest National Education Policy 2020, have been in place in India since its independence.

Each nation's ability to advance depends on the quality of its educational system, which can only carry out its mandates with the help of the proper teaching personnel. Teachers are the ones who put all educational ideas into action and help pupils learn. As a result, the instructors have the greatest impact on any educational institution. The only profession where students are shaped into better citizens of the future is teaching. As teachers are said to as nation builders, it is their duty to instill in the next generation of people the necessary skills and a good outlook. Teachers are the leaders in fostering a learning society, national unity, and social cohesion. Such instructors are prepared or taught in teacher training institutions whether by face-to-face method or through distance mode, and they are competent of producing and transferring information in accordance with the wants and expectations of the community. As teacher education has shown that instructors can also be produced, the idea that teachers are born and not made has entirely transformed. It is a professional programme that strives to help teachers grow both as individuals and as agents of social change. The major goal of teacher education is to support student instructors in making judgments about how to apply fundamental educational ideas to actual classroom circumstances without ignoring the learner characteristics. Consequently, pedagogy and the effective use of instructional resources must be a part of secondary teachers' professional education. In order to assist student teachers, develop the knowledge and abilities needed to succeed as instructors of young students, the secondary level teacher education programme places a strong focus on this. The department of employment's glossary of training terms from 1971 defined a teacher as "systematic development of attitude, knowledge, skill, and behavior patterns required by an individual in order to perform adequately a given job or task."

5.1 IMORTANCE OF TEACHER EDUCATION POLICIES

A teacher must carry out several tasks as part of their job, organizing co-curricular activities, teaching, guiding and counseling the students, evaluating, communicating. Concerns about teacher policies have grown in recent years as a result of the significant economic and social changes that are taking place as well as the necessity for schools to provide the groundwork for lifelong learning. Major curriculum reforms have been implemented across the board in educational systems, and they have strengthened the emphasis on gender equality in the classroom, the use of ICT, and increased inclusion of kids with special needs. These changes need a reconsideration of the function of teachers as well as their training, jobs, and professional paths.

5.2 REVIEW OF LITERATURE

Kumar and Azad (2016) conducted a study on "Teacher education in India: Some Policy issues and Challenges". It is a study problem including educational challenges, worries, questions, and circumstances. It is an area of worry for declining values and concerns about the purpose and aims of education for society. The policies, issues, and proposed solutions for teacher education are covered in this essay. The fact that the (CTET/State TET) fail to demonstrate even the most fundamental knowledge base needed of a teacher indicates that there are some fundamental issues with the system that need to be addressed. I type "issues of teacher education" into Google. Developing high-quality teachers takes on different forms in different countries. When a country guarantees the admittance of brilliant people into the teaching profession, efforts are Among today's top worldwide issues are sustainable global development and their status, training, working conditions, retention, and recruiting.

Tatto (2009) conducted a study on "Teacher policy: a framework for comparative analysis". This article provides an international and comparative approach for analysing policy studies that are teacher-focused. The article reviews major empirical studies that highlight the influence of policy on addressing issues including teacher recruitment, education, selection, retention, and development by using the idea of the professional life cycle of teachers. The framework is helpful in recognising the strengths and flaws in the conceptualization and design of teacher-focused policy and research, the study claims in its conclusion. It also offers suggestions for how to create robust studies that will help shape future policy in this area.

Chang (2014) conducted a study on "TEACHER EDUCATION POLICIES AND PROGRAMS IN PAKISTAN: THE GROWTH OF MARKET APPROACHES AND THEIR IMPACT ON THE IMPLEMENTATION AND THE EFFECTIVENESS OF TRADITIONAL TEACHER EDUCATION PROGRAMS". In this study, the implementation of conventional post-baccalaureate teacher education programmes provided by state universities in a southern region of Pakistan was evaluated along with the value of traditional and off-campus programmes and the implications of market techniques. Results indicate that there is a disproportionately high demand for new teachers in the system compared to the number of people enrolling in market-model off-campus teacher education programmes. Both conventional and off-campus programmes have low programme implementation quality indicators. They came to the conclusion that many opportunistic companies now see teacher education as a commodity and a lucrative business.

Mallik conducted study on "National Education Policy 2020 and Its Comparative Analysis with RTE ". This essay focuses on emphasising NEP

2020's innovations and new adoptions as well as its advantages over current policy, ramifications, and improvements. India-centered education is the main objective of the 2020 National Education Policy. The policy was written with consideration for the nation's age, history, culture, traditions, and values. A diverse and interdisciplinary liberal arts education is the goal of this policy. This policy, as predicted, has many positive aspects, but it still has to be enhanced, according to the researcher. NEP 2020 may end up being the finest policy in the area of education and human resources with ongoing revisions to its policies.

Sing (2019) conducted a study on "A COMPARATIVE STUDY ON TEACHER EDUCATION IN "NATIONAL POLICY ON EDUCATION" (NPE-1986) AND "NATIONAL EDUCATION POLICY" (NEP-2019). The purpose of the current study is to compare the guidelines for teacher preparation in the "National Policy on Education" (1986) and the draught National Education Policy (2019). This investigation is qualitative. The purpose of this study is to compare and contrast the teacher education suggestions made in the NEPs of 1986 and 2019 in order to determine their parallels and differences. The results of this study show that NPE-1986 and NEP-2019 both addressed teacher education, and there are parallels in the fields of teacher education development, administrative structure, faculty, and four-year integrated B.Ed course pre-service and in-service teacher education. Differences exist in the field of Elementary level teacher education, NCTE's multimodal teacher education responsibilities, and faculty cadre qualifications. There are differences in the fields of transdisciplinary teacher education, primary level teacher preparation, NCTE responsibilities, faculty qualifications, and teacher education cadre.

DHOKE (2021) "COMPARATIVE STUDY OF OLD (1986) AND NEW (2020) NATIONAL EDUCATION POLICY". similarities and differences between the two education policies, the previous education policy (NPE 1986) and the new education policy (NEP 2020) were compared. Focusing on the contrasts will make it easier to comprehend the key goals of the new policy. According to the study's findings, NPE

1986's educational goals were to develop human resources generally, foster international cooperation and peace, and advance socialism, secularism, and democracy, while NEP 2020's educational goals are to maximise human potential and advance national development. To accomplish these goals, the curriculum is more likely to foster critical thinking. This goal is to enhance the talent and human resource base in India.

Avanaki and Sadeghi (2014) "conducted a study on A Comparative Study of Teacher Education in Iran and the UK". This paper contrasts the UK and Iranian systems for teacher education in a concise manner. It points out the primary contrasts, which are mostly those in policy and practice, between Iran and the UK, where teacher education used to be more or less decentralized but has since become centralized Secondly, how each event may improve them. Hence, the main goal of teacher education planning was to enhance classroom practices. According to the study, Iran's teacher training desperately needs to balance theory with practice. It follows that considerably more practice is required. As a result, research on the teaching tactics utilized in the two systems is now necessary, along with teacher training for the transfer of effective and useful teaching methods, mostly from the English system to a Iranian system.

JOSHI (2022) conducted "A COMPARATIVE STUDY OF NATIONAL EDUCATION POLICY 1986 AND 2020 IN CONTEXT TO THEIR STRUCTURE". to research and contrast the educational policies of 1986 and 2020. To differentiate between the two policies. To evaluate the performance of their structure. We may state that the new Education Policy 2020 appears to be more comprehensive and successful in the current year after examining the structures of both Policies. Quality In every nation, higher education plays a crucial role in the growth of the economy, social standing, acceptance of new technologies, and optimal human performance. The national education policy of any nation determines its growth rate and universal value. The National Education Policy of India 2020 is working towards reaching this goal by implementing cutting-edge policies to enhance the quality, appeal, affordability, and supply by opening up higher education to the private sector and at the same time expanding the supply at the same time, each higher education institution is subject to strict monitoring to preserve quality.

Akhtar, Hashmi, and Naqvi (2010) "conducted a study on A comparative study of job satisfaction in public and private school teachers at secondary level " . The goal of the current study was to compare the work satisfaction of instructors in public and private schools. The term "job satisfaction" describes how people feel and behave towards their jobs. Job satisfaction is shown by positive and favorable views about the job. Job discontent is indicated by negative and unfavorable attitudes about the position. According to studies, one of the key factors influencing teachers' favorable attitudes about their jobs is how satisfied they are with their jobs. The intricate link between a person's work happiness and satisfaction with other parts of his or her life has also attracted a lot of attention. A comparison of teachers' work satisfaction in public and private schools was predicted to show

Gupta and Achuth (2021) conducted a study on "National Education Policies of India: A Comparative Study with respect to Higher Education. In this study". An analysis of comparative studies in higher education. In this study, the National Education Policy (NEP) 2020 modifications have been compared directly to the National Policy of Education (NPE) 1986 changes in higher education in India. The discrepancies are reported together with the related comparative aim. In an effort to comprehend the impact, extent, and significance of those modifications on the higher education industry in India, a number of extracts from interviews with specialist academics on the NEP 2020 have also been mentioned. The goal of the current study is to examine the standard of higher education that future generations might anticipate by having readers use their own personal justifications in light of the findings. Through the observations made in these results of the research, if the recommended adjustments and alterations in the NEP 2020 are implemented successfully and efficiently at all levels, they have the potential to revolutionize and reshape India's education system and position it as a global leader.

5.3 OBJECTIVES

1. To know the status of Teacher Education in NPE 1968
2. To know the status of Teacher Education in NPE 1986
3. To know the status of Teacher Education in NEP2020
4. To study the evaluation of teacher education in India with reference to 1968,1986, 2020 policies.

5.4 METHODOLOGY

The qualitative research was used to expedite the comparative analysis of NPE'S

5.5 SOURCE OF DATA

The data is gathered from draughts of the NPE'S 1968, 1986 and 2020. While the secondary data is gathered from publications, websites, and books.

1. Overview of NPE-1968, NPE-1986, NEP-2020 policies:

It was a significant milestone for our educational system. The National Policy on Education (NPE), developed by the Government of India to promote and govern education in India, was the policy that we were previously adhering to. The policy encompassed both rural and urban India's primary and secondary education as well as higher education. Prime Minister Indira Gandhi issued the country's first NPE in 1968; Prime Minister Rajiv Gandhi issued the second in 1986; and Prime Minister Narendra Modi issued the third in 2020.

5.6 TO KNOW ABOUT THE NPE-1968 POLICIES FOR TEACHER EDUCATION

The policy recognized the importance of teachers in raising educational standards and advancing the country. It emphasized the need to enhance the position and working circumstances of teachers and advocated for academic freedom for them to conduct research, publish their own findings, and share their opinions on important national and international topics. Moreover, in-service teacher education received attention

5.7 TO KNOW ABOUT THE NPE-1986 POLICIES FOR TEACHER EDUCATION

Elementary teacher education

Professional education for teachers to work in elementary and secondary schools is required in all sections of the country. where teacher education is mostly conducted to begin the process of restructuring education, NPE recommended. It is intended that certain institutions would've been developed as District Institutes of (DIET), Education and Training both for pre-service and in-service courses of teachers in primary schools and for continuing education of the teachers. This would give special importance to the training of teachers in primary schools.

Secondary teacher education

Colleges of Teacher 'Education connected with universities would still be in charge of providing secondary teacher education. In addition to the standard B.Ed./M.Ed. courses, some colleges of teacher education will be formed as complete organizations that offer primary teacher education programmes and, maybe, four-year integrated courses following higher secondary stage. Moreover, facilities and personnel would be made available to these comprehensive institutions in order to support the work of the (SCERT). State Councils of Educational Research and Training Good universities' departments of education and colleges will also be granted autonomy in order to encourage innovations and experimentation.

In-service education for teachers

in-service education programmes for primary teachers will be the District Institutes of Education and Training, with support from the district's school complexes. The programmes would be expanded for secondary school teachers through teacher preparation programmes and Centers for Continued Education. The District Education Officer will assist in the smooth running of the programmes. All in-service education programme cannot be performed in a face-to-face format because to the sheer volume of participants. With the assistance of broadcasting organisations, distance inservice education will be produced and expanded. SCERTs would be given the tools they need to create instructional materials other than printed ones. For each SCERT, the very minimum necessary equipment to capture audio and video programmes will be made available. In a staggered basis, production facilities will also be made available to DIETs and the comprehensive college of education. The DIETs and universities' production facilities might not be of a professional calibre that would develop content that could be used in its own training programmes and shared with other sister organizations

Cadre of teacher education

For the hiring of employees in SCERTs, secondary teacher education programmes, and DIETs, a distinct cadre will be established. Those chosen for this cadre will receive benefits including lodging and placement at a better salary range. To guarantee that these people continue their education, special measures will be made. Also, a collaboration between teaching and teacher preparation will be organised. There will be enough reserve and supernumerary jobs developed in schools to allow members of this cadre to work as teachers for 1-2 years every 4-5 years.

5.8 TO KNOW ABOUT THE NPE-2020 POLICIES FOR TEACHER EDUCATION

By 2030, such interdisciplinary HEIs' 4-year integrated B.Ed. programme will be the required degree for instructors in public schools. The 4-year integrated B.Ed. will be a dual-major holistic Bachelor's degree, with majors in Education and other subjects.

The 4 years integrated B.Ed programme with multidisciplinary institution and environment by implemented in 2030.

The Department of Universities has been advised by NEP to improve and expand the areas for research and innovation in education. The Department will arrange for pre-service training and ongoing (CPD) continuous Professional Development for teachers in both higher education and school settings. Additionally, it advocated for adequate funding, capacity planning for teacher education by RUSA in conjunction with state and federal governments, faculty strength in teacher education, the availability of online courses, interdepartmental cooperation for special subjects, research-based teacher preparation, postgraduate and doctoral programmes in education, and research-based teacher preparation.

From teacher education institutes, a good teacher may develop an excellent teacher. In this regard, NEP has suggested that hiring professors with specialty in areas of curriculum and pedagogy, basic areas of education technology, and research in education, which requires that they hold Masters' and PhDs in a variety of relevant fields, be done. Not everyone is required for the execution of the faculty profile. At least 50% of the faculty has a Doctorate, but it will be highly recognised if they also have teaching and field research experience. "It is also preferred, but not required, for professors to hold at least one degree in education (M.Ed., Masters, or PhD in Education). A minimum number of hours of practical teaching experience, acquired through teaching assistantships and other opportunities, will also be required of Ph.D. candidates. For this reason, Ph.D. programmes at colleges across the nation will be reoriented.

5.9 SIMILARITIES

- The three has been suggested by policies that teacher education should be developed.
- Three policies faculty and administrative organisation of the teacher education institution, policies have been proposed.
- 1986 and 2020 the policies have proposed for the four-year integrated B.Ed. course for teacher education.
- Pre-service and in-service teacher educations have been included in three policies.

5.10 DIS SIMILARITIES

- Overall, the NPE of 1986 produced a pool of educated and skilled people who contributed toward the value chain; but the NEP of 2020 aspires to produce people who will produce value propositions.
- The qualifications of the faculty at Teacher Education Institutions have been proposed by NEP-2020; however, nothing has been indicated in NPE-1968, NPE-1986.

5.11 CONCLUSION

The similarities and differences between NPE-1986 and NEP-2019, these two programmes are crucial for improving teacher education. As a result, much like a relay race, NPE-1986 has given the torch of teacher education to NEP-2019. The quality of teacher education has been proposed by NEP-2019, although it is unclear how and to what extent this recommendation may be put into practice in the educational system.

References

1. Aithal, P. S., & Aithal, Shubhrajyotsna (2020). Analysis of the Indian National Education Policy 2020 towards Achieving its Objectives. International Journal of Management, Technology, and Social Sciences (IJMTS), 5(2), 19-41. DOI: http://doi.org/10.5281/zenodo.3988767

2. Avalos, B. (1998). School-based teacher development the experience of teacher professional groups in secondary schools in Chile. Teaching and Teacher Education, 14(3), 257–271.

3. Brumfit, C.J. (1986). ESP for the University. Oxford: Pergamon Books Ltd, British Council.

4. Coppock, D. (1997). Respectability as a Prerequisite of Moral Character: the Social and Occupational Mobility of Pupil Teachers in the Late Nineteen and Early Twentieth Centuries. in History of Education, 26(2), 165-186.

5. Document on National Policy on Education 1986: https://www.education.gov.in/sites/upload_files/mhrd/files/ upload_document/npe.pdf

6.   Draft National Education Policy 2019: https://www.education.gov.in/ sites/upload_files/mhrd/files/Draft_ NEP 2019 EN Revised.pdf

7.   University of Mumbai, (2016). Concept of teacher education. Retrieved   fromarchive.mu.ac.in/myweb_test/ma%20edu/ Teacher%20Education%20-%20IV.pdf retrieved on14.11.2016

8.   K. Vinothkumar. (2018) Earlier National Education Policies of India- A Review, International Researc Journal of Engineering and Technology (IRJET), 5(12), 1148-1151.

9.   National Education Policy 2020, Ministry of Human Resource Development, Government of India https:// www.education.gov. in/sites/upload_files/mhrd/files/ NEP_Final_English_0.pdf

10.   National Policy on Education 1986, Ministry of Human Resource Development, Government of India https://www.education.gov. in/sites/upload_files/mhrd/ files/upload_document/npe.pdf

11.   National Policy on Education 1968, Ministry of Human Resource Development, Government of India https://www.education.gov. in/sites/upload_files/mhrd/   files/document-reports/NPE   1968. pdf

Evaluation of National Education Policies: Post-Independence to Present

H. Malsawmdawnga*

Dr. Pooja Walia**

ABSTRACT: *The education policies are framed to regulate and promote the education system of any country. The Ministry of Education, Government of India, has published three National Education Policies since its independence. The first education policy was introduced in 1968, emphasizing compulsory education for children up to the age of 14 years. It gave a new direction to standardize education within the country. It was instrumental in creating a structure of 10+2+3. The second education policy, i.e., the National Policy of Education (NPE) 1986, focused on removing the disparity between diverse social groups. Various educational schemes were started under NPE (1986). The NPE (1986) gave its recommendations almost on every aspect of our education with a plan of action to translate the suggestion into action. The NPE 1986 was modified in 1992, adopting a new policy based on the 'Common Minimum Program. 'The third education policy was introduced in 2020, called the 'National Education Policy (NEP).'The NEP 2020 emphasized a holistic approach with multidisciplinary courses and students, facilitating them with a bucket of choosing subjects of interest. The NEP 2020 is recommended to replace the 10+2+3 structure with the new 5+3+3+4 structure. The aim of the policies is perfect in many ways, but it is the implementation that lies the key to success. Thus, this paper focuses on evaluating the critical aspects of the National Education Policies since the evaluation results will be helpful for future education.*

Keywords: National Education Policy, Objectives, Implementations, and Outcomes.

*Research Scholar, Department of Education, Mizoram University, Aizawl. Mobile No.: 9874551819, Email: emesdonga2011@gmail.com

**Assistant Professor, Department of Education, Mizoram University, Aizawl. Mobile No.: 8529201718, Email: mzut273@mzu.edu.in

6.0 INTRODUCTION

The education policies are framed to regulate and promote the education system in any country. The Ministry of Education has launched three National Education Policies since its independence in India. Firstly, National Policy on Education (NPE) was launched in 1968, covering 18 years; it was known as NPE 1968. The second educational policy was launched in 1986, known as National Policy on Education (NPE) 1986; modified in 1992, the policy covered 34 years. The period of the NPE 1968 and 1986 had gone, and though their aims and objectives still needed to be fully achieved, favorable changes were achieved to develop national education. The third policy, 'National Education Policy (NEP) 2020', is recently launched in the country. This paper evaluates the critical aspects of the NPE 1968 and 1986 and the newly introduced NEP 2020 towards achieving its aims and objectives.

6.1 NATIONAL POLICY ON EDUCATION 1968

The first National Policy on Education was introduced in 1968 based on the report and recommendations of the Kothari Commission (1964-1966), aiming at restructuring and providing equal educational opportunities to all. It was the first time the nation had such a policy to establish national growth, a sense of common citizenship and culture, and strengthen national integration.

NPE1968 recommended that children up to 14 receive free and compulsory education. The program suggested that all the enrolled children in the school should complete the prescribed course satisfactorily, aiming at reducing the prevailing wastage and stagnation in schools. The program was developed to remove the barriers to quality education across all parts of the nation. Great efforts were put into providing free and compulsory education to all children up to the age of 14 years. Suitable programs were developed to ensure that every child who enrolled in the schools should complete the prescribed course. Although great efforts were put into trying to achieve the goal, the goal of universal education still needed to be ascertained. However, the first attempt at universal education paved the way for the future (MHRD, 1968 &OIS, 2021).

The policy recommended prioritizing science education and research to accelerate the growth of the national economy. Accordingly, Science and Mathematics were getting more priority under NPE 1968 as the two subjects were recommended to be an integral part of general education till the end of school education (GKtoday, 2016).

The NPE 1968 recommended a standard education structure in the form of 10+2+3. It was introduced across the country, and the new education pattern was accepted across all parts of the country. From that time, the country got a uniform schooling pattern of 10+2+3. Introducing the new education structure 10+2+3 was certainly successful under the NPE 1968(MHRD, 1968 & OSI, 2021).

Further, the NPE 1968 focused on the need to promote the condition of teachers. More importance was given to teachers' emoluments and service conditions because of professional competence. The policy gave more importance to teachers' qualification and their training programs.

The NPE 1968 recommended promoting a 'three language formula'- using Hindi, English, and one regional language. It was criticized instant across the country on the ground that Hindi was thrust upon the students. It was also criticized that the policy needed to give detailed guidelines for its practical implementation. However, people welcomed the policy because it was India's first-ever national education policy (Sharma, 2004). Despite various criticism, the NPE 1968 was known as the first systematic attempt to promote Indian education. Implementing the three-language formula was successful under NPE 1968(Manjunatha, 2016).

The policy developed Hindi as a national language and promoted Hindi as a common language for all Indians, including non-Hindi-speaking states, given national integration. At the same time, the policy inspired me to realize the value of ancient Sanskrit. The policy promoting Hindi and Sanskrit was somewhat successful (Singh, 2023).

In order to promote national education, the NPE 1968 suggested using 6% of the national income for education. However, the policy struggled to reach the targeted 6% due to the country's GDP fluctuation due to the war with Pakistan, hyper-increased expenditure on defense, etc. However, there was a favorable impact on the investment rate of GDP on education positively (OSI, 2021).

The policy did not succeed in bringing about the change that was expected because of the following drawbacks:

i. *Lack of proper action plan:* The policy needed a series of proper action plans. The authorities could not give special consideration to some issues and specific transactions.

ii. *Deficiency of funds*: India was suffering from a deficiency of funds as a result of *the Indo-Pak War of 1965, other border disputes, increase in defense spending(Mamoon, 2017).*

iii. *Problem concerning the constitution of India*: Education was on the state list during that time, but the center could not control the education policy of states (21st Constitutional Amendment, 1967). However, in addition to achievement in certain items, the policy put forward a valuable lesson for the following national education policy.

6.2 NATIONAL POLICY ON EDUCATION 1986

Ministry of Education, Government of India launched the second National Policy on Education in 1986. The National Policy of Education (NPE) 1986 focused on removing the disparity between diverse social groups. The NPE 1986 was modified in 1992, adopting a new policy based on the 'Common Minimum Program.'

The policy's objectives focused on providing education to whole sections of society, particularly on ST, SC, and OBC. The policy highlighted the promotion and gradation of the role of IT in education. The achievement in restructuring teacher education, early childhood care, women's empowerment, and adult literacy was remarkable. 216 DIETs were established in various parts of the country during the period (Education for All India, 2020). Open schools were established by 1990 in a phased manner. IGNOU is also the result of the NPE.

The commission led by Acharya Ramamurti assessed the impact of the NPE 1986 in 1990, and the Central Advisory Board of Education led by N. Janadhana Reddy reassessed the impact of the policy for the second time suggesting some modifications in NPE. The National Program of Action (NPA) of 1992 came out after the Central Advisory Board of Education submitted its report in 1992, and the NPA focused on the 'Common Minimum Program' The NPA was implemented, emphasizing quality enhancement and aiming at the considerable transformation of the Indian educational system. More importance was given to developing moral values among students, along with stress on bringing education closer to life (Ranganathan, 2007).

Remarkably, the NPE 1986 brought various government programs and schemes such as SSA, Mid-Day Meal Scheme, Nadodaya Vidyalayas, and Kendriya Vidyalaya. Besides, Under the NPE 1986, IT was started in education, recognizing its usefulness in the teaching-learning process. During 2002-2003 and 2008-2009, 1,48,492 new primary schools and 1,33,277 new upper primary schools were opened under the SSA scheme. In addition to this, an additional 8,00,000 classrooms were built, significantly expanding access to the elementary level (Joint Review Mission, 2009).

In order to continue and accelerate the ongoing program of the first NPE on free and compulsory education for children in the age group of 6-14 years, the government introduced the Right to Education Act (2009) on April 1, 2010. The RTI Act (2009) has been implemented under the 42nd constitutional amendment. According to the 42nd constitutional amendment, education and four other subjects were transferred from the State list to the Concurrent list. The movement was more successful when compared to the previous movement under the NPE 1968. However, the RTE encountered several hurdles at the implementation level because of the following;

1. It covered children aged between 6-14 years only.
2. The Act was gender-neutral.
3. The act did not discuss the right to education for children with disability.
4. Act was silent about the post-elementary stage.
5. School management was dishonest and manipulated while executing the act (MHRD, 1998).

Despite all government efforts in light of NPE 1986, the goal of universalizing education has yet to be realized. Overall, NPE 1986 brought various transformations in every field of education viz, school education, teacher education, and higher education; however, it failed to improve the quality of education in terms of creating graduates with employability skills and failed to generate research output in terms of patents and scholarly publication (Aithal & Aithal, 2020).

6.3 NATIONAL EDUCATION POLICY 2020

After 34 years, the third education policy was launched on July 29, 2020, after lengthy deliberations since its inception in 2015. The draft was prepared under former Indian Space Research Organization (ISRO) chief Krishnaswamy Kasturirangan. The final draft consisted of 63 pages containing 27 chapters in 4 sections. The primary focus areas are School Education; Higher Education; Teacher Education; Professional Education; Adult Education; Vocational Education; and Technology Integration in Education System. It proposes more comprehensive targets for the growing young population of India. It aims *to bring reformation in schools and colleges to prepare India as a global knowledge superpower. The government is moving forward to implement the policy in a phased manner.*

NEP 2020 envisions a massive transformation in a school education system that creates an equitable and vibrant knowledge society inculcated with a value system that enables them to be aware of Bharat's cultural and knowledge heritage. Policy attracted the concentration of educationists towards the knowledge treasure of India available in Vedas, Upanishads, manuscripts, etc., written in the Sanskrit Language. A significant policy recommendation is a change in the national education system, i.e., from 10+2+3 to 5+3+3+4. *The new structure will involve five years of the foundational stage, three years of the preparatory stage, three years of the middle stage, and four years of secondary education.*

The execution of the new education structure will need several new school buildings. Parting classes I and II from Primary school and setting up the Foundational stage will give rise to several new rooms. Again, there can be hurdles concerning the combination of classes 9 to 12, i.e., high schools and higher secondary schools, concerning administrative matters; some states like Mizoram have experienced such problems. In the meantime, a detailed action plan is still awaited, including how all these things will be done. On the other hand, the NEP 2020 emphasized a more holistic approach with multidisciplinary courses, and students are facilitated with a bucket of choosing subjects of their interest. *It envisages flexibility in a student's choice of subjects removing the distinction between the streams- science, commerce, and arts; students will have a more significant number of choices in the subject. The new policy is expected to give better educational careers to more students nationwide.*

Further, NEP 2020 emphasized the inculcation of core values and principles that enhance the foundational skills of literacy and numeracy, higher-order thinking skills such as critical thinking and problem-solving, and soft skills such as social and emotional skills. It is directly associated with the quality of teacher education. Teacher quality is the most critical factor in school factor influencing school achievement (Mishra, 2021). *The NEP 2020 envisages that the minimum educational qualification for teachers would be a four-year duration integrated B.Ed. Degree by 2030, irrespective of the stages aiming at the up gradation of schools and the teaching profession.* According to NEP 2020, teacher education must move into multidisciplinary colleges and universities by 2030. Only educationally sound, multidisciplinary, and integrated education programs will be in force by 2030. The admission to pre-service teacher preparation programs shall be through suitable subject and aptitude tests conducted by National Testing Agency. All stand-alone

Teacher Education Institutions (TEIs) will be required to convert to multidisciplinary institutions by 2030 to offer a 4-year integrated teacher preparation program. The NCTE will prepare a detailed action plan for implementing the critical aspects of NEP 2020 related to TEIs, including how TEIs will move to multidisciplinary colleges and universities by 2030 in a phased manner. (NCERT, n.d.).

Under NEP 2020, the government aims to achieve a Gross Enrolment Ratio (GER) of 50% in higher education by 2035 and 100% in primary and secondary education by 2030. The target for GER is commendable and very challenging for the country. However, it is a hard target because the present Indian GER in higher education is only 26.3% and only 73.79% in secondary education. How realistic are these high targets amidst the considerable dropout level across the country? Such setbacks are visible clearly in some states like Bihar (Kansal, 2023). Meanwhile, such issues should be considered while setting a high target for GER.

The policy put forward an enlargement of the scope of the Right to Education so that; the Education Department will reserve 25% of seats in private unaided schools across the country; for children from socially and economically weaker sections without giving proper incentives to private schools. Private schools are being run on profit motive and business-oriented; they dislike admitting children from low-income families and even disabling them because they cannot pay school fees properly.

The increase in the investment rate, i.e., 6% of the GDP in the education sector, will have a desirable result in the field of education. The expected rate will equal the prevailing rate in some countries like the USA (6%), New Zealand (6.4%), UK (6.2), etc. if achieved (World Bank, 2022). The government needs to find more revenues to fund this movement. Will the central government bear the burden, or will the states bear the same? One needs to answer.

The NEP 2020 has supported the three Language Policy. It was first incorporated into NEP 1968 in Hindi-speaking states: English, Hindi, and a modern Indian language in Non-Hindi speaking states, English, Hindi, and One of the Indian languages. According to the NEP 2020, schools will use their mother tongue/

regional language till Class 5, wherever possible. The aim is desirable from its appearance. However, problems arise, including which mother tongue will be chosen for a particular place with more than one mother tongue. Children with a parent with transferable jobs can face more problems with the imposition of their mother tongue. Further, NEP 2020 provides for setting up a Gender Inclusion Fund (GIF) to build the nation's capacity to provide equitable quality education for all girls and transgender students. The fund will focus on ensuring 100% enrollment of girls in schooling. *However, it remains to be seen how effectively the government can implement this policy, as one of the most significant problems in India is the implementation of laws and policies.*

As a result of the low level of investment in research and innovation, the National Research Foundation (NRF) is soon to be set up as an autonomous body envisaged under the New Education Policy 2020(The Indian Express, 2020). The government of India proposes to set up National Research Foundation with a total outlay of Rs. 50,000 crores over five years to strengthen the research ecosystem in the country (NCES, 2022). In academic institutions, particular focus will be given to universities and colleges where research capacity is developing. The aim of the policy is laudable if achieved.

6.4 CONCLUSION

All three national education policies set a similar expenditure goal on education at 6% of the GDP. However, the actual expenditure on education during the previous two National Education Policies needed to improve. The percentage of GDP has stayed stagnant at 2.9% since 2019. *During NPE 1968 and 1986, the 10+2 structure was successfully implemented across all parts of the country; the people accepted it without any problem, and there was a clear distinction between subject streams with minimal choice. However, the NEP 2020 proposes to use a new structure, i.e., 5+3+3+4. Accordingly, flexibility in choosing the subjects will facilitate students a lot. In the meantime, the new structure will have different requirements for teachers, resource persons, infrastructure, and administrative management.*

Despite significant efforts, the universal education program's goal was unsuccessful due to some mistakes like the absence of a proper action plan under the NPE 1968. The second attempt at the universal education program was successful to a great extent under NPE 1986 with the help of the 42nd constitutional amendment and the lessons from the previous NPE. The NEP 2020 proposes to ensure universal access to school education at all levels by providing infrastructure support and tracking students' progress and learning levels. On the other hand, NPE 1968 emphasized in-service teachers' education more, while NPE 1986 focused on the importance of both pre-service and in-service teachers' education. The NEP 2020 is quite different from the previous policies concerning teacher education; it proposes B.Ed. Degree as a minimum qualification for teachers irrespective of the stages with setting up of multidisciplinary integrated teachers' training institution. Such that, B.Ed. degree will be required to be a teacher even at the lowest level, i.e., the foundational stage. B.Ed. degree is recommended from foundational to secondary stage; it is a matter of significant issue.

Implementing the three-language formula was concluded satisfactorily under the NPE 1968(Manjunatha, 2016). The same was focused on by the NPE 1986, and the NEP 2020 also focuses on the three-language formula with a slightly different structure from one policy to another. *The NPE 1968 and 1986 contributed a lot to the up gradation of national education. In comparison to the 1968 policy, the 1986 policy performed better. Again, the NEP 2020 is much broader in scope when compared to NPE 1986(Sundaram, 2020). The government should control many issues like excessive privatization of education, corruption, mismanagement in education, bureaucratic control, etc., to avoid possible setbacks in achieving the goals of the NEP 2020. Otherwise, the expected change will become a distant dream. We must learn things from our history.*

References/ Bibliography

1. Aithal, R. S., &Aithal, S. (2020). Analysis of the Indian National Education Policy 2020 towards Achieving its Objectives.

International Journal of Management, Technology and Social Sciences (IJMTS), 5(2), 19-36. https://doi.org/10.5281/zenodo.3988767

2. Ministry of Human Resource Development, Government of India. (2020). National Education Policy 2020. https://www.education.gov.in

3. Ministry of Human Resource Development, Government of India. (1998). National Education Policy 1986. https://www.education.gov.in

4. Ministry of Human Resource Development, Government of India. (1968). National Education Policy 1968. https://www.education.gov.in

5. Gupta, A. (2022). Critical Analysis of NPE-1986 and NEP-2020. *International Journal of Sciences and Research (IJSR), 11*(4), 148-153. https://doi.org/10.21275/MR22321203711

6. National Council of Educational Research & Training, Delhi(n.d.). National Education Policy, 2020: Teacher and Teacher Education. https://www.education.gov.in

7. Kansal, K. (2023). Critical Evaluation of Nation Educational Policy, 2020. *Legal Service India E-Journal, 1*(1). 1–14. https://www.legalserviceindia.com

8. Singh, B.M. (2023). The Significant Shift in the Education Policy of India. *IUJ Journal of management. 2*(12), 1–6. http://journal.iujharkhand.edu.in

9. Janardhana Reddy Committee (1992). The Implementation of the National Policy on Education 1986.https://jinitha.weebly.com/national-policy-on-education

10. Sundaram, K.M. (2020). National Education Policy 1986 Vs. National Education Policy 2020- A Comparative Study. *International Research Journal on Advanced Science Hub. 2*(10), 127-131. https://rspsciencehub.com

11. Komal. (2021). Impact of National Education Policy on Teaching Recruitment 2022. *Byju's Exam Prep.1*(30), 1–5. https://byjuexamprep.com/national-education-policy-impact-on-teaching-recruitment-i

12. Mamoon, D. (2017). Missing the Peace Train in 2006 Economic and Political Dynamics of India Pakistan Hostility. *Munich Personal Repec Archive. 3*(10), 1–10. https://mpra.ub.uni-muenchen.

13. Govt. of India: Ministry of Human Resource Development. (1998). New Education Policy 1986 as Modified in 1992. https://www.education.gov.in

14. The Economic Survey of India 2022-23. (2023). https://m.economictimes.com

15. World Development Indicator. (2021). https://databank.worldbank

16. National Centre for Education Statistics. (2022). Online Education Database. https://nces.ed.gov

17. The Indian Express. (2020, September 11). PM Modi Speech on NEP 2020 Highlights. https://indianexpress.com

18. GKtoday. (2016, October 1). National Education Policies 1968 and 1986. https://www.gktoday.in/topic

19. Online Schools India. (2021). Key Highlights of the National Policy of Education 1968. https://onlineschoolsindia.in

20. Joint Review Mission. (2009). Rashtriyamadhyamik Shiksha Abhiyan (RMSA).https://www.education.gov.in

21. Ranganathan, S. (2007). Educational Reform and Planning Challenge, Kanishka Publishers, Distributors, New Delhi. http://14.139.82.46:8080/newgenlibctxt

22. The Twenty-first Amendment of the Constitution of India: The Constitution (Twenty-first Amendment) Act, 1967. https://legislative.gov.in

23. Education for All India. (2020). District Institute of Education and Training (DIETs). https://educationforallinindia.com

Gandhiji's Educational Legacy and NEP 2020

L.K Lalbiakfeli* & Dr. Muttu Vemula**

*Research Scholar, Department of Education, Mizoram University,
Mizoram- 796004
Email: biakfeli96@gmail.com
**Assistant Professor, Department of Education, Mizoram University,
Mizoram- 796004
Email: drmuttuedu@gmail.com

ABSTRACT: *Gandhiji proposed the Wardha System of Basic Education in 1937, which was based on his ideas on education. He believed that education plays an important role in forming an ideal citizen who has a harmonious development of all four aspects of human personality. He advocated activity-centered methods and medium of instruction in Mother Tongue, craft-centered education, and a link between education and vocational training. He also proposed that industrialization should be slowed down and modified in accordance with a strategy for social and political advancement. His Utopia envisioned the ideal citizen as a hard-working, self-respecting, and giving person who lived in a small town. This is the mental model that drives his instructional strategy.*

Keywords: *National Education Policy 2020, holistic development, mother tongue.*

7.0 INTRODUCTION

Gandhiji's Basic Education was the culmination of his educational philosophy. His fundamental education takes on the difficult task of educating young students to become morally upright, self-reliant, socially positive, economically productive, and responsible future citizens, which can help to solve the unemployment problem by empowering youth to become self-employed through skill training. Gandhiji was convinced that in order for a child to properly develop into a human being, education should encourage that child's full potential. This is how one can realize the Truth of God, which is the ultimate aim of existence when one's personality is fully and harmoniously developed. Gandhiji has stated this himself: "I define education as the process of bringing out the greatest qualities in a child's or a man's body, intellect, and spirit. Neither the start nor the end of education is literacy. This is merely a method for educating a person, male or female."

7.1 REVIEW OF RELATED LITERATURE

Vaishnav, Harmik (2019) conducted a study on "Gandhi's Nai Talim and Liberal Studies: A Comparative Study of the two models of Education" and concluded that the two models ultimately aim to realize the overarching goals of education by creating microcosmic individuals who then create microcosmic societies and microcosmic worlds.

Bhattacharya, and Dr. Nirupama. (2019) conducted a study on "The Concept of Ideal State and Freedom in Gandhi's Philosophy and Underlying Relation" and concluded that only when there is social, political, and economic concord can the perfect state be created. This study aims to be as intellectual and analytical as possible while correlating many concepts to show how well they work together. It is evaluated how Gandhi's ideas of swaraj, Sarvodaya, man, truth, god, and ramrajya apply to education reform and the whole development of human personality under the influence of soul, truth, and nonviolence. One of Gandhi's main philosophical tenets is the idea of freedom, which inspires the idea of an ideal state.

Bajaj, Dr. Abhilasha. (2020) conducted a study on "Finding NAI TALIM in the Vision of NPE 2020: Exploring the Resemblance" and concluded that Gandhi's philosophy of education is a cohesive synthesis of pragmatism, naturalism, and idealism. His "Nai Talim" was distinctive in that it advocated imparting education through folkcraft. The goal was to make teaching a craft the focal point of the entire curriculum. Gandhi's educational principles are in line with NEP 2020.

Jha, Dr. RK (2020) conducted a study on "The Impact Of Gandhian Educational Ethics in Shaping National Education Policy,2020" and concluded that Gandhi's ideas served as a significant inspiration for the NEP, 2020 while developing its policies. India is a democratic country, and one of education's main goals is to meet the requirement and wants of the vast majority of its citizens. Education should place a strong emphasis on Swadeshi, social, cultural, and individual values. The growth of the intellect and body have to be prioritized as well. A key concern is economic development. NEP 2020 was developed to fulfill the needs of the populace and create a thriving India while keeping in mind the nation's diversity.

Pandey, Pramod Kumar, Ghosh, Amatava., Lahiri, Biswajit. (2020) conducted a study on the Educational Thoughts of Mahatma Gandhi" and concluded that Gandhi's Education-related concepts evolved for both the present and the years to come. His educational approach was activity-centered, craft-focused, life-focused, and society-focused. He believed that education was a powerful force for human emancipation, as well as for personal, social, and national growth.

Sharma, Sarika (2021) conducted a study "A Study on Similarities between Gandhiji's Basic Education and New Education Policy 2020" and concluded that in the context of our current educational reform, it is entirely appropriate to assert that the fundamental concepts of basic education are still applicable and productive. They are pertinent to be applied as the foundational ideas of contemporary education. Gandhiji's desire for education has been realized in many ways by our NEP 2020.

Thirugnanam, Balasubramanian, Venkatraman, V., Dhanalakshmi, N. (2021) conducted a study on "Gandhi's view on Swadeshi Nationalism" and concluded that Gandhi developed an entire approach that essentially addressed every part of human life since his life was holistic and undivided. And that is the most distinctive aspect of his thinking, which has the potential to become a tenet of the resurrection of humanity. He even went so far as to emphasize the unity of all creation, including sentient and non-sentient beings. Unfortunately, independent India was unable to recognize the revolutionary nature of its views and rejected them during the early years of independence. It is now clear that India, and perhaps the entire world, will have to follow Gandhi's example in order to effectively handle the challenges.

Panda, Ranjan. (2022) conducted a study on "Making of a Man: A Reading of Gandhi's Philosophy in the 21st Century and concluded that we must think carefully about Gandhi's many interactions and experiments that reveal the truth by if we want to truly comprehend this basic fact of human life, we must follow the road of nonviolence. Gandhi's commitment to truth and nonviolence has immense epistemic power to awaken us to a world of self-knowledge that would aid humanity in becoming the kind of man that a successful civilization requires.

Sutradhar, Dhananjoy (2022) write an article on "Educational Philosophy of Mahatma Gandhi" and concluded that Gandhiji made significant contributions to education. His pedagogical philosophy was a mix of naturalism and idealism. He proposed ideas for shaping the education system in such a way that it secured an individual's overall growth.

Roy, Dr. Deepa., Mitra, and Joyita. (2022) conducted a study on "Modern Era of Gandhi's Philosophy & Education" and concluded that on the one hand, education is viewed as an investment in the potential for productivity that should enhance the social and economic aspects of society. True education eliminates all barriers and makes society transparent. Gandhi's idea of education is mirrored in today's society in which we live. It appears that Gandhi's theory is still relevant in light of this modern society.

Sahu, Nirmala., Behera, and Harekrushna. (2022) conducted a study on the "Relevance of Gandhian Thought of Education in Present Day Context" and concluded that education was not education if character development was not a goal. He believed that a good citizen's cornerstone is a strong character. Gandhiji aspired to create small, self-sufficient villages with hard-working, self-respecting, and charitable residents who shared a sense of community. In order for children to develop their minds, body, and spirit in a way that is harmonious and also meets the needs of their future lives, he desired that certain local handicrafts would be produced as a means of instruction.

7.2 GANDHI'S EDUCATIONAL PHILOSOPHY

Gandhiji's pedagogical approach has received widespread acclaim and acceptance. Gandhi had a very pragmatic perspective on education and thought it should assist a person grow in all areas, not only his ability to read and write. He spoke extensively about the type of education Indian schools should provide for their kids. Gandhi argued that the most crucial element for development is education. He thought that education is a crucial tool for enabling individuals to achieve freedom and independence. A new generation that is more socially conscious and committed to making India a better place for all has benefited from his teachings and way of life.

The Immediate Aim includes a number of things, including sociological growth, moral development, vocational development, and cultural development.

Ultimate Aim in which Gandhiji held the view that a learner should develop the virtues of truth and ahimsa and self-realize God.

According to Mahatma Gandhi, education should serve as a springboard for action. These are the tenets around which Mahatma Gandhi's educational philosophy for India was built:

1. Education should be free, required, and available to every child from the age of 7 to 14 years.
2. Local language should be used as the medium of teaching.
3. English should not be taught to children as a subject.
4. Literacy alone does not constitute education.
5. Education should also instill human values in children.
6. Education should help children develop their full potential in accordance with the society of which they are an essential part.
7. Education should promote the child's balanced growth of their body, mind, heart, and soul.

8. Crafts should be emphasized in education to help children develop their financial independence.

9. All education must be delivered through a useful craft or industry, and there must be a useful connection to that industry.

10. Moreover, all courses should be taught using some locally produced crafts.

11. The industry should allow children to gain valuable work experience through hands-on work.

12. Education should be made financially independent by engaging in some useful work.

13. Education should promote financial security and independent living.

14. School should be a place of activity where the child can become involved in numerous activities and get new experiences that will lead to new research.

15. Citizens should be useful, accountable, and dynamic as a result of their education.

7.3 NATIONAL EDUCATION POLICY 2020:

The National Education Policy, 2020, which succeeds the NPE, 1986 after 34 years, is the first new education policy to be launched in India in the twenty-first century. Prior educational strategies have mostly concentrated on concerns of access and equity, but as the global economy and job market change, it is more crucial than ever for kids to learn not just what to learn but also how to learn. Hence, education must shift away from teaching subjects and towards teaching students how to be innovative. By 2035, the Gross Enrolment Ratio will have increased to 50%, with the goal of achieving holistic productivity, equitable access, and inclusive education for all students, regardless of social or economic background. NPE 2020 wants to create:

1. Good people who can think and act rationally, have compassion and empathy, courage and tenacity, a scientific disposition, and a creative imagination.

2. A good educational institution is one in which every student is welcomed and cared for, in which there is a safe and stimulating learning environment, in which a diverse range of learning experiences are available, and in which all students have access to good physical infrastructure and appropriate learning resources.

3. Empathy, respect for others, cleanliness, civility, democratic spirit, spirit of service, regard for public property, scientific temper, liberty, responsibility, pluralism, equality, and justice are all values that should be cultivated.

4. Fostering multilingualism and the value of language in education;

5. Life skills, including resilience, cooperation, teamwork, and communication;

6. Focus on routine formative assessment for learning rather than summative evaluation, as the coaching culture of today encourages.

7. A heavy reliance on technology for educational planning and management, language barrier removal, and access for Divyang students;

8. bearing in mind that education is a contemporaneous subject, respecting diversity and the local context in every curriculum, pedagogy, and policy;

9. For all students to thrive in the educational system, true fairness and inclusion must be at the heart of all educational decisions.

10. Curriculum coordination at all educational levels, from prekindergarten through secondary school higher education.

11. The significance of instructors and professors in the educational process, including their recruitment, continued professional development, and favorable working and service conditions;

12. A minimal but severe regulatory environment to ensure honesty, openness, and resource efficiency in the educational system through public openness and audit, while stimulating innovation and innovative thought through autonomy, good governance, and empowerment.

7.4 ANALYSIS OF GANDHI'S EDUCATIONAL LEGACY AND NEP 2020

Although the National Education Policy (NEP) 2020 and Gandhi's philosophy are two separate ideas, there are some parallels between them. Here are some potential parallels:

1. GANDHIAN PRINCIPLES AND THE EMPHASIS ON HOLISTIC DEVELOPMENT IN NEP 2020:

Gandhi did not place as much weight on armchair thinking in education as other educationalists did. He stated that "Sa Vidya Ya Vimuktaye"—education is that which liberates or leads to freedom—was the definition of education. According to him, true education involves a person's physical, mental, and spiritual growth. Literacy was not the end in and of itself; it was merely a tool for delivering instruction. Gandhiji placed a priority on the development of each person's character when it came to education. Nobody can excel in any area of life without having a strong character. Without upholding a moral code of conduct, education cannot transform a man into a man of character. Truthfulness in behavior and non-violence are two crucial conditions for character development.

The National School Policy (NEP) 2020 emphasizes the need for holistic development in schools. This is consistent with Mahatma Gandhi's principles, who believed that education should be a tool for personal, social, and national development. By emphasizing students' complete development, the NEP 2020 also encourages holistic development. It seeks to offer a well-rounded education that combines academic learning with the growth of social-emotional learning, moral and ethical values, and life skills. The policy encourages the inclusion of sports and other physical activities in the curriculum and places a strong emphasis on the value of physical health and mental well-being.

2. NEP's ATTENTION TO MOTHER TONGUE: A RECALL OF GANDHI'S APPROACH TO THE LANGUAGE ISSUE:

In the early years of schooling, according to the National Education Policy (NEP) 2020, the medium of instruction should be the student's mother tongue or a regional language. This is a reminder of Mahatma Gandhi's response to India's linguistic problem, as well as a practical strategy to improve learning outcomes.

Gandhiji believed that supporting mother tongue education was necessary for India's growth and that language was a crucial component of culture, identity, and unity. He underlined how crucial it is for kids to study in their native language in order to preserve their culture as well as to perform better academically. Gandhi's goal is echoed in the NEP's emphasis on mother language education, which also values maintaining India's linguistic variety. It also accepts that instruction in a language that kids can comprehend and feel at ease with helps them learn.

The NEP ensures that children should have a solid foundation in their first language and equips them with the skills necessary to master other languages by encouraging mother tongue education. They will be able to interact and communicate with people from other cultures and backgrounds, promoting cultural diversity and national cohesion.

3. VOCATIONAL EDUCATION IN THE NEP AND GANDHI'S SUCCESS MANTRA:

The importance of vocational education in providing students with useful skills and knowledge is highlighted in India's National Education Policy (NEP), which was recently modified in 2020. The NEP recognizes that traditional academic training may not be sufficient to effectively prepare students for the demands of the modern workforce and that vocational training may be extremely valuable in developing employability and entrepreneurship.

Gandhi, on the other hand, stressed the value of independence and self-sufficiency as a strategy for success. He held that in order to succeed, people should concentrate on honing their own abilities and talents rather than relying on outside variables like riches or social standing.

The emphasis on vocational education and giving students control over how and what they desire to study is another area of emphasis in NEP. Many entry and exit points for higher education, as well as a wide range of topic possibilities, all support the creation of a workforce that is both marketable and capable of creating new jobs. These are also the tenets that guided Gandhiji's views on education. Gandhi said that education shouldn't only be about getting kids to memorize a bunch of numbers and facts since that just encourages laziness and inaction. What a student learns in school or college and what he practices at home truly have no relation to one another.

Both Gandhi's mantra of self-reliance and self-sufficiency and the NEP's emphasis on vocational education is grounded in the notion that education should be useful and directed toward educating students for the challenges of the real world. By emphasizing practical skills and self-development, people can increase their chances of success in both their personal and professional lives.

4. TO PRODUCE DYNAMIC AND RESPONSIBLE CITIZENS AND SOCIAL WORKERS: Mahatma Gandhi thought that education is a potent weapon for transforming society and producing responsible, active citizens. To realize this objective, the National Education Policy (NEP) 2020 was created.

The NEP 2020 places a strong emphasis on the necessity of an inclusive and all-encompassing approach to education that prioritizes the growth of students' cognitive, social, emotional, and ethical qualities. Additionally, it acknowledges the value of community involvement and experience learning in producing responsible and vivacious citizens.

Gandhiji believed that the ultimate purpose of education was to produce obedient, brave, and responsible Indian citizens. Our NEP 2020 supports this educational goal as well. In the NEP 2020 (MHRD) report, at point

9.1 According to the section titled "Quality Universities and Colleges: A New and Forward-looking Vision for India's Higher Education System," "higher education plays an enormously important role in encouraging human development as societal well-being and in building India into the democratic, just, socially conscientious, culturally and humane society that upholds liberty, equality, fraternity, and justice for all that its Constitution envisions."

5. EDUCATION FOR ALL:

National Education Policy (NEP) 2020 and Education for All Gandhi are two significant educational policies in India. Here's a brief overview of both:

Education for All Gandhi: In order to provide all children in India, especially those who are economically and socially underprivileged, access to high-quality education, the Indian government launched EFA Gandhi in 2010. The goal of the policy is to increase basic education access while lowering dropout rates and raising educational standards. It focuses on enhancing teachers' skills, supporting the educational system, and expanding opportunities for girls and marginalized groups.

National Education Policy (NEP) 2020:

The National Education Policy 2020 is the Indian government's most current educational endeavor. The policy's objective is to completely transform India's educational system and bring it into the twenty-first century. All kids must receive a top-notch education that attempts to develop students' social, emotional, and cognitive skills as well as their creativity and critical thinking.

Some key features of the NEP 2020 are:

1. Early childhood education, as well as core literacy and numeracy, are prioritized in the policy.
2. It proposes a 5+3+3+4 curricular and pedagogical structure, which replaces the current 10+2 structure.

3. The policy aims to reduce content overload in the curriculum and focus on essential learning.

4. It promotes multilingualism and offers flexibility in the choice of languages.

5. The policy aims to bridge the digital divide and promote online and blended learning.

6. The policy also emphasizes teacher education and development, as well as the use of technology in the classroom.

Gandhiji believed that every student should have a basic education. He emphasized numerous times in his address that providing for a child's education, which is a fundamental human right, falls on both the nation and the parent.

Both Education for All Gandhi and National Education Policy 2020 seek to raise educational standards and advance equity in India. Although NEP 2020 calls for massive changes to the entire educational system, from early childhood to higher education, EFA Primarily concentrates on elementary education.

7.5 CONCLUSION

Gandhi's educational proposals made through Basic Education in 1937 are consistent with the NPE 2020. Basic Education concerned the education that should be given to a kid between the ages of 7 and 14. pre-basic education and post-basic education were the two main sub-components. The Gandhian model of elementary education generally corresponds to the NPE timetable of 5+3+3+4. The NEP's emphasis on the mother tongue resonates with Gandhi's comparable principles. Gandhi stressed character development, which NPE's emphasis on values mirrors. Although Basic Education has never been able to fit into the traditional educational system until now, this educational program is matchless and distinctive among other programs. Nonetheless, the NPE 2020 education strategy acknowledged the significance of Gandhi's since it amply demonstrates the integration of some of the fundamental components of Basic Education.

A comparison of the NPE 2020 and Gandhi's educational theories reveals a startling similarity.

Reference

1. Thirugnanam, B, Venkatraman, V., Dhanalakshmi, N. (2021) "Gandhi's view on Swadeshi Nationalism" Kala: The Journal of Indian Art History Congress ISSN: 0975-7945, Volume. 27, No. 1 (XIII): 2021, p.64,65

2. Vaishnav, Dr. M. (2019) "Gandhi's Nai Talim and Liberal Studies: A Comparative study of the two models of Education" International Journals and Reviews in Social Sciences, ISSN-2357-5415, DOI: 10.5952/2454-2687.2019. 00039. X, Vol. 07/ Issue-03, July-September 2019.

3. Pandey, P (2020) Finding Gandhi in the National Education Policy 2020https://www.outlookindia.com/website/story/opinion-finding-gandhi-in-the-national-education-policy-2020/361300

4. Sharma, S (May 2021) A study on similarities between Gandhiji's basic education and New Education Policy 2020, JETIR May 2021, Volume 8, Issue 5, p. 158-162https://www.jetir.org/papers/JETIR2105274.pdf

5. Sutradhar, D (September 2022) Educational Philosophy of Mahatma Gandhi, https://yoursmartclass.com/educational-philosophy-of-mahatma-gandhi/

6. Dr. Bajaj, A (November 2020) Finding NAI TALIM in the Vision of NPE 2020: Exploring the Resemblance, IOSR Journal of Humanities and Social Science (IOSR-JHSS) Volume 25, Issue 11, Series 7 (November. 2020) 31-37 e-ISSN: 2279-0837, p-ISSN: 2279-0845. p.31-37

7. Dr. Roy, D & Mitra, J (June 2022) MODERN ERA OF GANDHI'S PHILOSOPHY & EDUCATION, International Journal of Educational Science and Research (IJESR) ISSN (P): 2249-6947; ISSN (E): 2249-8052 Vol. 12, Issue 1, Jun 2022, 155–164 © TJPRC Pvt. Ltd, p.155-163

8. Dr. Jha, R.K (2020) THE IMPACT OF GANDHIAN EDUCATIONAL ETHICS IN SHAPING NATIONAL EDUCATION POLICY, 2020, JOURNAL OF CRITICAL REVIEWS ISSN- 2394-5125 VOL 07, ISSUE 03, 2020 p. 1857-1859

9. Sahu, N &Behera, H (June 2022) Relevance of Gandhian Thought of Education in Present Day Context, International Journal for Research in Applied Science & Engineering Technology (IJRASET) ISSN: 2321-9653; IC Value: 45.98; SJ Impact Factor: 7.538 Volume 10 Issue VI June 2022 p.4565-4570

10. Phukan, K.T (2021) The Educational Philosophy of Mahatma Gandhi and It's Necessity on Present, Context, Quest Journals Journal of Research in Humanities and Social Science Volume 9 ~ Issue 12 (2021) pp: 16-18 ISSN(Online):2321-9467 p. 16-18

11. Asopa, S (2019) Importance of Gandhian Philosophy, International Journal of Political Science (IJPS) Volume 5, Issue 3, 2019, PP 44-48 ISSN 2454-9452 p. 44-48

12. Kumar, A. (2021). New education policy (NEP) 2020: A roadmap for India 2.0. In W. B. James, C. Cobanoglu, & M. Cavusoglu (Eds.), Advances in global education and research (Vol. 4, pp. 1–8). USF M3 Publishing. https://www.doi.org/10.5038/9781955833042

13. Dar, R.A (January, 2023) Educational Philosophy of Mahatma Gandhi and his Educational Relevance to Contemporary World, Journal of Xi'an University of Architecture & Technology Volume XIV, Issue 4, 2022, ISSN No: 1006-7930, p. 93-96

14. Bhattacharya, Dr. N. (2019) "The Concept of Ideal State and Freedom in Gandhi's Philosophy and Underlying Relation" DOI:10.36344/ccijhss.2019.v05i01.003 , January 2019,https://www.researchgate.net/publication/360177736_The_Concepts_of_Ideal_State_and_Freedom_in_Gandhi%27s_Philosophy_and_Underlying_Relation

15. Tiwari, D. (2022) "Towards new Education: An analysis on Gandhian Philosophy of Education" International Journal

of Law Management & Humanities, ISSN 2581-5369, Volume-5, Issue-1, 2022. DOI: https://doij.org/10.10000/IJLMH.112551.p.1247,1248

16. Jena, Dr.P.K. (2020) "Mahatma Gandhi and Basic Education" "Mahatma Gandhi From Holy Deeds to Unholy Death (Part-1)" Anu Books, 2020, ISBN-978-81-947224-7-2, Chapter-9, Pages-(57-63) (https://anubooks.com/product/mahatma-gandhi-from-holy-deeds-to-unholy-death/

Gandhian Pragmatic Educational Philosophy

Rebecca Lalchhuanawmi* & Nitu Kaur**
*Research Scholar, School of Education, Mizoram University
**Assistant Professor, School of Education, Mizoram University

ABSTRACT: *This paper explores the educational philosophy of Mahatma Gandhi through the lens of pragmatism and examines how it aligns with the educational ideas of John Dewey and Benjamin Bloom. Gandhi's "Basic Education" or "Nai Talim" is analyzed in depth, revealing its pragmatic features such as learning by doing, a focus on productive activities, and the integration of practical and theoretical knowledge. The paper also discusses the National Education Policy (NEP) 2020 in India and its emphasis on multidisciplinary education and experiential learning, which resonates with both Gandhi's and pragmatist educational principles. Overall, the paper highlights the enduring relevance of Gandhi's educational philosophy in the context of contemporary education and its alignment with pragmatic ideals.*

8.0 INTRODUCTION

General discussion concerning educational philosophies in the academic circle may often not include Mahatma Gandhi, mainly because he is regarded as much more, a national leader, a freedom fighter, and a social reformer, amongst other things. Some may also see him as existing in another timeframe in Indian history, when India was in a much worse state than today. More than 70 years has passed since his death and Indian independence. We have come a long way since then, we have seen much changes and development as a nation, as well as in the sphere of our education. Despite the passage of time and age, Gandhi's stance on education and how it holds up in today's context, is still a significant question (Pandey, 2020). However, we can subsequently find our answer through the newest education policy.

The National Education Policy (NEP, 2020) is intimated with a vast array of educational concerns. Not only a lot of traces of Gandhi's ideas are reflected, it can be said that Gandhi's visions, many of which had failed in the past, can be fulfilled finally, if the policy is implemented satisfactorily according to its intention (Thakur, 2020). Few examples include the NEP's insistence upon the use of mother tongue "…. until at least Grade 5, but preferably till Grade 8 and beyond..", inclusion of The Socially and Economically Disadvantaged Groups (SEDGs) to make education more inclusive and equitable, emphasis on no hard separation between various streams, curricular and extracurricular activities, academic and vocational education, to make education in more holistic way and eliminate harmful hierarchies among different areas of learning, promoting ethics and human values to ensure character building, producing engaged citizens for building equitable and inclusive society, etc.

As a great educational reformer, Gandhi has made a significant contribution by planting vital concepts to bring about social reconstruction through education that has influence us even till today. Our concern about his educational philosophy in current time is therefore justified. In this paper, we will look at his educational philosophies through the lens of pragmatism, and see how well ahead of time he is, and how his thoughts and ideas resonate with other great thinkers from around the world, like John Dewey and Benjamin Bloom.

8.1 PRAGMATISM

Despite the existence of various forms of pragmatism, the common thread that binds them together is the fact that they are all concerned with the effectiveness of thinking and doing, which were viewed as impossible to separate. "Direct experience gained through immersion in the situation of concern" is given due importance (Simpson, 2018). Reality is dictated by individual sense experience, we as a human are not able to truly 'know' anything beyond what we experienced (Kumar, Pandey, and Gupta, 2015). Connection between an individual experience and their thoughts in relation to actions is the focal point (UK Essays, 2018).

Doubt is considered as an important initiator, and is to be followed by inquiry (Simpson, 2018). This is especially significant for solving problems. We have doubts when we face problems, in such situation, pragmatists believed that inquiry should be the tool to produce and refine answers (Tallise Aikins, 2005). Pragmatism does not confine itself to any beliefs. In other words, it does not believe in fixed or absolute truth, values or standard, as they believed these things to be always changing (Tallise and Aikins, 2005; Rai and Lama, 2020; Sharma, Devi, Kumari, 2018; Shawal, 2017). There is no truth that can stay true for every single circumstance, they can vary depending on the contexts, and is dependent on what we observe and experience, (Tan, 2006; Rai and Lama, 2020) and therefore need to be revised (Tan, 2006). It concerned itself more with the integrity of belief. Consequently, inquiry and experimentation are considered as the proper methods for revision and correction. Those beliefs that survived the inquiry are then considered worth keeping (Talisse and Aikins, 2005). Therefore, instead of searching for universal truths or ideas, pragmatism prefer to test beliefs through their practical consequences, or in otherwords, their usefulness in achieving the desired outcome or what it set out to do (Tan 2006; UK Essays, 2018). Hence, utility is emphasized.

From the above discussion, we can see that pragmatism is more concerned with experimentation, action and experience, rather than metaphysical concepts. In addition, they are also concerned with improvement of society, and therefore give due concern to the societal aspect of phenomena such as education. They considered 'knowing' to be a social and situated accomplishment that shapes the lived experience of knower, and simultaneously is shaped by the same (Simpson 2018).

8.2 IN THE CONTEXT OF EDUCATION

Pragmatists are against the traditional method of the education, that is, where the teacher assume the active role of teaching and giving lecture, and the pupil assuming the role of being a passive recipient of knowledge. Instead, they believe in making the students assume more active role in their learning –i.e., not only active in thinking, but through actual action.

Activity therefore is considered as the foundation of the educative process. In addition to activity, continuous real-life experiences and experiments are considered educative, through which one can gain real knowledge as well as a constant reconstruction of experiences. They believe that education should be an ever-evolving process of revision, reconstruction and integration of experiences. The child is placed at the centre of the educative process. Their needs as well as freedom for discovery should be given due importance. Therefore, education according to pragmatism should be child centred. (UK Essays, 2018)

Pragmatists believed that the world is in a constant motion (Simpson, 2018) therefore, everything is subjected to change. This includes the society as well as individuals, along with their views and experiences. Therefore, it is important that the individual is armed with a resourceful and adaptable mind that will be able to solve problems he will face throughout his life. Therefore, problem solving should be given importance in education. (Kumar, Pandey, and Gupta, 2015; UK Essays, 2018).

Pragmatists perceive education as a social process. Through interaction with the environment, that is, though interaction with various people, one can gain more knowledge and develop qualities and attitudes that are acceptable to society, which will promote his welfare and happiness. (UK Essays, 2018). Therefore, education should have a social function, it should help the students to adjust themselves effectively in their social surroundings, and it should help them to become an efficient contributing member of society. (Sharma, Devi, Kumari, 2018).

The social process continues throughout life as individuals experience various things and continue to reflect upon those experiences, naturally making necessary changes and adjustments in their attitudes, thinking and actions accordingly. Therefore, education according to pragmatism has 'no end beyond itself'; it is its own end. (Educational System, 2013).

A pragmatic education is a practical in nature, it stresses on effective preparation of students for future lives. It also emphasizes instilling democratic values through education, they believed that education should prepare the students for democratic living. Pragmatists believe in collective responsibility, equipping individuals with skills, attributes and traits which will make them well-fit in the society. (Kumar, Pandey and Gupta, 2015; Tan, 2006; Educational System, 2013).

When it comes to curriculum, pragmatists are opposed to dividing the curriculum into specialized and theoretical subjects, and believed that it should be inter-disciplinary, integrated and action-oriented (Tan 2006). When developing curriculum, principles such as principle of utility, principle of interest, principle of experience and principle of integration are to be followed. The subjects may include languages, health education, physical education, geography, history, agriculture, natural and domestic science, and mathematics (UK Essays, 2018; Educational System, 2013; Sharma, Devi and Kumari, 2018).

When it comes to method of education, they give importance to such methods that will allow active participation by the students, and these methods should not be fixed and rigid, but should rather be dynamic and flexible. They therefore emphasize methods that are project based which may have an individual or social character, problem based, activity based, and experience-based. 'Learning by doing' therefore is the chief method of learning. (Shawal, 2017; Kumar, Pandey and Gupta, 2015; Rai and Lama, 2020).

Thus, the well-known quote of Confucius, "I hear and I forget, I see and I remember, I do and I understand" is most appropriate for summarizing the pragmatic way of education. (UK Essays, 2018).

8.3 GANDHI'S "BASIC EDUCATION" AND ITS PRAGMATIC FEATURES

Mahatma Gandhi spent years to develop his philosophy and system of education, called "Basic Education. "Basic Education" is also known as "Nai Talim" or "Wardha Scheme of Education". Gandhi first experimented his philosophy of education in South Africa and continued at his Ashram in India. (Periaswamy, 1969). The Satyagraha Ashram, (later known as the

Sabarmati Ashram) was founded on the 25th of May, 1915. (Gandhi 1927, as cited in Periaswamy, 1969), and the Sevagram Ashram was founded in April 1935. Through this scheme of education, Gandhi aimed at reconstructing the existing educational system in India. It was based on the cultural, social, spiritual and economic needs of the country (Deb, 2021). Education was an integral part in his endeavour of societal reform, as he believed that social progress and educational reconstruction are closely connected. He hoped to put an end to the prevailing inequality based on caste and class by making his Basic Education universal and compulsory for all children, particularly through productive activity (Sailakshmi, 2018).

Basic Education has clearly reflected Gandhi's ideals of education as well as his philosophy. Dr. M.S. Patel observed that, "Gandhiji's philosophy of education is naturalistic in its setting, idealistic in its aim and pragmatic in its method and programme of work." (Singh,2019). Looking at his educational philosophy, we can indeed see many elements of pragmatism embedded in many of its features.

In Gandhi's Ashram, activities are used as a medium for education. Practical work in the field is the foundation for the theory classes. Through the same activities, they learn different things from different knowledge areas or subjects. For example, through working in the garden, they learn how to calculate the area of the plot, write letters to ask price quotations, read poetry in praise of some flowers, inquiry into the varieties of soil, utility of fertilizers, etc. Therefore, it is clear that there is no precise separation between knowledge areas or subjects. In addition, there is no distinction between the hours of activity and the hours of learning, as the learning happened through the activities (Periswamy, 1969). This tells us that it followed the pragmatic belief of practical and activity centred education, interdisciplinary and integrated education along with its preferred principles of curriculum, such as principle of integration, experience, and also of utility, since these activities are functional. It also showed that the students are at the centre of the education process and play an active role, unlike in a traditional setting.

Gandhi insisted on making craft as the focal point of education. He said, "Only every handicraft has to be taught not merely mechanically as is done today but scientifically, i. e, the child should know the why and the wherefore of every process" (Basic Education, n.d.). This implies making use of individual's sense experience, as Gandhi believed that the child does not learn exclusively with his mind or with his body, but with the combination of the two. The pupils learn more quickly by actually doing things instead of passively listening to the teacher. This again reflects the method of learning by doing, which was the main method of learning in pragmatic education. Connection between direct individual experience and their thoughts in relation to action, which was given due significance in pragmatic thinking has also been highlighted here.

Gandhi's educational concepts came from his direct observation and perception of the nation, its situation and needs. He believed that education has been cut off from the reality of life and he want to rectify this, (Periswamy, 2019), he believed in concrete education, (Dehury, 2006) and advocated learning by living (Singh, 2019) which reflected his practical and pragmatic ideals. He therefore wants to fix this by making the school to be a place of experimentation and discovery. (Periswamy, 1969).

Gandhi also recognizes the importance of education through manual work. He is of the opinion that students learn dignity of labour by working with their hands. It also pragmatic as it prepares the child for real life, equipping him with knowledge and skills.

Gandhi's Basic education is also co-operative and democratic in nature, as the teacher and students plan the learning activities together, and the students learn through various activities together (Periswamy, 1969). Gandhi also gives due importance on the social development of the child. He wants the child to learn how to live in the society, to learn social awareness, responsibility and service and develop democratic values, civic sense and adjustment with the environment which will make child fit for later life and will become useful member of society. (Sahu and Behera,

2022). This resonates with pragmatic ideals of democratic values and social function of education.

8.4 JOHN DEWEY AND BENJAMIN BLOOM

When discussing pragmatism, it is impossible not to mention John Dewey, as he extensively systematized the pragmatic stance. Dewey's system of education has much resemblance with Gandhi's Basic Education. Dewey's system was often summarized as "Learning by doing", and Gandhi's system as "Learning by living" or "Education for life, through life, and throughout life" (Link, 1962). Despite their differences in various details, they are both practical thinkers and believed in pragmatic education.

Both of them rejected the traditional education which places importance on subjects and methodologies, and merely acknowledging the learners as empty vessels that need to be filled. They both came up with their own educational ideals and systems, placing the learners right at the centre of education, being actively engaging and taking responsibility in their own learning.

Gandhi heavily focused upon practical work and found a way to balance it with theory classes, likewise, Dewey also stressed upon active learning and learning by doing, which he believed will help in harmonize theory and practice. (Austin and Bonaventure, n.d.)

Dewey gave due emphasis on active involvement in a specific activity. For Gandhi, the activities should be functional or have productive value. For Dewey, activities have social notion and function, he stresses upon learning through direct and real-life activities with other people, and connecting school activities and life experiences of the child. Activities that call for the exercise of reflective thought should also be provided in education. For young children, activities that are already familiar to in their home, (Austin and Bonaventure, n.d.) and activities that are related to the child's immediate social and natural environment is important (Link, 1962).

Dewey also has a unique concept which he called "occupations", which stands for activities which are significant beyond school context. (Austin and Bonaventure, n.d.). These are not mere activities or work to keep children out of mischief, but "reproduces, or runs parallel to, some form of work carried on in social life. "The activities representing this may include shop work with wood and tools, cooking, sewing, textile work, etc. The point of "occupations" is to maintain a balance between the intellectual and the practical sides of experience, as it involves the use of physical organs like eyes and hands and also the mind. In this way, Dewey, like Gandhi's use of craft and labour for its productive and educative value, also give importance to manual training which is not merely for production of objects or mastery of tools but for its educative as well as utility value (Dewey, 1915).

Like Gandhi, Dewey had his own conception of his Laboratory or Experimental School in Chicago. He believed that learning was "an organic cycle of doubt, inquiry, reflection, and the re-establishment of one's sense of understanding" which he practiced in his school. Like Gandhi, Dewey stressed upon the connection between society and education. He believed that "education proceeds by participation of the individual in the social consciousness" (Bantock, 1965, as cited in Periaswamy, 1969). Therefore, he considered school and education to be crucial for bringing about social progress and reconstruction. (Periaswamy, 1969).

Like Gandhi, Dewey also believed in democracy, it was his dominant ideal (Periaswamy, 1969). Gandhi let the students learn democracy in action through labor (Link, 1962). While Dewey based his very own concept of education in the principles of democracy. (Park, 1958, as cited in Sullivan, 1966). In a foreward to Dewey's book "Democracy and Education", the former NCERT Director, Krishna Kumar mentions that "Dewey's interest is in a democratic way of life, not merely as a system of good governance". This democracy should also be reflected in the school or classroom.

Benjamin Bloom is another popular figure in the field of education. He is most well-known for his taxonomy of educational objectives. Bloom identified three domains of educational activities, namely cognitive, affective and psychomotor. The cognitive domain involves intellectual skill, the affective domain involves emotions, feelings and attitudes, and the psychomotor domain involves physical functions, reflex actions and motor skills area (Bloom's Taxonomy, n.d.). It can be said that the three domains are in parallel with Gandhi's concept of the 3H's (head, heart and hand). Gandhi is of the opinion that all three are important for the all-round development of the child (Singh, 2019). While cognitive domain has to do with the head, the affective domain with the heart, and psychomotor with the hand. It is seen that learning is long lasting when it takes into account the learners' the entire three domains in holistic way and when things are learned by doing it. Shields (2006) mentions that using that the student has knowledge and comprehension of the subject matter as a raw material to build up his/her conceptual framework for the analysis and synthesis to take place. These levels of cognition are necessary before the analysis and synthesis of recognizing and building a conceptual framework can occur. Conceptual frameworks are built upon the premise and practice of a careful, thoughtful and reflections on knowledge and understanding of subject area of concern. Students are thus expected to draw upon the wisdom and insights of the available understanding and their experience to develop a plan or map to guide their inquiry. Blooms perhaps made his thinking on a similar plan to present his hierarchies of learning level and their sequential arrangement. Thus, to a lot extent his approach was pragmatic, as was that of Gandhi on unification of 3Hs.

8.5 THE PHILOSOPHY OF MULTIDISCIPLINARY IN NEP 2020

The National Education Policy 2020 focuses on proceeding towards cognitive development, character building, and producing holistic and well-rounded individuals. It emphasizes on getting rid of the traditional rote-based education and moving towards a holistic and multidisciplinary education. Instead of relying on mere examination-oriented education, developing the student's intellectual, aesthetic, social, physical, emotional, and moral in an integrated manner is necessary. This is also in accordance with the kind of education Gandhi had envisioned for the country. He described education as "all-round drawing out of the best in child and man-body, mind and spirit" (Basic education, n.d.), therefore stressing upon the total development of the individual through education. Bloom's emphasis on the cognitive, affective and psychomotor domains of the child is also in accordance with producing a well-rounded individual.

In order to have this kind of education, experiential learning is recommended, where there is a meaningful interaction between teachers and students in the teaching and learning process, with direct experiences, hands-on learning, collaborative and exploratory activities. This is the kind of education the pragmatists like John Dewey emphasized. If we want to produce well-rounded students that able keep up with the needs and requirements of the country, we cannot rely on mere verbal lessons and theory-heavy classes, as we are doing right now. It is vital that we provide opportunities to students so they can learn by being active and engaged in their own learning, we have to provide activities and experiences so that they can by doing things themselves, instead of spoon feeding them everything, we have to let them re-learn 'how to learn'.

As the NEP 2020 had pointed out, we therefore have to remove rigid boundaries between various knowledge areas and subjects, and move towards multidisciplinary education. Flexible curriculum where the students can have a choice of subject to study, particularly in secondary school is emphasized. No hard separation among 'curricular', 'extracurricular', or 'co-curricular', among 'arts', 'humanities', and 'sciences', or between 'vocational' or 'academic' streams, emphasized by the Policy, is also realized and practiced by Gandhi in his Ashram, as previously mentioned. This is necessary for bringing us closer to our aim of holistic development of our students.

The Policy also stressed upon flexible curricular structure for higher education, which will allow creative combinations of disciplines for study to ensure possibilities for life-long learning. This is also not only in accordance with Gandhi's ideals, but is very much the need of the hour to move towards a holistic education that is appropriate for keeping up with the needs and requirements of the 21st century society.

8.6 CONCLUSION

Gandhi's educational philosophy certainly has left its mark on Indian education. His contributions were far reaching and crucial for the reformation of education as well as the society as a whole. His ideas of making education accessible, practical and self-supporting are well aging and still in consistent with today's educational concerns. His insistence on activities, direct sense experience and craft as an educational process has highlighted the fact that he's on par with some of the most influential educators and scholars around the world. His aim towards all round development through education showed the comprehensiveness of his ideal education.

References

1. Austin, M. A., and Bonaventure, U. (n.d.). *John Dewey's Pragmatic Approach to Education, A Philosophical Analysis.* [Doctoral dissertation]. Nnamdi Azikiwe University.https://phd-dissertations.unizik.edu.ng/onepaper.php?p=841

2. *Basic Education.* (n.d.). https://www.mkgandhi.org/edugandhi/basic1.htm

3. *Bloom's Taxonomy of Learning Domains.* (n.d.). Vikaspedia.https://vikaspedia.in/education/teachers-corner/bloom-s-taxonomy-of-learning-domains

4. *Bloom's Taxonomy: Understanding the Framework and Its Importance in Education.*Educere centre.(n.d). https://educerecentre.com/what-are-the-three-domains-of-blooms-taxonomy/

5. Deb, P. R., (2021). Educational philosophy of Mahatma Gandhi and its present day implications. *International Journal of Creative Research Thoughts (IJCRT)* Volume 9, Issue 12 | ISSN: 2320-2882

6. Dehury, D., (2006). Mahatma Gandhi's Contribution to Education. *Orissa Review*, pp11- 15.

7. Dewey, J. (1915). "The Psychology of Occupations. "Chapter 6 in *The School and Society* (Revised edition). Chicago: University of Chicago Press: 131-137.https://brocku.ca/MeadProject/Dewey/Dewey_1907/Dewey_1915c.html

8. Dewey, J. (2004). *Democracy and Education. An Introduction to the Philosophy of Education.* (Indian ed.). Aakar Books. (Original work published in 1915).

9. Educational System, (2013). *Implications of Pragmatism in educational System.*https://educational-system.blogspot.com/2013/02/implications-of-pragmatism-in.html

10. Essays, UK. (November 2018). *Pragmatism in Education Lecture.* UK Essays.https://www.ukessays.com/lectures/education/approaches/pragmatism/?vref=1

11. Kumar, H., Pandey S.K., Gupta, A., (2015). *Philosophical Foundation of Education.* Vikas Publishing House, Pvt. Ltd. New Delhi.

12. Link, E. P. (1962). John Dewey and Mohandas K. Gandhi as Educational Thinkers. *Comparative Education Review, 5*(3), 212–216. http://www.jstor.org/stable/1187088

13. Ministry of Human Resource Development, (2020). National Education Policy.https://www.education.gov.in/sites/upload_files/mhrd/files/NEP_Final_English_0.pdf

14. Pandey, P. (2020). *Finding Gandhi In The National Education Policy 2020.*https://www.outlookindia.com/website/story/opinion-finding-gandhi-in-the-national-education-policy-2020/361300

15. Periaswamy, A (1969). *School and Society According to John Dewey and Mahatma Gandhi: A Retrospective Critique.* [Master's Theses]. 2593. https://ecommons.luc.edu/luc_theses/2593

16. Rai, P.C., Lama, R. (2020). Pragmatism and Its Contribution to education. *International Journal of Creative Research Thoughts (IJCRT)* Volume 8, Issue 3 | ISSN: 2320-2882.

17. Sailakshmi, B, (2018) Educational Philosophy of Gandhiji – A Study. *Journal of English Language and Literature*, Vol. 5, Spl Issue 2. VEDA Publications.

18. Sharma, S., Devi, R., Kumari, j., (2018). Pragmatism in Education. *Conference Proceeding of International Conference on New Frontiers of Engineering, Science, Management and Humanities* (ICNFESMH-2018) at OM Institute of Technology & Management, 12 KM stone, Hisar-Chandigarh Road, Hisar India. ISBN: 978-93-87433-11-3

19. Shawal, M. (2017) 'Pragmatism in Education: Study Notes.' http://www.yourarticlelibrary.com/education/pragmatism-in-education-study-notes/69152/

20. Shields, P. M. (2006). *Using pragmatism to bridge the gap between academe and practice.* Paper Presented at the 2006 Conference of the American Society for Public Administration, Denver, Colorado, April 1-4

21. Simpson, B. (2018). Pragmatism: a philosophy of practice. In C. Cassell, A. L. Cunliffe, & G. Grandy (Eds.), *SAGE Handbook of Qualitative Business and Management Research Methods: History and Traditions* (Vol. 1, pp. 1-26).

22. Singh, N., (2019). Mahatma Gandhi's Thoughts on Education in India. http://dx.doi.org/10.2139/ssrn.3484176

23. Sullivan, P., (1966). John Dewey's Philosophy of Education. *The High School Journal, Vol. 49, No. 8 (May, 1966), pp. 391-397.*: University of North Carolina Press. http://www.jstor.org/stable/40366240

24. Talisse, R.B., Aikins, S.F., (2005). Why Pragmatists Cannot be Pluralists. *Transactions of the Charles S. Peirce Society Winter (Vol. XLI, No. 1, p 106).*

25. Tan, C (2006). Philosophical perspectives on education. In Tan, C., Wong, B., Chua, J.S.M. & Kang, T. (Eds.), *Critical Perspectives on Education: An Introduction (pp. 26).* Singapore: Prentice Hall.

26. Thakur, A. (2020). *Resemblance of Gandhi's 'Nai Talim' in NEP 2020 is Unmissable.*https://www.thequint.com/news/education/resemblance-of-mahatama-gandhis-nai-talim-in-nep-2020#read-more

A Study on Knowledge and Cognitive Skills of Secondary School Teachers on Classroom Communication and Integration of Information and Communication Technologies (ICTS)

Dr. Shekhar Pasaragonda[1] and Dr. T. Vijaya Kumar[2]

[1]ICSSR Doctoral Fellow, Assistant Professor, R. G. R. Siddhanthi College of Education (Co-Education), Affiliated to Osmania University, Approved by NCTE, Sy. No. 703. Opp. Tivoli Gardens, Bolton Road, Near JBS, Secunderabad-500003, T. S. (India), Email ID: shekhar16.education@gmail.com, Mobile No: 9951123418.

[2]Associate Professor, NIRD-NERC, Guwahati, Assam, India, Email ID: tvkumar.edn@gmail.com, Mobile No: 7731007799·

ABSTRACT: *The present research study attempts to determine knowledge and cognitive skills of secondary school teachers on classroom communication and integration of information and communication technologies (ICT) in the classrooms of Sircilla Rajanna district, Telangana, India. This is descriptive research in which 300 teachers were selected through simple random sampling technique in 36 selected secondary schools. The data was collected by administering the questionnaire and analyzed by using descriptive statistics. The results indicate that teachers' knowledge and cognitive skills in terms of integration of ICT in classroom communication process is found to be low levels. The female teachers' knowledge and cognitive skills were slightly higher than male teacher's knowledge and cognitive skill on classroom communication and integration of ICT. The teachers from language and non-language teaching subjects are on the same level of their knowledge and cognitive skills and noticed that there is "no difference" in their level of "knowledge and cognitive skills".*

Keywords: *Integration of ICT in Classroom Communication; Knowledge and Cognitive Skills on Classroom Communication (KACSOCC); Secondary School Teachers.*

9.0 INTRODUCTION

As part of the in the present scenario, knowledge and cognitive skills on classroom communication and integration of ICTs are inevitable of secondary school teachers for dynamic changing of secondary school classrooms, teaching-learning strategies for an effective teaching. The range of ICTs tools are readily available for teaching in classrooms through "audio-video conferencing", "computer-based teaching", "Google Classrooms", "online teaching software", "podcasts", "smart boards", "wiki grade blogs", "interactive whiteboards", "digital projectors", "mobile devices", "social media", and "digital content". It has become an essential and indispensable aid for classroom communication and it can provide an effective and flexible way for improving teachers' training programs, and also promotes professional development among teachers. Hence, there is an ever-growing demand on educational institutions to integrate ICTs to teach in classrooms to need for in this connection the present study envisaged to find out the teachers' knowledge and cognitive skills on classroom communication and integration of ICTs.

"The new information and communication technologies (ICT) challenge traditional conceptions of both teaching and learning and, by reconfiguring how teachers and learners gain access to knowledge have the potential to transform teaching and learning processes. ICT provides an array of powerful tools that may help in transforming the present isolated, teacher-cantered, and text-bound classrooms into rich, student-focused, interactive knowledge environments. To meet these challenges, schools must embrace the new technologies and appropriate the new ICT tools for learning. They must also move toward the goal of transforming the traditional paradigm of learning (The 1998 UNESCO World Education Report)".

To enable teachers to include this tool in classroom communication updated knowledge and skills on ICTs for training needed. In different many countries, educational systems are adopting new technologies. In such manner, the teaching profession shifts from teacher-centered to learner-centered learning environment. Since the integration of ICT enables student-teacher interaction along with a better accepting of the use of technology in the classroom.

"Integration of information and communication technologies (ICTs) is understood as the usage of technology seamlessly for educational processes like transacting curricular content and students working on technology to do authentic tasks" (Kainth and Kaur). The researcher says "ICTs facilitate not only the delivery of content but also the learning process itself." This embrace "computer-based technologies", "digital imaging", "the internet", "file servers", "data storage devices", "network infrastructure", "desktops", "laptops", and "broadcasting technologies" which are used as instructional tools by teachers in secondary classrooms.

Therefore, the students are being shifted to beyond textbooks and use more and more digital and physical resources in the classrooms. Because of the above backdrop, the researcher says "information and communication technologies can play a crucial role to enhance the teaching-learning environment". Subsequently within a short period of time, one of the basic building blocks of modern society. Now a days, understandings for need of ICT into the classrooms and mastering basic knowledge and skills have become a part of the core of education alongside the "3 R". The three 'R' refers to three basic skills taught in schools "reading", "writing", and "arithmetic".

However, secondary school teachers are required for rich knowledge and cognitive skills on classroom communication and integration of ICT in secondary school classrooms for an effective teaching-learning process. According to North Star Digital Library, "secondary school teachers' be skillful on the essential computer skills (basic computer skills, Internet basics, using E-mail, windows 10, and MAC OS), essential software skills (MS-word, Excel, and PowerPoint), and using ICT in daily life (social media, information literacy, career search skills, and your digital footprint)". Those skills are integrated into the teaching-learning process; teaching is very effective, clearly understanding the instructional objectives as well as academic standards perceived in secondary school teaching subjects.

9.1 STATEMENT OF THE PROBLEM

The statement of the problem is "A Study on Knowledge and Cognitive Skills of Secondary School Teachers on Classroom Communication and Integration of Information and Communication Technologies (ICTs)".

After the review of the literature, the researcher came to know there is a need for a study on teachers' knowledge and cognitive skills on classroom communication and integration of ICTs among urban, rural, and tribal populations located in secondary classrooms. Significantly very few attempts have been made previously by some researchers but they are not updated, upgraded, and properly not connected with the teaching-learning taxonomy in secondary education.

9.2 THE OBJECTIVE OF THE STUDY

1. To ascertain the knowledge and cognitive skills of secondary school teachers' usage on the integration of ICTs and classroom communication.

Concerning for: gender, age, teaching experience, educational qualifications and subject of teaching

9.3 RESEARCH QUESTION OF THE STUDY

1. Knowledge and cognitive skills of secondary school teachers do influence the teaching of integration of ICT in classroom communication?

9.4 REVIEW OF RELATED LITERATURE

Abbas PourhoseinGilakjani (2017) studied on "the integration of technology into the learning and teaching of English language skills at Iran". The researcher revealed that the integration of technology into the classrooms considerably improves the learning and teaching of English language skills.

ManasRanjanPanigrahi (2016) investigated on "trends and challenges in ICT integrated teacher education in commonwealth Asia". The investigator probed that the successful implementation of ICT is certainly a powerful means of improving quality of education in general and teacher education in particular.

Bulut and Delen (2011) and Costely (2014) conducted on "the impact of ICT use in mathematics and science classes by investigating the effect of such integration on grade three students' attitude towards ICT use, and their achievement in mathematics and science". The researcher concluded that "information and communication technology have a great impact on learners' learning and should be incorporated in language teaching".

HadiSalehi and ZeinabSalehi (2012) examine "the challenges for using ICT in education: teachers' insights". Researcher examined that "insufficient technical supports" at schools and "little access to internet" and ICT prevent teachers to use ICT in the classroom. Shortage of class time and time needed to learn using ICT were reported as two other key barriers for teachers to integrate ICT into the curriculum.

9.5 METHODOLOGY

Study Area and Population

The present study is confined to the Rajanna Sircilla district in the Indian state of Telangana. It was a part of the Karimnagar district before the reorganization of districts in the state.

Population and Sampling

The respondents for the present study consisted of all secondary school teachers to teach 8th, 9[th,] and 10th classes of Govt High Schools and ZPHS school teachers from Rajanna Sircilla district (Urban/Rural/Tribal) whereas using simple random sampling technique the sample was drawn from the thirty-six randomly selected secondary schools among selected 300 secondary school teachers.

Data Collection Instruments

The instrument used "secondary school teachers' Questionnaires on Classroom Communication and Integration of ICT (CCAIICT), which has five dimensions, Dimension 1 was on classroom communication, which contains 10 Items, dimension 2 was on ICT Hardware, which contains 10 items, dimension 3 was on ICT software, which contains 10 items, dimension 4 was on ICT applications and usage, which contains 10 items and dimension 5 was on digital literacy skills, which contains 10 items.

9.6 RESULTS

Table 1

Comparison of Means of Teachers' Knowledge and Cognitive Skills on Classroom Communication and integration of ICT (Gender Wise)

Gender	N	Mean	SD	95% Confidence Interval for Mean
Male	193	25.77	7.202	24.75 To 26.79
Female	107	28.05	6.888	26.73 To 29.37
Total	300	26.59	7.164	25.77 To 27.40

Note: N (No. of Respondents), SD (Standard Deviation)

Table1 shows the mean scores of male and female teachers' knowledge and cognitive skills on classroom communication and integration of ICT. The total sample mean scores of secondary school teachers' knowledge and cognitive skills were 26.59 with SD 7.164. The obtained mean scores of female teachers were 28.05 and SD 6.888 and male teachers were 25.77 with SD 7.202, this shows that the mean scores of female teachers were slightly higher than the male teachers' knowledge and cognitive skills on classroom communication and integration of ICT.

Table 2

Teachers' Knowledge and Cognitive Skills Levels on Classroom Communication and Integration of ICT (Gender Wise)

Gender	High	Moderate	Low	Total
Male	18 (9.3%)	77 (39.9%)	98 (50.8%)	193 (49%)
Female	14 (13.1%)	55 (51.4%)	38 (35.5%)	107(51%)
Total	32 (10.7%)	132 (44%)	136(45.3%)	300(100%)

Table 2 reveals that the knowledge and cognitive skills levels of male and female teachers' usage on the integration of ICT and classroom communication. It shows that out of 300 teachers, the majority (136, 45.3%) of teachers have low knowledge and cognitive skills on classroom communication and integration of ICT, followed by (132, 44%) of teachers having moderate knowledge and cognitive-skills and (32, 10.7%) teachers have high knowledge and cognitive skills. It is also indicated in the table 2 that the majority (98, 50.8%) of male teachers were having low-level knowledge and cognitive skills, followed by (77, 39.9%) male teachers and (55, 51.4%) female teachers were having moderate knowledge and cognitive-skills of usage on the integration of ICT and classroom communication. Whereas (14, 13.1%) female teachers and (18, 9.3%) male teachers were high-level knowledge and cognitive skills of usage on the integration of ICT and classroom communication.

Further, to examine whether there is any significant differences in secondary school teachers' knowledge and cognitive skills among male and female teachers. The data were subjected to the Independent Sample t-Test, and the result of the Independent Sample t-Test is given in Table 3.

Table 3

Independent-Samples t-Test

Teachers' Knowledge and Cognitive Skills on Classroom Communication and Integration of ICT (Gender Wise)

Source of Variation	Levene's Test for Equality of Variances		t-Test for Equality of Means		
	F	Sig	t	df	Sig (2-tailed)
Equal Variances Assumed	.179	.673	-2.666**	298	.008*
Equal variances not assumed			-2.700**	227.324	.007*

*Not significant at 0.05 levels

**Negative sign indicates that the low scores were tabulated first in the SPSS

The result of the Independent-Samples T-Test in Table 3 reveals that there is no significant difference between male and female teachers' scores on knowledge and cognitive skills on classroom communication and integration of ICT at 0.05 levels. Therefore, it can be concluded that gender has no significant influence on teachers' knowledge and cognitive skills on classroom communication and integration of ICT.

Table 4

Comparison of Means of Teachers' Knowledge and Cognitive Skills on Classroom Communication and Integration of ICT (Age Wise)

Age Group	N	Mean	SD	95% Confidence Interval for Mean
22-30 Yrs	2	26.00	4.242	-12.11 To 64.11
31-40 Yrs	57	29.28	6.656	27.51 To 31.04
41-50 Yrs	133	26.51	7.389	25.245 To 27.77
51-58 Yrs	108	25.27	6.862	23.96 To 26.58
Total	300	26.59	7.164	25.77 To 27.40

Note: N (No. of Respondents), SD (Standard Deviation)

Table 4 reveals that the comparison of mean scores of teachers' knowledge and cognitive skills belonging to different age groups. It shows that the total mean score of secondary school teachers' knowledge and cognitive skills is 26.59 with SD 7.164, The mean scores of 31-40 age group was 29.28 with SD 6.656 was slightly higher when compared to other age categories in the study, followed by mean scores of 41-50 age groups were 26.51 with SD 7.389 and the mean score (26.00 with SD 4.242) of 22-30 age group. Whereas the mean score of 51-58 years age group was found slightly lower 25.27 with SD 6.862 when compared to other age group of teachers in the study.

Table 5

Teachers' Knowledge and Cognitive Skills levels on Classroom Communication and integration of ICT (Age Wise)

Age Group	High	Moderate	Low	Total
22-30 Yrs.	0(0%)	1(.3%)	1(.3%)	2(0.7%)
31-40 Yrs	09 (3%)	27(9%)	21(7%)	57(19%)
41-50 Yrs	15 (5%)	56(18.66%)	62(20.66%)	133(44.3%)
51-58 Yrs	8 (2.6%)	48(16%)	52(17.33%)	108(36%)
Total	32(10.7%)	132(44.0%)	136(45.3%)	300 (100%)

Table 5 reveals that the knowledge and cognitive skills of teachers on classroom communication and integration of ICT from different age groups. It shows that out of 300 teachers, the majority (136, 45.3%) of teachers has low knowledge and cognitive skills on classroom communication and integration of ICT, followed by (132, 44.0%) of teachers are having moderate knowledge and cognitive-skills and (32, 10.7%) teachers have high knowledge and cognitive skills on classroom communication and integration of ICT.

Further, to examine whether there is any significant difference among teachers coming from different age group' knowledge and cognitive skills, the data were subjected to One-way Analysis of Variance (ANOVA), and the result of ANOVA is given below Table 6

Table 6

Analysis of Variance

Teachers' knowledge and Cognitive Skills on Classroom Communication and integration of ICT (Age Wise)

Source of Variation	Sum of Squares	df	Mean Square	F	Sig.
Between Groups	600.161	3	200.054	4.016	.008*
Within Groups	14746	296	49.816		
Total	15346.570	299			

*Not Significant at 0.05 levels

The findings of ANOVA in Table 6 reveal that the F value (4.016) is found to be not significant; this indicates that "there is no significant difference among teachers' knowledge and cognitive skills from different age groups."

Table 7

Comparison of Means of Teachers' Knowledge and Cognitive Skills on Classroom Communication and Integration of ICT (Teaching Experience Wise)

Years of Teaching Experience	N	Mean	SD	95% Confidence Interval for Mean
Up to 10 Yrs	21	31.76	7.063	28.54 To 34.97
11-20 Yrs	141	26.70	6.946	25.54 To 27.85
21-30 Yrs	128	25.89	7.149	24.64 To 27.14
31-35 Yrs	10	23.00	6.218	18.55 To 27.44
Total	300	26.59	7.164	25.77 To 27.40

Note: N (No. of Respondents), SD (Standard Deviation)

Table 7 presents the mean scores of teachers' knowledge and cognitive skills on classroom communication and integration of ICT having different years of teaching experience. The total sample mean scores of teachers' knowledge and cognitive skills scores is 26.59 with SD 7.164 The obtained mean scores among teachers having up to 10 years of teaching experience were higher (31.76 and SD 7.063) when compared to other teaching experience categories of teachers in the study. Followed by 11-20 years of teaching experience teachers mean score is 26.70 with SD 6.946 and the mean scores of teachers having 21-30 years teaching experience is 25.89 with SD 7.149. Whereas the mean scores of teachers' knowledge and cognitive skills from 31-35 years teaching experience having teachers was found lower 23.00 with SD 6.218 when compared to other experience group of teachers.

Table 8

Teachers' Knowledge and Cognitive Skills on Classroom Communication and integration of ICT (Teaching Experience Wise)

Teaching Experience	High	Moderate	Low	Total
Up to 10 Yrs.	6 (2%)	11 (3.7%)	4 (1.3%)	21 (7%)
11-20 Yrs	16 (5.3%)	58 (19.3%)	67 (22.3%)	141 (47%)
21-30 Yrs	10 (3.3%)	59 (19.7%)	59 (19.7%)	128 (42.7%)
31-35 Yrs	0	4 (1.3%)	6 (2%)	10 (3.3%)
Total	32 (10.7%)	132 (44%)	136 (45.3%)	300 (100%)

Table 8 reveals that knowledge and cognitive skills of secondary school teachers are having different years of teaching experience on classroom communication and integration of ICT in secondary classrooms. Of the 300 secondary school teachers, the majority (136, 45.3%) of secondary school teachers have low knowledge and cognitive skills, followed by (132, 44%) of teachers having moderate knowledge and cognitive-skills, and (32, 10.7%) teachers have high knowledge and cognitive skills. The majority of teachers (67, 22.3%) from 11-20 years of teaching experience were having low knowledge and cognitive skills, followed by (59, 19.7%) teachers from 21-30 years of teaching experience were low knowledge and cognitive-skills. Few of the teachers (6, 2%) having up to 10 years of teaching experience has high knowledge and cognitive skills. Whereas the majority (4, 1.3%) of the teachers from 31-35 years teaching experience were having low knowledge and cognitive-skills, the same majority of teachers from up to 10 years of teaching experience were high knowledge and cognitive skills on classroom communication and integration of ICT. No one of the teachers from 31-35 years of teaching experience was having high knowledge and cognitive skills on classroom communication and integration of ICT.

Table 9

Analysis of Variance

Teachers' Knowledge and Cognitive Scores on Classroom Communication and Integration of ICT (Teaching Experience Wise)

Source of Variation	Sum of Squares	df	Mean Square	F	Sig.
Between Groups	753.591	3	251.97	5.095	.002*
Within Groups	14592.979	296	49.301		
Total	15346.570	299			

*Significant at 0.05 levels

The result of ANOVA in Table 9 reveals that the F value (5.095) is found to be significant at 0.05 levels (F=5.095, p<0.05); this indicates that there is a significant difference among secondary school teachers' knowledge and cognitive-skills having from different years of teaching experience.

Table 10

Comparison of Means of Teachers' Knowledge and Cognitive Skills on Classroom Communication and Integration of ICT (Educational Qualification Wise)

Educational Qualification	N	Mean	SD	95% Confidence Interval for Mean
Graduation with B. Ed	66	25.16	6.833	23.48 To 26.84

PG with B. Ed	212	26.92	7.065	25.97 To 27.88
PG with M. Ed	22	27.59	8.721	23.72 To 31.45
Total	300	26.59	7.164	25.77 To 27.40

Note: N (No. of Respondents), SD (Standard Deviation)

Table 10 presents the mean scores of teachers' knowledge and cognitive skills on classroom communication and integration of ICT having different educational qualifications. The total sample mean of teachers' knowledge and cognitive-skills is 26.59 with SD 7.164.

The obtained mean scores among teachers having PG with M. Ed educational qualifications were higher (27.59 and SD 8.721) when compared to other educational qualification categories of teachers in the study. Followed by PG with B. Ed educational qualification teachers mean score is 26.92 with SD 7.065 and the mean score of teachers' educational qualification having Graduation with B. Ed is 25.16 with SD 6.833. Whereas the mean score of teachers' educational qualification Graduation with B. Ed teachers was found lower 25.16 with SD 6.833 when compared to other educational qualification categories of teachers.

Table 11

Teachers' Knowledge and Cognitive Skills on Classroom Communication and integration of ICT (Educational Qualification Wise)

Educational Qualification	High	Moderate	Low	Total
Graduation with B. Ed	2 (0.7%)	29 (9.7%)	35 (11.7%)	66 (22%)
PG with B. Ed	25 (8.3%)	97 (32.3%)	90 (30%)	212 (70.7%)
PG with M. Ed	5(1.7%)	6 (2%)	11 (3.7%)	128 (42.7%)
Total	32 (10.7%)	132 (44%)	136 (45.4%)	300 (100%)

Table 11 reveals the knowledge and cognitive-skills of teachers having different educational qualifications on classroom communication and integration of ICT. Of the 300 teachers, the majority (136, 45.3%) of teachers have low knowledge and cognitive skills, followed by (132, 44%) of teachers having moderate knowledge and cognitive skills, and (32, 10.7%) teachers have high knowledge and cognitive skills. The majority of teachers (97, 32.3%) from PG with B. Ed educational qualification were having moderate knowledge and cognitive skills on this present study, followed by (90, 32.3%) teachers from same educational qualification were low knowledge and cognitive skills and (25, 8.3%) also the same educational qualifications were having high knowledge and cognitive skills. Few of the teachers (2, 0.7%) having graduated with B. Ed educational qualification were high knowledge and cognitive-skills and the teachers (6, 2%) having PG with B. Ed educational qualification were having moderate knowledge and cognitive-skills.

So, it may be concluded that the majority of teachers (97, 32.3%) from PG with B. Ed educational qualification were having moderate knowledge and cognitive skills, followed by (90, 32.3%) teachers were low knowledge and cognitive-skills and (25, 8.3%) were having high knowledge and cognitive-skills of PG with B. Ed educational qualifications on classroom communication and integration of ICT when compared to other two categories i.e. graduation with B. Ed and PG with M. Ed educational qualifications.

Further, to examine whether there is any significant difference among teachers having different educational qualifications in knowledge and cognitive skills, the data were subjected to One-way Analysis of Variance (ANOVA), and the result of ANOVA is given in table 12.

Table 12

Analysis of Variance

Teachers' Knowledge and Cognitive skills Scores on Classroom Communication and Integration of ICT (Educational Qualifications)

Source of Variation	Sum of Squares	df	Mean Square	F	Sig.
Between Groups	183.146	2	90.073	1.764	.173*
Within Groups	15166.424	297	51.065		
Total	15346.570	299			

*Not significant at 0.05 levels

The result of ANOVA in Table 12 reveals that the F value (1.764) is found to be insignificant; this proves that "there is no significant difference among secondary school teachers' knowledge and cognitive skills on classroom communication and integration of ICT having a different educational qualification at 0.05 levels (F=1.764, p>0.05).

Therefore, it can be concluded that educational qualifications have no significant influence on teachers' knowledge and cognitive skills on classroom communication and integration of ICT.

Table 13

Comparison of Means of Teachers' Knowledge and Cognitive Skills on Classroom Communication and Integration of ICT (Teaching Subject Wise)

Teaching Subject	N	Mean	SD	95% Confidence Interval for Mean
Mathematics	64	27.17	7.486	25.30 To 29.04
Physical Science	36	28.33	6.247	26.21 To 30.44
Biological Science	48	26.39	6.967	24.37 To 28.41
Social Studies	40	27.52	6.360	25.49 To 29.55
English	40	25.90	7.765	23.41 To 28.38
Telugu	42	25.80	6.971	23.63 To 27.98
Hindi	30	24.33	8.05	21.32 To 27. 34
Total	300	26.59	7.164	25.77 To 27.40

Note: N (No. of Respondents), SD (Standard Deviation)

Table 13 presents the mean scores of teachers' knowledge and cognitive skills on classroom communication and integration of ICT on different subject teaching teachers. The total sample mean of teachers' knowledge and cognitive skills score is 26.59 with SD 7.164. The obtained mean scores of Physical Science teaching teachers were higher (28.33 and SD 6.247) when compared to other teaching subject teachers in the study. Whereas the mean score of Hindi teachers was found lower 24.33 with SD 8.05 when compared to other subject teaching teachers.

Table 14

Teachers' Knowledge and Cognitive Skills on Classroom Communication and integration of ICT (Teaching Subject Wise)

Teaching Subject	High	Moderate	Low	Total
Mathematics	11(3.7%)	20(6.7%)	33 (11%)	64 (21.3%)
Physical Science	6 (2%)	19 (6.3%)	11(3.7%)	36 (12%)
Biological Science	4(1.3%)	21 (7%)	23 (7.7%)	48 (16%)
Social Studies	3 (1%)	22 (7.3%)	15 (5%)	40 (13.3%)
English	4 (1.3%)	17 (5.7%)	19 (6.3%)	40 (13.3%)
Telugu	4 (1.3%)	17 (5.7%)	21 (7%)	42 (14%)
Hindi	0	16 (5.3%)	14 (4.7%)	30 (10%)
Total	32 (10.7%)	132 (44%)	136 (45.4%)	300 (100%)

Table 14 reveals that the knowledge and cognitive-skills of different teaching subject teachers on classroom communication and integration of ICT. Of the 300 teachers, the majority (136, 45.4%) of teachers have low knowledge and cognitive-skills, followed by (132, 44%) of teachers having moderate knowledge and cognitive skills and (32, 10.7%) teachers who have high knowledge and cognitive skills. The majority of Mathematics teachers (33, 11%) were having low knowledge and cognitive skills followed by (22, 7.3%) Social studies teachers were moderate knowledge and cognitive-skills and (11, 3.7%) Mathematics teachers were having high knowledge and cognitive skills on classroom communication and integration of ICT. No one of the Hindi teaching subject teachers was high knowledge and cognitive-skills on classroom communication and integration of ICT.

Table 15

Analysis of Variance

Teachers' Knowledge and Cognitive Scores on Classroom Communication and Integration of ICT (Teaching Subject)

Source of Variation	Sum of Squares	df	Mean Square	F	Sig.
Between Groups	365.264	6	60.877	1.191	.311*
Within Groups	14981.306	293	51.131		
Total	15346.570	299			

*Not significant at 0.05 levels

The result of ANOVA in Table 15 reveals that the F value (1.191) is found to be insignificant; at 0.05 levels (F=1.191, p>0.05), this indicates that there is no significant difference among teachers in knowledge and cognitive-skills belonging to different teaching subject teachers.

The researcher found that research question 2, knowledge and cognitive skills of secondary school teachers influenced on teaching of integration of ICT in classroom communication.

9.7 CONCLUSION

This present research paper concludes that the secondary schools' teachers in the sample schools are having low level of knowledge and cognitive skills in relation to classroom communication and integration of ICT with respect to gender, age, teaching experience, educational qualifications and teaching subject. The result of this study differs with the findings of Yavuz Akbar (2011) obtained comparisons for each indicator revealed that males' evaluations were significantly more positive than those of females in terms of e-learning, policy, special education, and technical assistance. Further the study concludes that teachers need lot of training on knowledge of ICT applications along with the skills to utilize in the classrooms. The entire demographic variables studied in the present research paper do not have any influence on the knowledge and cognitive skills of the teachers on classroom communication and integration of ICT. Further in the sample schools the ICT facilities do not make any difference on the levels of knowledge and cognitive skills of the teachers.

References

1. Anderson, R., & Speck, B. (2001). *Using technology in K-8 literacy classrooms*. Upper Saddle River, N.J.: Prentice-Hall.

2. Bhavna Sukla, *ICT in Education Vision and Realities*. Bookman: 2016.

3. Christensen, N. (2006). The nuts and bolts of running a lecture course. In A. DeNeef & C. Goodwin (Eds.), *the academic's handbook, 3rd edition*, pp. 179-186. Durham, NC: Duke University Press.

4. Chami-Sather, G. & Kretschmer, R. (2005). Lebanese/Arabic and American children's discourse in group- solving situations. *Language and Education, 19*(1), 10-22.

5. Cohen, E., Brody, C., & Sapon-Shevin, M. (2004). *Teaching cooperative learning*. Albany, NY: State University of New York Press.

6. Dutta, Indrajeet & Dutta Neeti. *(2012). Blended Learning- A Pedagogical Approach to Teach In Smart Classrooms. Edu tracks, Vol.11, No.10.*

7. Dimitar Trajanov, Verika Bakeva, *ICT innovations in 2017*

8. Diaz-Rico, L.T. (1995). Cross-cultural, language and academic development handbook. New York: Allyn & Bacon.

9. Gayathri Rathod Vaibhav Jadav, *ICT Integration in Education: The Indian Schools Perspective*

10. Information and Communication Mapping Report RMSA Technical Cooperation Agency November 2013.

11. Johnson, L. (2017). Cultivating communication in the classroom: future-ready skills for secondary students. SAGE.

12. Louis Cohen, Lawrence Manion, Keith Morrison and Dominic Wyse, (2010). *A Guide to Teaching Practice*, (5th Edition.), New York and London: Rutledge Taylor & Francis Group.

13. Mrunalini, Ramakrishna, *Information & Communication Technology (ICT) in Education,* Neel Kamal Publishers, 2016.

14. Ministry of Human Resource Development National Policy on Education 2016: *Report of Committee for Evolution of the New Education Policy.*

15. NCERT, *National Policy on Information and Communication Technology (ICT) In School Education Department.* India: 2009.

16. National Educational Policy 2020

17. Roffey, S. (2011). The new teacher's survival guide to behavior, London: Sage Publishers

18. Robert G. Powell & Dana L. Powell (2010). *Classroom communication and diversity: Enhancing instructional practice* (2nd Edition.), New York and London: Rutledge Taylor & Francis Group.

19. R. Budhiraja, Sachdeva, *E-readiness assessment.* India: 2011.

20. Renshaw, P. (2004). Dialogic teaching, learning, and instruction: Theoretical roots and analytic perspectives. In J. van der Linden & P. Renshaw (Eds.), *Dialogic learning: Shifting perspectives to learning, instruction, and teaching.* Norwell, MA: Kluwer Academic.

21. Razack, S. (1998). *Looking White people in the eye: Gender, race, and culture in courtrooms and classrooms.* Toronto, Ontario: University of Toronto Press.

22. Rosenfeld, P., Lambert, N., & Black, A. (1985). Desk arrangement effects on pupil classroom behavior. *Journal of Educational Psychology, 77* (1), 101-108.

23. Singh, *Advanced Educational Technology.* Lotus: Saurabh Publishers, 2011.

24. S. K. Mangal, Uma Mangal (2009), *Essentials of Educational Technology*: PHI Learning Private Limited, Delhi.

25. Teaching and Learning Strategies for the Thinking Classroom:*A Publication of the Reading and Writing for* critical Thinking Project, Alan Crawford, Wendy Saul, Samuel R. Mathews, and James Makinster.

Article Journals

1. Abdullah Alenezi (2019), A Teacher's Perspective of ICT Integration in Saudi Secondary Schools, *International Journal on Integrating Technology in Education (IJITE)* Vol.8, No.2, June 2019.

2. Abu-Obaidah Alazam, A. R. Bakar, R. Hamzah, S. Asmiran (2012), teachers' ICT skills and ICT integration in the classroom: the case of vocational and technical teachers in Malaysia, *Creative Education* 2012. Vol.3, Supplement, 70-76, DOI:10.4236/ce.2012.38b016.

3. Amina safdar(2011), effectiveness of information and communication technology (ICT) in teaching mathematics at secondary level, *International Journal of Academic Research,* Vol. 3. No. 5. September, 2011, I Part, www.ijar.lit.az

4. Albert Sangrà and Mercedes González-Sanmamed(2010), The role of information and communication technologies in improving teaching and learning processes in primary and secondary schools, *ALT-J, Research in Learning Technology* Vol. 18, No. 3, November 2010, 207–220.

5. Albirini, A. (2006). Cultural perceptions: The missing element in the implementation of ICT in developing countries. *International Journal of Education and Development using ICT [Online], 2*(1). Retrieved from http://ijedict.dec.uwi.edu/viewarticle.php?id=146

6. Athryn Geldard and David Geldard, (2004), 2nd Edn., Counselling Adolescents, Sage Publications.

7. Baniabdelrahman, A. A. (2013). Effect of using Internet tools on enhancing EFL students' speaking skill.*American International Journal of Contemporary Research, 3*(6), 79-87. Retrieved from http://www.iier.org.au/iier20/mansfield.pdf

8. Baytak, A., Tarman, B., & Ayas, C. (2011). Experiencing technology integration in education: children's perceptions. *International Electronic Journal of Elementary Education, 3*(2), 139-151.

9. Bulut, O., & Delen, E. (2011). The relationship between students' exposure to technology and their achievement in science and math. *The Turkish Online Journal of Educational Technology, 10*(3), 311-317.

10. Billings, E., & Mathison, C. (2011). I get to use an iPod in school? Using technology-based advance organizers to support the academic success of English Learners. *Journal of Science Education Technology, 21*(4), 494-503. https://doi.org/10.1007/s10956-011- 9341-0

11. Bee Theng Lau (2008), exploring the extent of ICT adoption among secondary school teachers in Malaysia, *International Journal of Computing and ICT Research*, Vol. 2, No. 2, pp.19- 36; http://www.ijcir.org/volume2-number2/article

12. Braul, B. (2006). *ESL teacher perceptions and attitudes toward using computer-assisted language learning (CALL): Recommendations for effective CALL practice.* MA Dissertation, Department of Secondary Education, Edmonton, Alberta.

Indian Educational System: An Overview of the Ancient Indian Education

Dr.Burri Umashankar, Assistant Professor (P), Department of Human Resource Management, Kakatiya University, Warangal, Telangana

ABSTRACT: *This paper offers a comprehensive overview of the ancient Indian education system, emphasizing its holistic approach to nurturing students both spiritually and intellectually. It explores the diverse educational methods employed in ancient India, including gurukuls and temple-based learning, highlighting inclusivity and the profound guru-student relationships. The paper delves into the philosophical foundations of this system, emphasizing the importance of action (Karma) and mental control (Chitti-Vrittinirodha). It showcases how knowledge transmission was achieved through oral traditions and guru-student interactions, covering a curriculum that encompassed various subjects. Ultimately, it underscores the enduring significance of ancient Indian education in shaping holistic development and contributing to knowledge and societal well-being.*

10.0 INTRODUCTION

India has a rich tradition of learning and education right from the antiquity. These were handed over generations to generations either through oral or written medium. A single feature of ancient Indian or Hindu civilization is that it has been molded and shaped in the course of its history more by religious than by political, or economic influences. The fundamental principles of social, political, and economic life were welded into a comprehensive theory, which is called Religion in Hindu thought. The total configuration of ideals, practices, and conduct is called Dharma (Religion, Virtue or Duty) in this ancient tradition. Indian culture is suffused thoroughly by religious values. The approach of our forefathers to life, their subtle analysis and codification of duties, all indicate their cherished spiritual values. Their political as well as social realities were not circumscribed within the narrow geographical bounds. Their attitude to life was characterized by width of vision and they identified their duty with devotion to the ideal of 'summum bonum' of mankind. Multi-dimensional progress of all mankind became the sole objective of her civilization.

In ancient India, both formal and informal ways of education system existed. Indigenous education was imparted at home, in temples, pathshalas, tols, chatuspadis and gurukuls. There were people in homes, villages and temples who guided young children in imbibing pious ways of life. Temples were also the centres of learning and took interest in the promotion of knowledge of our ancient system. Students went to viharas and universities for higher knowledge. Teaching was largely oral and students remembered and meditated upon what was taught in the class.

Gurukuls, also known as ashrams, were the residential places of learning. Many of these were named after the sages. Situated in forests, in serene and peaceful surroundings, hundreds of students used to learn together in gurukuls. Women too had access to education during the early Vedic period. Among the prominent women Vedic scholars, we find references to Maitreyi, Viswambhara, Apala, Gargi and Lopamudra, to name a few. During that period, the gurus and their shishyas lived together helping each other in day-to-day life. The main objective was to have complete learning, leading a disciplined life and realising one's inner potential. Students lived away from their homes for years together till they achieved their goals. The gurukul was also the place where the relationship of the guru and shishya strengthened with time. While pursuing their education in different disciplines like history, art of debate, law, medicine, etc., the emphasis was not only on the outer dimensions of the discipline but also on enriching inner dimensions of the personality.

The Indian education system continued in the form of ashrams, in temples and as indigenous schools. During the medieval period, maktabas and madrassas became part of the education system. During the pre-colonial period, indigenous education flourished in India. This was an extension of the formal system that had taken roots earlier. This system was mostly religious and spiritual form of education. Tols in Bengal, pathshalas in western India, chatuspadis in Bihar, and similar schools existed in other parts of India. Local resources via donations supported education. References in texts and memoirs inform that villagers also supported education in southern India. As we understand, the ancient education system of India focused on the holistic development of the students, both inner and outer self, thus preparing them for life. Education was free and not centralised.

Our present-day education system has a lot to learn from the ancient education system of India. Therefore, the stress is being laid on connecting learning to the world outside the school. Today educationists recognise the role and importance of multilingual and multicultural education, thereby connecting the ancient and the traditional knowledge with contemporary learning.

10.1 PHILOSOPHY OF LIFE IN ANCIENT INDIA

The outstanding characteristics of the ancient philosophy of life in India are that while no great significance is attached to the physical existence in the world, yet the importance of action in this material world is not overlooked. The doctrine of action (Karma) occupies a very significant place in the Indian system of life and of education. Action or Karma should not be for the redemption of mankind. This has been the ideal of the doctrine of karma as also of the educational system of ancient India. Hence, the ultimate object of devotion for an individual is the Brahma and not this world. The material world is the lab of the human soul where the individual has to receive systematic education for bringing about self-development. The ancient Aryan culture of India lays the greatest emphasis on plain living and high thinking as the moral basis of education for self-development. Consequently, the individual has been bidden necessarily to gain both kinds of knowledge, materialistic and spiritual.

10.2 FUNDAMENTALS OF ANCIENT INDIAN EDUCATION

Ancient Indian Education had been evolved strictly on the foundations of Indian epistemological and philosophical traditions. The idea of the ephemerality of life and the world, the concept of ultimate death and the futility of mundane pleasures had provided them with a special angle of vision. The entire educational tradition originated in these principles. Thus, the Indian sages devoted themselves to the study of a Supra-sensible world and spiritual powers and molded their life accordingly. The ultimate aim of education emerged as the Chitti-Vrittinirodha (the control of mental activities connected with the so-called concrete world). However, education did not neglect the development of the pupil's powers for his all-sided advancement.

10.3 KNOWLEDGE RELATED TO LIFE

During the ancient times in India, the pupil away from the haunts of din and distractions of the material world, amidst beautiful natural surroundings, sitting at the feet of his teacher, would comprehend all the intricate problems of life through listening and meditation. He would not remain contended with mere bookish learning but acquire fairly practical knowledge of the world and society through close contact with the people. An attempt was made to make the student capable of experiencing the Supreme truth himself and mould the society accordingly.

10.4 EVOLUTION OF EDUCATION IN THE RIGVEDA

The Rig-Veda, in the form in which we have it now, is a compilation out of old material, a collection and selection of 1,017 hymns out of the vast literature of hymns, which have been accumulating for a long period. When the Rigvedic texts was thus fixed and appropriated for purposes of the Samhita, its editors had to think out the principles on which the hymns could be best arranged. These show considerable literary skill, originality of design, and insight into religious needs. Rishis were chosen, who were seers of truth. Their works were utilized to constitute six different Mandalas. These Rishis are Gritsamada, Visvamitra, Vamadeva, Atril, Bharadvaja, and Vasistha. When the highest knowledge was thus built up by these Seers and revealed and stored up in the hymns, there the methods were then necessarily evolved by which such knowledge could be acquired, conserved, and transmitted to posterity. Thus, every Rishi was a teacher who would start by imparting to his son the texts of the knowledge he had personally acquired and such texts would be the special property of his family. Each such family of Rishis was thus functioning like a Vedic school admitting pupils for instruction in the literature or texts in its possession. The relations between teacher and taught was well established in the Rig Veda. The methods of education naturally varied with the capacity of pupils. Self-realization by means of tapas would be for the few. It is believed that these sages, by virtue of their Tapas or asceticism and Yoga, were gifted with the vision of a clairvoyant, capable of knowing about the past, present and the future.

Curriculum plays an essential role in the education system. It was dynamic and not static; it was made up of different stages. The fundamental goal of building a good curriculum was to develop students physically and mentally. The curriculum consists of four Vedas, six vedangas, Upnishads, darshanas, Puranas, Tarka Shastra. The six vedangas were Shiksha, Chhandas, Vyakarana, Nirukta, Jyotisha, and Kalpawhile the darshanas were Nyaya, Baiseshika, Yoga, Vedanta, Sankhya, Mimasa. Algebra, Geometry, and grammar were also given more importance at that time. Panini was famous in the domain of grammar at that time. The curriculum of the Buddhist system consists of pitakas, Abhidharma, and sutras. Besides this medicine, Vedas were also given importance. Hindu learning was a part of Buddhist learning, although more emphasis was given to Buddhist learning. Both the systems were going hand in hand at that time. The education was totally through orals and debates, and the exams were conducted every year. The education system of the ancient period focused on subjects like warfare, military, politics, religion.

10.5 CONCLUSION

Thus, the ideal of the Vedic education was lofty. Ample opportunities were provided to the pupil for the development of his personality. The preceptors took personal care of the pupils, which resulted inevitably in a multi-dimensional development. The educational system of Vedic period achieved a pronounced success in connection with character formation, development of personality, and contribution to knowledge in all branches of learning as well as social well-being and material prosperity. The Vedic education was essentially spiritual and religious in character, yet it did not ignore the material aspect, the evidence whereof is available in the Yajurveda and the Atharvaveda. Thus, it points unmistakably to the future evolution of Aryan culture.

References:

1. Altekar, A.S., Education in Ancient India, (5th edition), 1957, Varanasi: Nand Kishore and Bros.
2. Chaube, S.P. History and Problems of Indian Education, Agra: Vinod Pustak Mandir.
3. Harshananda Swami, An Introduction to Hindu Culture: Ancient & Medieval, 2007.
4. Ifrah Georges, The Universal History of Numbers, p 421-423. Mukherjee, R.K., Hindu Civilization Longman, Green and Co. London, p. 111 1936.

NEP 2020 Towards Multidisciplinary and Holistic Approach in Higher Education: Problems and Challenges

Malsawmkimi, Research Scholar,

Dr. F. Lalrinzuali, Assistant Professor,

Department of Education, Mizoram University.

ABSTRACT: *The National Education Policy 2020 emphasizes a holistic and multidisciplinary approach to education in India. The policy aims to shift the focus from rote learning and standardized testing to a more well-rounded approach that takes into account the diverse needs and interests of students. The policy advocates for a flexible and student-centric education system that encourages critical thinking, creativity, and problem-solving skills. It also recognizes the importance of integrating different subjects and disciplines to provide a more comprehensive and interconnected understanding of the world. Overall, the holistic and multidisciplinary approach in higher education proposed by the NEP 2020 will enable students to develop into well-rounded individuals with a broad range of skills and knowledge. This will not only enhance their employability but also contribute to the overall development of the country. While the holistic and multidisciplinary approach advocated in NEP 2020 has the potential to transform education in India, it also faces several challenges, and there are challenges of institutional restructuring as large investment is required for a single discipline institution to convert into a multidisciplinary institution. However, partially the curricular restructuring will enable multidisciplinary teaching in Indian higher education; this paper will reflect on the salient features of NEP 2020 on holistic and multidisciplinary education and the problems and challenges faced for the implementation and suggestions for effective implementation of a holistic and multidisciplinary approach in higher education.*

Keywords: *NEP-2020, Holistic and Multidisciplinary Approach, Higher Education.*

11.0 INTRODUCTION

Realizing one's full potential, creating a fair and just society, and advancing global progress all depend on education. The secret to India's continuous rise and leadership on the international stage in terms of economic growth, social justice and equality, scientific advancement, national integration, and cultural preservation is ensuring that everyone has access to high-quality education. The best method to develop and utilize our nation's many talents and resources for the benefit of the individual, society, the nation, and the world is through universal high-quality education. India will have the most population of young people in the world over the next ten years, and the future of our nation will depend on our capacity to offer them chances for high-quality education.

The landscape of knowledge is changing quickly on a global scale. Many low-skilled jobs could be replaced by machines due to dramatic scientific and technological advancements like the rise of big data, machine learning, and artificial intelligence. As a result, there will be a growing demand for skilled workers with expertise in mathematics, computer science, and data science as well as cross-disciplinary skills in the natural and social sciences as well as the humanities. The way we meet the needs of the world for energy, water, food, and sanitation will significantly change as a result of climate change, raising pollution, and the depletion of natural resources. This will once again lead to a need for new skilled workers, particularly in the fields of biology, chemistry, physics, agriculture, climate science, and social science. The increasing frequency of epidemics and pandemics will necessitate joint research in managing infectious diseases and vaccine development, and the ensuing socio-economic challenges will increase the need for interdisciplinary education. As India grows closer to being a developed nation and one of the three greatest economies in the world, there will be a rising demand for humanities and arts.

Prior educational policies have mostly dealt with concerns of access and equity in their implementation. This Policy adequately addresses the unfinished business of the National Policy on Education (NPE 1986), revised in 1992. The Right of Children to Free and Compulsory Education Act of 2009, which established the legislative foundations for achieving universal elementary education, was a significant step since the previous Policy of 1986/92. The National Education Policy 2020 was adopted by the Union Cabinet, which is presided over by Prime Minister Shri Narendra Modi, paving the way for extensive, paradigm-shifting changes in both school and higher education sectors. The new strategy aims to open the door for fundamental changes in the nation's school and higher education sectors. The National Policy on Education (NPE), 1986, which had been in place for 34 years, is replaced by this, the first education policy of the twenty-first century. The National Education Policy 2020 (NEP 2020), which aspires to answer the numerous expanding developmental imperatives of our nation, is the first education policy of the twenty-first century. To construct a new system that is in line with the aspirational goals of 21st-century education and builds on India's traditions and value systems, this Policy proposes the modification and revamping of all parts of the educational structure, including its regulation and governance.

11.1 SALIENT FEATURES OF NEP 2020: HOLISTIC AND MULTIDISCIPLINARY EDUCATION

- A holistic and multidisciplinary education would aim to develop all capacities of human beings -intellectual, aesthetic, social, physical, emotional, and moral in an integrated manner.

- Such a holistic education shall be, in the long term, the approach of all undergraduate programmes, including those in professional, technical, and vocational disciplines.

- Even engineering institutions, such as IITs, will move towards more holistic and multidisciplinary education with more arts and humanities. Students of arts and humanities will aim to learn more science and all will make an effort to incorporate more vocational subjects and soft skills.

- The policy aims to increase the GER to 100% in preschool to secondary level by 2030 whereas GER in Higher Education including vocational education from 26.3% (2018) to 50% by 2035.

- Imaginative and flexible curricular structures will enable creative combinations of disciplines for study, and would offer multiple entry and exit points.

- Departments in Languages, Literature, Music, Philosophy, Indology, Art, Dance, Theatre, Education, Mathematics, Statistics, Pure and Applied Sciences, Sociology, Economics, Sports, Translation and Interpretation, etc. will be established and strengthened at all HEIs.

- Curricula of all HEIs shall include credit-based courses and projects in the areas of community engagement and service, environmental education, and value-based education.

- The undergraduate degree will be of either 3 or 4-year duration, with multiple exit options within this period, with appropriate certifications, e.g., a certificate after completing 1 year in a discipline or field including vocational and professional areas, or a diploma after 2 years of study, or a Bachelor's degree after a 3-year programme. The 4-year multidisciplinary Bachelor's programme, however, shall be the preferred option.

- An Academic Bank of Credit (ABC) shall be established which would digitally store the academic credits earned from various recognized HEIs so that the degrees from an HEI can be awarded taking into account credits earned.

- The 4-year programme may also lead to a degree 'with Research' if the student completes a rigorous research project in their major area(s) of study as specified by the HEI.

- Model public universities for holistic and multidisciplinary education, at par with IITs, IIMs, etc., called MERUs (Multidisciplinary Education and Research Universities) will be set up and will aim to attain the highest global standards in quality education.

- HEIs will focus on research and innovation by setting up start-up incubation centres, technology development centres, centres in frontier areas of research, greater industry academic linkages, and interdisciplinary research including humanities and social sciences research.

11.2 OBJECTIVES

With reference to NEP 2020, this paper intends to examine the following:

1. To highlight the vision and salient features of NEP 2020 towards a multidisciplinary and holistic approach in higher education.
2. To highlight the problems and challenges for the successful implementation of holistic and multidisciplinary approach in higher education.
3. To give suggestions for effective implementation for successful implementation of holistic and multidisciplinary approach in higher education.

11.3 TOWARDS A MULTIDISCIPLINARY AND HOLISTIC APPROACH IN HIGHER EDUCATION

With the NEP-2020, the nation's educational system is expected to undergo a paradigm shift and a revolutionary transformation. The primary goal of this initiative is to enhance the educational system by making it more accessible, holistic, multidisciplinary, and productive. It aims to foster multidisciplinary education at all higher education institutions, including universities, colleges, and standalone educational institutions like IIMs, IITs, and NITs. It intends to implement a multidisciplinary and holistic approach to education, initially in schools and later also in higher education institutions. It encourages interdisciplinary studies through many academic institutions. Collaboration between academic institutions, colleges, research institutions, and other organizations falls under this category. Students can learn sciences, technology, and math while also studying liberal arts, humanities, languages, social sciences, professional skills, vocational skills, ethics, morals, human values, and other topics through the creative teaching method known as multidisciplinary and holistic learning. This will enable them to become more well-rounded citizens and prepare them for the future. Further, it promotes the inclusion of conventional Indian knowledge systems in contemporary curricula. By giving pupils a more holistic understanding of many subjects, serves to enrich the learning experience. In addition, a multidisciplinary approach to education also helps learners explore subjects from various perspectives, allowing them to develop their own beliefs and viewpoints. The NEP 2020 seeks to establish interdisciplinary education as the standard in India at all educational levels. This method of learning will be more accessible to students by being incorporated into the core curriculum and has the potential to inspire the development of a new generation of creative thinkers.

The ambitious revisions included in the new NEP 2020 have the potential to fundamentally transform the educational system. Although it is a commendable and ambitious attempt to modernize, advance, and make equal India's educational system, nonetheless, effective implementation and execution are crucial here. To successfully implement this policy, decision-making processes must be drastically simplified, and budgetary resources must be reprioritized in the months and years to come. This

According to the All-India Survey on Higher Education (AISHE) 2019 report, 3.85 crore students are enrolled in roughly 1,000 universities, 39,931 colleges, and 10,725 standalone institutions in India. Further, from 3.85 crores in 2019–20, the number of students enrolled in higher education has surged to around 4.14 crore in 2020-21. Around 72 lahks more students enrolled during 2014–15, according to AISHE 2020-2021. The aim of NEP 2020 is to increase the overall GER in higher education including vocational education from 26.3% (2018) to 50% by 2035. Consequently, NEP demands a massive implementation on a scale that has never been attempted before in the globe. To achieve the purposes of the NEP 2020, it may be claimed that before moving further in this direction, the government must not only determine the solutions to the aforementioned issues but also guarantee that adequate safeguards are in place to secure the welfare of higher education students in particular and the educational system as a whole. To execute all the necessary suggestions for reforming education, establishing new institutions, funding, infrastructure (in both urban and rural areas), regulatory mechanisms, grievance redress cells, professionally trained teachers, and other things are required for the government to carry out the provisions in their true spirit.

11.4 PROBLEMS AND CHALLENGES OF MULTIDISCIPLINARY AND HOLISTIC APPROACH IN HIGHER EDUCATION:

While the holistic and multidisciplinary approach advocated in NEP 2020 has the potential to transform education in India, it also faces several challenges. Some of these challenges are:

1. **Limited institutions**

To achieve the aim of increase in the overall GER in higher education to 50% by 2035, according to the policy, one new university shall be established each week for the following 15 years. Rather than being pushed to be multidisciplinary, a sound education system will require a variety of institutions. There should be a variety of institutions available to students. The plan runs the risk of bringing about a brand-new institution-mandated isomorphism.

2. **Learning or certificate/degree**

Although multiple exits is a significant step for reducing the number of dropouts in higher education, concern remains over the worth and value of these diplomas and certifications. So, to put the new system into place, we must first do away with the outdated notion that getting a degree is a need for landing a job. This is a risky worldview that discredits and dissuades a person's other natural abilities.

3. **Funding**

Given the limited resources available, it will be a challenge to completely implement NEP 2020's recommendations for the higher education sector. For students from low-income strata to be admitted, private universities must provide more scholarships, but the NEP does not address how this might be done. This suggests that higher education needs more public funding, which in reality does not fit well with the current situation. Simply put, the implementation requirements cannot be met by the rise in the education budget from 3% to 6% of GDP.

4. Educational restrictions/Pedagogical limitations

The policy mentions adaptability, variety, and experimentation. It acknowledges the diversity of pedagogical needs in higher education. If it is a required option within a single institution, this will be a setback since designing a curriculum for a class that includes both students pursuing one-year diplomas and those pursuing four-year degrees dilutes the institution's character and identity.

5. Higher education that crosses disciplines calls for a change in culture/culture shift

The NEP 2020's emphasis on interdisciplinary learning is a highly positive development for higher education. For many years, education in India has been relatively repetitive and secluded. It is difficult to see the entire higher education system is made up of "exceptions" teachers who respect, are interested in, and lean towards other fields of study while being experts in their own. During the next 15 to 20 years, this calls for a cultural change throughout the entire higher education ecosystem.

6. Implementation

Implementing a holistic and multidisciplinary approach to education requires significant changes in the existing education system, including curriculum development, teacher training, and assessment strategies. Implementing these changes effectively and efficiently on a large scale will be a major challenge.

7. Resourcing

The holistic and multidisciplinary approach requires additional resources, including funding, materials, and facilities, to support the integration of multiple disciplines and the development of new teaching methodologies. Ensuring adequate resources are available for implementation can be a significant challenge.

8.   **Teacher training**

The implementation of the holistic and multidisciplinary approach requires significant teacher training to enable them to teach across multiple disciplines and employ new pedagogical methods. Ensuring the availability of high-quality training opportunities for all teachers can be a challenge.

9.   **Assessment**

The current education system in India relies heavily on standardized testing, which is not well-suited to the holistic and multidisciplinary approach. Developing new assessment strategies that accurately measure student learning across multiple disciplines will be a significant challenge.

10.   **Equity**

While the holistic and multidisciplinary approach has the potential to benefit all students, ensuring that it is accessible to all students, regardless of their socio-economic background or geographical location, will be a significant challenge. The policy needs to ensure that no student is left behind in the implementation of the new approach.

11.   **Establishment of Multidisciplinary Education and Research Universities (MERUs)**

To set up MERUs, requires several initiatives and necessitates ensuring consistency on matters of curriculum, pedagogy, and assessment across institutions and programs. To encourage and support students from socio-economically disadvantaged backgrounds, the need to establish universities and colleges with high-quality support centers requires adequate funds and academic resources. Given the limited resources and funding available as aforementioned, it will be a challenge to attain successful implementation. In addition, to provide professional academic and career counseling to all students, as well as counselors to ensure students' physical, psychological and emotional well-being, the present severe shortage of trained counselors in India is already a challenge. Furthermore, the inability to uphold effective and functional counseling cells at HEIs at present will require extensive transformation.

Overall, the implementation of a holistic and multidisciplinary approach to education in India will require significant effort and commitment from all stakeholders, including the government, educators, and the wider community. Addressing these challenges will be critical in ensuring the success of NEP 2020 in achieving its goals.

11.5 SUGGESTIONS FOR EFFECTIVE IMPLEMENTATION OF A HOLISTIC AND MULTIDISCIPLINARY APPROACH:

The National Education Policy (NEP) 2020 emphasizes the importance of a multidisciplinary approach in higher education. Here are some suggestions for the effective implementation of this approach:

1. **Curriculum Design:** Revision of the curriculum to integrate different disciplines and provide opportunities for interdisciplinary study. Encourage students to take courses outside their major field of study, and create opportunities for team-based projects and research.
2. **Faculty Development:** Providing training to faculty members on interdisciplinary teaching methodologies and encouraging them to collaborate with colleagues from different disciplines. This will help to promote interdisciplinary research and pedagogy.
3. **Infrastructure:** Investing in infrastructure to facilitate interdisciplinary research, including laboratories, libraries, and collaborative spaces. Create opportunities for students to engage in interdisciplinary research projects, internships, and community outreach programs.
4. **Assessment and Evaluation:** Develop an assessment tool that can measure students' understanding of interdisciplinary concepts and

skills. Use feedback mechanisms to evaluate the effectiveness of the multidisciplinary approach.

5. **Partnerships:** Collaborating with industry, NGOs, and government agencies to create opportunities for interdisciplinary research and development. Engage with alumni and other stakeholders to promote interdisciplinary learning and research.

By implementing these strategies, universities can promote a multidisciplinary approach in higher education and prepare students for the complex challenges of the future.

11.6 CONCLUSION

The NEP 2020 has not yet been put into action. Reviving the Indian educational system with a contemporary perspective is a bold effort. The NEP 2020 drafting committee has made a thorough effort to create a policy that takes into account many points of view, international best practices in education, practical experience, and stakeholder feedback. The vision is aspirational, but the execution plan will determine if it will promote an inclusive education that prepares students for the workplace and the future. No matter how appealing this may seem, the actual implementation of any policy is crucial. A policy can become a big success with effective execution, or it can become a huge disaster with poor implementation. The most crucial three elements, infrastructure, funding, and a well-thought-out plan strategy, are still lacking in actuality. Further, it must be considered that this move towards holistic education does not result in the commercialization of education since government institutions lack the necessary infrastructure to offer practical education, which allows private companies to profit from the situation. To achieve the goal of comprehensive and multidisciplinary education, it must be ensured that international universities and local private institutions collaborate with governmental institutions. NEP 2020, in a nutshell, is a blueprint for a new India with substantial changes in the educational landscape.

References

1. All India Survey on Higher Education, MHRD, Govt. on India: www.aishe.gov.in
2. National Education Policy 2020.
3. https://www.education.gov.in/sites/upload_files/mhrd/files/nep/NEP_Final_English.pdf
4. Gurchal, M. G., & Yamdagin, P. (2022) Multidisciplinary and Holistic Approach in Higher Education with Reference to NEP : 2020. *International Journal of Advanced Research in Science, Communication and Technology (IJARSCT)*. ISSN (Online) 2581-9429 https://ijarsct.co.in/Paper3561.pdf
5. NEP Higher Education Guideline. https://iucee.org/wp-content/uploads/2021/05/NEP-HE-Guidelines.pdf

NEP-2020 and E-Learning Problems and Perspectives

*Dr. M. Saraswathi_*

ABSTRACT: *India, a global leader in technology and space, is embracing digital transformation through initiatives like Digital India. The National Education Policy (NEP) 2020, launched in July 2020, is a comprehensive framework aimed at revolutionizing education in India by 2040. NEP 2020 focuses on affordability, accessibility, quality, equity, and accountability. It underscores the importance of E-Learning, digital infrastructure, and online teaching platforms like NPTEL, MOOCS, Swayam, and Deeksha. The COVID-19 pandemic accelerated the adoption of E-Learning, prompting the government to prioritize foundational literacy and numeracy. NEP 2020 emphasizes multidisciplinary education, digital literacy, problem-solving, and vocational exposure to prepare the next generation for the digital age.*

Key Words: *E-learning, Traditional, Communication technologies, Emphasizes, Affordability, Accessibility, Quality, Equity, and Accountability.*

Asst. Professor, Dept. of Economics, GRP G.D.C Bhainsa Nirmal.
Email: saraswathiseerla@gmail.com 9989160243

12.0 INTRODUCTION

Education is an important indicator of social and economic development. Increase in higher education will brings industrialization, urbanization, better communication, increased trade and commerce and modernization. Improved education levels help in the growth of awareness, social skills and in the improvement of economic conditions. There has been a huge increase in the demand for higher education since independence. India's higher education system is the third largest in the world.

Education, in its broadest sense of development of youth, is the most crucial input for empowering people with skills and knowledge and giving them access to productive employment in future. Improvements in education are not only expected to enhance efficiency but also augment the overall quality of life.

The Digital India Campaign is helping to transform the entire nation into a digitally empowered society and knowledge economy. While education will play a critical role in this transformation, technology itself will play an important role in the improvement of educational processes and outcomes. Thus, the relationship between digital technology and education at all levels is bidirectional.

12.1 OBJECTIVES OF THE STUDY

1. To understand the key-reforms introduced in Indian Education System through NEP2020
2. To understand the role and importance of E-Learning system in education.
3. To analyze the impact of digitalization of education on Teachers and Students.
4. To discuss the problems and perspectives of online teaching methods in filling the gap in Face to face teaching and learning process.

12.2 METHODOLOGY

The methodology used in this paper with the help of the data from secondary Sources

12.3 HYPOTHESIS

The new policy framed a comprehensive framework to transform elementary education to higher education in India by through E-Learning Platform.

12.4 THE NATIONAL EDUCATION POLICY (NEP 2020)

Launched on 29 July 2020, outlines the vision of India's new education system. NEP 2020 focuses on five pillars: Affordability, Accessibility, Quality, Equity, and Accountability – to ensure continual learning. The new policy forms a comprehensive framework to transform both elementary and higher education in India by 2040.

National Educational Technology Forum (NETF), created to provide a platform for the free exchange of ideas on the use of technology to enhance learning, assessment, planning, administration, and so on, both for school and higher education.

Regulatory mechanisms of higher education would have "accreditation" conducted by an independent body amongst other key functions. Accreditation ensures Quality Assurance of Faculty, Infrastructure; Program Design; Training Management System.

The hosting of Quality Ed-Tech tools in all the dimensions of teaching-learning delivery would enable institutions of learning to adapt quickly. This will secure the 'personal privacy of individual students.

12.5 COVID-19 AND E-LEARNING

National Educational Technology Forum (NETF), will be created to provide a platform for the free exchange of ideas on the use of technology to enhance learning, assessment, planning, administration, and so on, both for school and higher education. The policy aimed to transform the education system to be digitalized. Using technology (ICT) in learning process improves the quality and accessibility.

The pandemic has triggered a significant increase in the use of technology for learning. To improve learning outcomes, the Government is focused on foundational literacy and numeracy (FLN) as recommended by the National Education Policy 2020

The New Education Policy (NEP) 2020 of the Govt. of India emphasizes on the importance of online and digital education using the advantage of technology, in order to explore the possibilities to meet the future challenges in providing quality education for all. The learners and tutors are required suitable training which is recognized by the Government in NEP-2020. The

NEP 2020 emphasizes the creation of virtual labs wherein students can practice their theoretical knowledge and make course content available in different languages. The newly renamed Ministry of Education proposes to set up a dedicated unit for promotion of digital learning. The dedicated unit will comprise experts from the field of education, educational technology, administration, and e-governance who will focus on online learning needs of both the school and higher education. More emphasis will be given to online assessment and examinations.

12.6 NATIONAL EDUCATION POLICY (NEP 2020) AND E-LEARNING

The NEP 2020 calls for key reforms in both school and higher education that prepare the next generation to thrive and compete in the new digital age.

The outlook of our class room has been transformed into new orientation, The modern class rooms adopted, Smart Classes/ Smart Boards, PowerPoint presentations Virtual Classrooms, Digital Library, Google Classrooms/ Zoom/Microsoft class etc. Devices like, Desktops, Laptops, Mobile.etc has taken place instead of Black Board and Chalk piece.

The infrastructure needs to Online teaching platform, Electricity, Internet, Data devices, Signals and it needs Hardware like Projectors, connectors etc. And also, there is a need of Education learning Apps i.e Byzus, Edu care etc. Search browsers like Google, Wikipedia etc. are giving more additive knowledge. The institutions are facing lot of Constraints in this area.

Skills must be adopted by the teacher and students like Training while using of ICT, Awareness about Software and Hardware technology and must be easy access to reach the required cites.

The technologies that facilitate the provision of courses over long distances are broadly termed as "Learning management System". Online education is only appearing to be solution to face-to-face interaction in classroom until Covid 19 brought under control and regular classes are resumed. This will enable inclusive education by facilitating learning across diverse geographies in India. Moreover, it will provide an opportunity for educators to come up with customized learning solutions for every student.

A massive open online course (MOOC) is an online course aimed at unlimited participation and open access via the web. India is considered to be the biggest market for MOOCs in the world after the USA.

NEP-2020 advocated the promotion of digital infrastructure, online teaching platforms, like NPTEL, MOOCS, Swayam, Deeksha etc. And also, the policy advocated to promoting content creation, digital repository, dissemination, digital divide, virtual labs, etc, for effective implementation of online teaching in the country.

Finally, we can state that the digital tools and platforms for teaching and learning are internet based. Internet has become an essential commodity. Hence, access to internet and Open Educational Resources has to be considered as a fundamental right to provide online education for all.

12.7 PROBLEMS AND CONSEQUENCES

Students and Staff not having the skills they need to use technology and they are not having good enough internet Connection. There are lot of difficulties delivering physical resources.

Power cut, poor internet signals and audio problems are becoming major problems in rural areas. There is lack of availability and affordability of physical resources mainly in Govt. Institutions, assessment also become difficult.

Students may misuse the sources; they may get radiation effect. There will be psychological Disorders in the Teachers and Students. Reading and Writing skills will not be improved, there might be no Motivation for learning, class room discipline may disturb. And it also degrades the communication skills and language proficiency among the students.

New Addictions found in students, like playing online Video Games, watching unhealthy websites etc. will affects badly. Students may become passive learners, and they may get fatigue due to long hours of attending classes.

12.8 STEPS TO IMPROVE ACCESSIBILITY AND QUALITY IN TRANSFORMATION

- More private channels to be encouraged like MANA TV.
- Free access to be provided like YouTube video lessons, education portals etc.
- More free Learning Portals, like Swayam, Udemy, etc. and apps like Byju's, Edu Care etc. to be introduced.
- Presently there are 10 online platforms in India and they are enabling the students to acquire the knowledge. They include; 1. SWAYAM online courses, 2. UG/PG MOOCs, 3. e-PG pathshala, 4. e-content courseware in UG subjects, 5. SWAYAMPRABHA, 6. CEC-UGC YouTube channel, 7. National Digital Library, 8. Shodhganga, 9. e- shodu sindhu, 10. Vidwan.
- E- Learning classes may be introduced through public media sources Door Darshan, Radio etc. They can give more access and can improve the quality of Digital Teaching and Learning process.

12.9 CONCLUSION

The present age is driven by digital technology and whole globe come under the influence of internet and World Wide Web. The internet equipped both the education seeker as well as education provider and laid them together under the virtual roof. Due to which the concept of virtual classroom is already popularized across the globe. Therefore, in the modern era, the role of online technology in providing the education is vital and with its flexible nature the online educational technology has gained popularity.

The online education is now more accessible to the less privileged groups in comparison to the centralized classroom education system.

References

1. Bhattacharya, B. (2008). "Engineering Education in India-the role of ICT" Innovations in education and teaching International, 45(2), 93-101.
2. Bhattacharya, Saumyajit. (2020). What Is Wrong with Online Teaching? Economic and PoliticalWeekly, Vol.55, Issue no.23, 6 Jun 2020
3. Misra, Kamlesh. (2020). Covid-19: Education System Big Shift from Classroom to Computers, India Today, daily newspaper, Delhi edition, May 12th, 2020
4. Duevi, S., Rizwan, M., & Chander, S. (2012). ICT for Quality Education in India. International Journal of Physical and Social Sciences, 2(6), 542-554.
5. Dainik Jagran 30 July 2020; Let us know why a new national.
6. Draft National Education Policy 2019. Committee for Draft.
7. Govt. of India (1968). National Policy on Education,1968.
8. Govt. of India (1986). National Policy on Education, 1986.

Savitribai Phule Contributions in the Field of Education and NEP 2020

Glory Lalthanpuii Darlong
Research Scholar
Department: Education,
Mizoram University, Aizawl
Email address: glorydarlong123@gmail.com
7005430669
Co-Author's Name: Jacob Lalrinawma
&
Rebec Lalramtiami
Research Scholar
Mizoram University

ABSTRACT: *Savitribai Phule was an important social reformer and Educationist. She was the first lady teacher of first girl's school in India. Not only a teacher she was a great social reformer. In nineteenth century, she was a power source of woman education and woman empowerment. She was also a founder of modern Marathi poetry. The present study aims to know Savitribai Phule's aims of Education, to know the contributions of Savitribai Phule's for women Education and women Empowerment, to understand the contributions of Savitribai Phule's in NEP 2020. Savitribai Phule's ideas and values should be incorporated in education because she has contributed many schools and fights against women rights which was unequal rights for the women. She also moved against untouchability and rule out the discrimination grounded on caste and gender. She tried to break the conservative education system that was prevailed in the society and wanted to reconstruct it as an open and universal education system of all. This study is a qualitative approach related with the historical study method. The method of historical study is adopted by the researcher to conduct her study. In this study, secondary data have been used i.e., published journals, articles, magazines and unknown sources from internet. As the NEP 2020 has focused about SEDGs young girl's education taking inspiration* *from Savitribai Phule contributions in the field of education we can reshape and motivated the young girls to get a better education.*

13.0 INTRODUCTION

Savitribai was born on January 3, 1831, in Naigaon (presently in Satara district) in British India in a farming family to Khandoji Neveshe Patil and Lakshmi as their eldest daughter. Girls in those days were married off early, so following the prevalent customs, the nine-year-old Savitribai was wedded to 12 years old Jyotirao Phule in 1840. Jyotirao went on to become a thinker, writer, social activist, and anti-caste social reformer. He is counted among the leading figures of Maharashtra's social reform movement. Savitribai's education started after her marriage. It was her husband who taught her to read and write after he saw her eagerness to learn and educate herself. She cleared third- and fourth-year examination from a normal school and became passionate about teaching. She took training at Ms Farrar's Institution in Ahmednagar. Jyotirao stood firmly by the side of Savitribai in all her social endeavours.

Savitribai Jyotirao Phule was a well-known Indian social reformer, educationist and poet who played an instrumental role in women education and empowerment during the nineteenth century. Counted among few literate women of those times, Savitribai is credited for founding the first girl's school in Pune in Bhide Wada with her husband Jyotirao Phule. She took great effort towards educating and emancipating child widows, campaigned against child marriage and sati pratha, and advocated for widow remarriage. A leading figure of Maharashtra's social reform movement, she is considered an icon of Dalit Mang caste along with likes of B. R. Ambedkar and Annabhau Sathe. She campaigned against untouchability and worked actively in abolishing caste and gender-based discrimination. For this activity in 16 November 1852 honored the Phule family for their contributions in the ground of education by the British government. The Pune City Corporation built a memorial in 1983 to pay homage to her. Government of India released a postal stamp to honour her on March 10, 1998. In 2015 The University of Pune changed the name of the university and it was renamed as Savitribai Phule Pune University. Google create Google doodle to celebrate her 186th birth anniversary on January 3, 2017.

13.1 STATEMENT OF THE PROBLEM

The Problem is "Educational Contributions of Savitribai Phule in the field of Education and NEP 2020". Educational Contributions of Savitribai Phule and her educational ideas in the present Indian Education System.

13.2 RELATED STUDIES

Thom Wolf (2011), published of Journal on "Comenius and Savitribai Phule". In this journal, he talked about changing education: a note on the "original and unusual" world voice, worldview, and world venue of Jan Comenius and Savitribai Phule.

Dipongpou Kamei (2013), had study "Women and Education: Contribution of Savitribai Phule and Pandita Ramabai for Women Education in India".

Suchismita Pai (2013), in her study "Savitribai, The Mother of Modern Girls' Education in India". She has discussed in her study, Savitribai Phule may not be as famous as Mahatma Gandhi or Swami Vivekananda.

Patel (2017), work on "Contribution of Savitribai Jyotirao Phule in Education Field". He mentioned here, Savitribai Phule was one of the most important women who has contributed greatly in adding glory to the work of the modern Indian social scenario.

Waghmare (2020), made the work on "Savitribai Phule: Women Empowerment in India". This work focus on Women's Education and Empowerment. One of the world's great puzzles that women, who make up half the world's population, have been so much discriminated against throughout history.

13.3 OBJECTIVES OF THE STUDY

The objectives of this study are to-

- To know Savitribai Phule's aims of Education.
- To know the contributions of Savitribai Phule's for women Education and women Empowerment.
- To understand the contributions of Savitribai Phule's and NEP 2020

13.4 METHODOLOGY OF THE STUDY

This study is a qualitative approach associated with the historical study method. In this study, secondary data have been used by the researcher. The secondary sources are collected from published journals, articles, and unknown source from internet (will include the link)

13.5 DISCUSSION OF THE OBJECTIVES

i) To Know Savitribai Phule's Aims of Education:

Savitribai Phule's has many aims in education during her life span. Here, I will highlight some few importance aims. Savitribai Phule's have a keen interest education as instrument to bring up humanism. About 170yrs ago during the British regime and people were not enough educated so, she wants to bring change through this education system so, that the other person can have humanity over another person. And she also believes that through this education, women of India able to develop her own, she can raise her own voice, against the inequality and discrimination. Furthermore, she also believes that education add permanent values like freedom, equality and fraternity should be developed through education. Personality should be developed and social equality should be established by the Education.

ii) To Know the Contribution of Savitribai Phule's for Women's Education and Women Empowerment:

After completing her teaching training, Savitrabai Phule, along with her husband Jyotirao's began to teach girl students in Pune. At a time when educating girls was unthinkable, Savitribai initiated a movement that enabled women to stand out in society as equals.

Some of the activity of Savitribai Phule for Women: -

- Phule couple started a shelter home- Balhatya
- Pratibandhak Griha for Brahmin widows in their own house.
- After realising the Caste discrimination prevailing among women, she started organising meetings and Til-Gur festivals. In these meetings and festivals women of all caste could participate.
- Mahila Mandal was formed in Pune in 1852 by her. This Mahila Mandal started working for the empowerment and liberty of the women.
- She has opened a care centre for the pregnant rape victims. The Centre was called 'Balhatya Pratibandhak Griha'.

The first indigenously-run school for girls in Pune (at that time Poona) was started by Jyotirao and Savitribai in 1848 when the later was still in her teens. Savitribai became the first teacher of the school. Jyotirao's and Savitribai later started schools for children from the Mang and Mahar castes, who were regarded as untouchables. Three Phule's schools were in operation in 1852. On November 16 1852, the British government honored the Phule family for their contributions in the field of education while Savitribai was named the best teacher. That year she also started the Mahila Seva Mandal with the objective of creating awareness among women regarding their rights, dignity, and other social issues. She was successful in organising a barber's strike in Mumbai and Pune to oppose the prevailing custom of shaving heads of widows. All the three schools run by the Phule's were closed by 1858. There were many reasons for this, including drying up of private European donations post the Indian Rebellion of 1857, resignation of Jyotirao from the school management committee due to difference of opinion on curriculum, and withdrawal of support from the government. Undeterred by the circumstances Jyotirao and Savitribai along with Fatima Sheikh, took charge of educating people from the oppressed communities as well.

Over the years, Savitribai opened 18 schools and taught children from different castes. Savitribai and Fatima Sheikh began teaching women as well as other people from downtrodden castes. This was not taken well by many, particularly the upper caste of Pune, who were against Dalits education. Savitribai and Fatima Sheikh were threatened by the locals and were also harassed and humiliated socially. Cow dung, mud and stones were thrown at Savitribai when she walked towards the school. However, such atrocities could not discourage the determined Savitribai from her goal and she would carry two saris. Savitribai and Fatima Sheikh were later joined by Saguna Bai who also eventually became a leader in the education movement. Meanwhile, a night school was also opened by the Phule couple in 1855 for agriculturist and labourers so that they can work in daytime and attend school at night. To check the school dropout rate, Savitribai started the practice of giving stipends to children for attending school. She remained an inspiration for the young girls she taught. She encouraged them to take up activities like writing and painting. One of the essays written by a student of Savitribai called Mukta Salve became the face of Dalit feminism and literature during that period. She conducted parent-teacher meetings at regular intervals to create awareness among parents on the significance of education so that they send their children to school regularly. In 1863, Jyotirao and Savitribai also started a care center called 'Balhatya Pratibandhak Griha,' possibly the first ever infanticide prohibition home founded in India. It was set up so that pregnant Brahmin widows and rape victims can deliver their children in a safe and secure place thus preventing the killing of widows as well as reducing the rate of infanticide. In 1874, While Jyotirao advocated widow remarriage, Savitribai worked tirelessly against social evils like child marriage and sati, pratha two of the most sensitive social issues that were gradually weakening the very existence of women. She also made effort in bringing the child widows into mainstream by educating and empowering them and advocated for their re-marriage. Such pursuits also met with strong resistance from the conservative upper caste society.

iii) To Understand the Contributions of Savitribai Phule's and Nep 2020:

In NEP Part-I sub-No.6.7 "It must be noted that women cut across all underrepresented groups, making up about half of all SEDGs. Unfortunately, the exclusion and inequity that SEDGs face is only amplified for the women in these SEDGs. The policy additionally recognizes the special and critical role that women play in society and in shaping social mores; therefore, providing a quality education to girls is the best way to increase the education levels for these SEDGs, not just in the present but also in future generations. The policy thus recommends that the policies and schemes designed to include students from SEDGs should be especially targeted towards girls in these SEDGs" (NEP Page-26)

As mentioned above, the NEP 2020 sub-No.6.7 has targeted towards girls' education specially Socio- Economically Disadvantages Group. About 170yrs ago, Savitribai Phule's has taken initiatives towards girl's education despite her struggles and obstacles. She motivated many young girls to go to school and encouraged them to fight the evils of society by taking education but also worked to open the doors of education for girls in India.

As mentioned in the second objective Savitribai Phule opened many schools and night school too so that the students could work in daytime. She also started the practice of giving stipends to children for attending school during those days. Even today's scenario, the government is running many schemes regarding the education and health of women, due to which women have become aware. But the campaign to educate women and make them stand on their own feet was started by Savitribai Phule who was social worker and teacher, who not only defeated the evils of society by taking education but also worked to open the doors of education for girls in India. Savitribai Phule stood firm in her struggle to educate women without grit and self-confidence, overcoming many obstacles and achieved success. Though she worked for women underrepresented groups, from my visit I came to see that we need to work more to encourage many young girls who are living in rural places who do not even have school near the village and there are so many young girls who do not aware this various scheme launched by Government.

Even Right to Education Act, mid-day meal schemes are is modern-day concept but Savitribai Phule and Jyotirao Phule has introduced it almost 170 years back by giving stipends to children to reduce the dropout rate in schools. They took initiatives to reduce malnutrition in children by taking care of the health of each child in school. They introduced the RTE and Mid-day Meal Schemes in 1850.

13.6 CONCLUSION

Savitribai Phule a social reformer, educationist and anti-abronist with her husband Jyotirao's immensely contributed in the field of education specially for the women. Though she was married in a very young age her husband understood her keen interest on studies, so he let to go to school and get a good education. After she completed her studies, she was well trained for a teacher with well equip knowledge. Later, on together with her husband they opened more than 18 schools and taught children from different castes. Savitribai and Fatima Sheikh began teaching women as well as other people from downtrodden castes. Savitribai took up the responsibility of educating other women as well. The study is relevant to the recommendation of NEP 2020 which talks about underrepresent group of girls providing a quality of education to them. Like, Savitribai Phule's we can also take initiatives to make them aware about the New Education Policy and help them to reach out the school. Through educating women, we can bring many changes in the future generations too. She felt that women must receive an education as they were in no way inferior to men; they were not the slaves of men. Savitribai Phule emphasized that education is the key to self-reliance and further to social reform.

References

1. W. Pramod, Pandharinath, (2020). Savitribai Phule: *Women Empowerment in India, Studies in Indian Place Names* (UGC Care

Journal), March, ISSN: 2394- 3114, Vol-40, Issue-38, P932- 939, 8p. 84

2. Das & Das. *Educational Contribution of Savitribai Phule in 21st Century India.* Published in International Journal of Trend in Scientific Research and Development Volume 5 Issue 4, May-June 2021, P-1281 & 1284.

3. Mangala, K. D. (2018). *Savitribai Phule: Revolutionary work and literature.* Indian journals.com. Vol 5, pp 71-75

4. Garaian, Sen (2021). *SAVITRIBAI PHULE THE FIRST LADY TEACHER AND SOCIAL REFORMER IN NINETEENTH CENTURY OF INDIA.* EPRA International Journal of Multidisciplinary Research (IJMR) - Peer Reviewed Journal Volume: 7 | Issue: 6 | June 2021||P-326. <u>1030pm 49. EPRA JOURNALS 7439.pdf</u>

5. https://learn.culturalindia.net/savitribai-phule.html

6. https://en.wikipedia.org/wiki/Savitribai_Phule

7. https://www.hercircle.in/engage/get-inspired/achievers/ remembering-savitribai-phule-and-her-contribution-to-women39s-education-in-india-4073.html

8. https://www.slideshare.net/sain23/contribution-of-savitribai-phule-in-education

Philosophical Perspective of Swami Vivekananda In NEP 2020

Lalrochami Ralte* & Lalbiakdiki Hnamte**

*Research Scholar, Department of Education, Mizoram University,
Mizoram- 796004

**Professor, Department of Education, Mizoram University, Mizoram- 796004
Email: diki233@gmail.com

ABSTRACT: Swami Vivekananda was a revolutionary thinker and an unconventional educator. He advocated the replacement of the educational system of his day with a comprehensive, harmonious model centred on the needs of students. Many aspects of his vision for education and the NEP 2020 are similar, such as the importance of mother tongue in subject teaching and the importance of learning Sanskrit and English for overall personality development. To meet the 2030 Sustainable Development Goals, NEP 2020 aims to develop whole people in the form of students who have moral and spiritual values, character, knowledge, skills, creative genius, innovation, and leadership abilities.

14.0 INTRODUCTION

Narendranath Datta who came to be popularly known as Swami Vivekananda was influenced by both Western and Indian civilizations. His exposure to Hindu god worship and Christian religion regularly conflicted with his beliefs - that is, up until he accepted Ramakrishna as his guru and became a monk. His broad cultural understanding also contributed to his success in advancing interfaith understanding and helped him win admiration for it. He believed this because he had heard from his guru that serving others can serve God.

Swami Vivekananda's journey into spirituality was an amazing one. He did quite well in school and he studied anything that piqued his interest, whether it was literature, philosophy, physics, history, or religion. He was also a voracious reader of all kinds of sacred writings, including the Vedas, the Bhagavad Gita, the Ramayana, the Mahabharata, and the Upanishads. At age 10, after spending two years in Raipur, his family returned to their birthplace, and he took the entrance exam for Presidency College. He was the sole student to receive grades in the first division. He was an all-rounder who had studied Indian classical music and took part in organized sports. His brilliance was evident in how he utilized it in daily life rather than only in books.

14.1 SWAMI VIVEKANANDA'S EDUCATIONAL IDEAS ENVISAGED IN NEP 2020

When one studies the fundamental ideas of The National Education Policy 2020, one will find many of Swami Vivekananda's concepts of education, some of which are listed below:

1. Holistic development: Swami Vivekananda stressed the importance of a person's holistic growth, which includes fostering their physical, mental, and spiritual facets. The NEP 2020 emphasizes the value of comprehensive education that fosters physical, mental, emotional, and social growth.

2. Value-based education: Swami Vivekananda held that moral and ethical ideals should be instilled in students through education. The NEP 2020 acknowledges the need of cultivating values like compassion, honesty, and respect and advocates value-based education.

3. Multidisciplinary education: Swami Vivekananda was a big advocator of a multidisciplinary approach to education. The NEP 2020 emphasizes the need for diverse education that fosters originality, creativity, and critical thought.

4. Education for social transformation: Swami Vivekananda strongly believed that education should promote both individual growth and social change. With a focus on minimizing gaps and advancing

social justice, the NEP 2020 seeks to establish an educational system that is open, equitable, and accessible to all.

5. The goal of NEP 2020 is to create a new and vibrant India with a vision of limitless, universal, and true human perfection. This goal is consistent with Swami Vivekananda's advice to "teach yourselves, teach everyone his real nature, call upon the sleeping soul and see how it awakens," which is to "bring about revolutionary changes and also have a notable impact on the rest of the world." When this sleeping soul is awakened to self-conscious activity, "power will come, glory will come, goodness will come, purity will come, and everything excellent will come."

6. Swami Vivekananda's statement that "true education" has not yet been conceptualized among us echoes the need for pupils to not only learn but also how to learn. It can be characterized as the growth of faculty rather than the accumulation of words, or as the instruction of people to will correctly and effectively. Students must be given the tools to become morally upright, logical, compassionate, and caring people through education.

7. The NEP places a high focus on imparting Indian traditions and value systems in education, as well as preserving India's vast cultural past. Swami Vivekananda expressed similar thoughts; we must develop in accordance with our nature. I don't criticize the institutions of other races; they serve their interests, not ours. We may naturally follow our bent and run into our grooves given our traditions and thousands of years of karma, and that is exactly what we must do.

8. According to the NEP, education for historically underrepresented, impoverished, and marginalized people shall be prioritized. Swamiji has constantly emphasized the importance of this essential national requirement. 'Educate and uplift the masses, and only then will a nation be feasible,' he implored. The entire flaw is here: the people who reside in the cottages have forgotten their manhood and individuality.

14.2 SWAMI VIVEKANANDA'S EDUCATIONAL IDEAS FOR HIGHER EDUCATION AS VISIBLE IN NEP 2020

India hasn't made any significant reforms to its educational system for the past several years. On July 31, 2020, the National Education Policy (NEP) was formally unveiled. The strategy intends to improve education for close to 300 million students in the nation through a variety of changes, increasing public spending on education from 4.4% of India's GDP to 6%. To achieve this, the policy lays out extensive reforms that will impact all students, from the youngest enrolling in kindergarten to the most ambitious graduate student seeking a Ph.D. program.

There is hardly much research being done at universities or colleges. There is far less opportunity to study any innovative or futuristic ideas. The division of higher education into two categories of institutions, one for teaching and the other for research is one of the main causes of the paucity of research. In comparison to other countries, research funding is also lacking. The NEP also addresses the issue of granting universities graded autonomy, a step that will phase out university affiliations over the next 15 years.

Swami Vivekananda's ideas for higher education which are reflected in NEP 2020 may be summed up in the following few paragraphs:

1. Innovation and research: Swami Vivekananda opined that education should encourage innovation and research. In NEP 2020, it is emphasized that institutions must promote a culture of research and innovation and that they should work in partnership with businesses and other stakeholders.

2. Technology-enabled learning: Swami Vivekananda thought that technology could be used to raise educational standards. Technology-enhanced learning has great promise, and NEP 2020 encourages institutions to take advantage of it to increase access and quality.

3. Swami Vivekananda has also expressed concern about treachery. 'As long as millions of people suffer from hunger and illiteracy, I

consider every man a traitor who, having been educated at their expense, pays no attention to them,' he stated. This reality must now be communicated throughout India, particularly among the younger generation. They understand Swamiji's saying to mean both "be" and "create," noting that our country's foundational ideals are "renunciation and service."

4. Swami Vivekananda had a lot of faith in the youth. Higher education is required to generate such a generation of youth. When our higher education institutions become such information custodians, comprised of competent students and instructors, the country will be transformed into the knowledge society envisaged by the NEP.

14.3 WOMEN'S EDUCATION ACCORDING TO SWAMI VIVEKANANDA AND NEP 2020

Swami Vivekananda was a strong advocate of women's education and held the view that it was crucial for the advancement of society. Vivekananda's plea for the empowerment of the oppressed masses, especially the long-neglected women, has received widespread support; yet, civilizations frequently alter education to suit their own interests, robbing the weak of the power to shape their own destiny. His female education system's main objective is to develop strong, courageous women who are aware of their chastity and dignity.

The NEP 2020 also envisioned an egalitarian and inclusive education for all children and youth, especially girls from economically and socially disadvantaged groups. The policy's focus is crucial since, despite attempts to educate women, girls drop out at an alarming rate after secondary school. Secondary and upper-secondary enrollment ratios are also declining. Menstruation and a lack of proper bathrooms are only two of the many reasons why ladies drop out before completing their education. The NEP 2020 intends to meet this challenge with its Gender Inclusion Fund. The fund will be utilized to ensure that all pupils get a good education. It is hoped that it will also be used to ensure the security of facilities, and clean bathrooms are surely on GIF's infrastructure checklist. In addition to restrooms, NEP has proposed hostel facilities for female students. This might be advantageous in locations where pupils must commute significant distances to school.

Women teachers were also overlooked, in addition to women's education. NEP 2020 attempts to solve the issue of gender disparity in rural teacher recruitment. The policy aims to apply novel techniques that will ensure that qualifications and merit are considered and that women teachers have access to the appropriate recruitment channels. It is a well-known fact that competent teacher training is required for high-quality education.

The policy has emphasized the need for educators, such as Anganwadi workers, to receive the appropriate training to provide guidance to the families of female students. This family's participation in therapy is important since the disparity between an educated girl child and her uneducated relatives creates a unique set of issues.

NEP's emphasis on skill-improvement classes would be a significant step forward for female students. Economic empowerment of women through education will surely be progressive, attracting female students to educational institutions and, ideally, changing how traditional families differentiate between male and female schools, considering the former as a more lucrative proposition.

The NEP 2020 has placed a strong emphasis on the value of women's education and empowerment, and it seeks to give women equal opportunity in both the classroom and the workplace. The goal of the policy is to advance gender equality in education by emphasizing the importance of providing safe and welcoming learning settings for women.

The NEP 2020 strives to give women the information and skills they need to become leaders in their industries because it acknowledges the significant role they can play in the growth of the nation. The goal of the program is to provide scholarships and other incentives to encourage women to seek higher education. It also encourages the development of more women's colleges and universities.

The various provisions laid down in NEP 2020 for the education of girls/women are found to be significantly related to Vivekananda's thoughts on the same.

14.4 ANALYSING SWAMI VIVEKANANDA'S PHILOSOPHY FROM NEP 2020

The NEP 2020 emphasizes the need for multidisciplinary education that integrates academic and vocational education and promotes critical thinking and problem-solving skills. Swami Vivekananda's emphasis on practical education and the application of knowledge in real-world situations is reflected in the NEP 2020's focus on experiential learning and internships.

According to Swami Vivekananda, education should emphasize the growth of moral and ethical principles, and the NEP 2020 acknowledges the significance of this kind of education. The policy places a strong emphasis on the value of fostering empathy, compassion, and respect for the difference via education.

The NEP 2020 emphasizes the significance of inclusive education that offers equal opportunity to all, regardless of their social and economic circumstances, because Swami Vivekananda felt that education should be available to all. The policy also acknowledges the significance of addressing the particular requirements and difficulties experienced by marginalized groups, especially girls and women. Swami Vivekananda thought that education should nurture a culture of research and innovation, and the NEP 2020 pushes institutions to do the same. The policy acknowledges the value of industry and academic cooperation in fostering innovation and entrepreneurship. The National Education Policy (NEP) 2020 guidelines echo his excellent pedagogical philosophies.

When delivering education, Vivekananda placed a strong emphasis on the importance of the mother tongue. With the same goal in mind, NEP wants to mandate mother tongue instruction for pupils in the primary grades. They would also have to learn any other language listed on the list of official languages. His emphasis on science and technology is noted in NEP with notable projects including the establishment of NRF, NETF, and school curricula that embrace ML, AI, and other technologies. His idea of transforming people into chance givers rather than opportunity seekers has echoed in NEP's emphasis on vocational education from the elementary school level up. With initiatives like Study in India-Stay in India and deeper connection with the top 100 institutes of the globe, NEP aims to give India back it's old standing as a Vishwa guru. NEP is driven by the goal to develop a person's character, refine his intellect, and equip him to stand on his own while contributing to the nation and the larger world, just as Vivekananda had noted the close relationship between national development and character transformation. With Vivekananda's vision looming large, it would be splendid if we could continue to make progress toward capacity-building, character-building, and nation-building.

The NEP 2020 charter states that it would 'make the educational system holistic, adaptable, multidisciplinary, and connected to the needs of the 21st century and the 2030 Sustainable Development Goals'. Students worldwide used to flock to places like Nalanda and Taxila to study the arts and sciences. NEP is an effort to bring India back to its previous grandeur and turn it into a hub of innovation, knowledge, and quality once more. According to the principles of Access, Equality, Quality, Affordability, and Accountability, it seeks to transform the country's educational environment into a thriving knowledge society.

"Do not believe that you are weak or small, you can do anything and anything," advised Swamiji. His emphasis on fostering self-confidence and self-esteem was a crucial part of his vision because, in his words, "education is not just filling the mind with a lot of facts". It needs to be a meaningful and purposeful exercise. NEP 2020 strives to develop pupils into people with excellent sportsmanship and teamwork, moral and spiritual values, character, knowledge, skills, and creative genius. The growth of both mental and physical power is something that Swamiji has always supported. Swamiji emphasizes physical health in his educational scheme because a sound mind resides in a sound body. He frequently quotes the Upanishadic dictum 'nayamatma nalahinena labhyah,' which means that the physically weak cannot realize the self. However, in addition to physical culture, he emphasizes the importance of focusing on mental culture. According to Swamiji, students' minds must be controlled and trained through meditation, concentration, and ethical purity practice. He advised having "iron muscles and steel nerves."

Swamiji believed that the solution to all social and international ills was education. He emphasized the urgent need to help people discover their spiritual selves since that is what education is all about. In Swamiji's opinion, the goal of all education is the creation of men. The first sentence of NEP 2020, "Education is fundamental for achieving full human potential" echoes Vivekananda's proposal for man-making education within the context of his larger Vedanta philosophy.

Along with other life skills like leadership, cooperation, communication, and teamwork that are crucial for developing a well-rounded personality, we must have life-building, man-making, character-making assimilation of ideas. NEP 2020 places a lot of emphasis on the development of each person's creative potential. It is based on the notion that in addition to developing students' cognitive abilities, education must also strengthen their social, ethical, and emotional abilities.

Starting in 2021–2022, the new strategy is supposed to be implemented progressively this decade. Every student, teacher, parent, and other stakeholder has an important role to play. Effective implementation of the new policy will only be a pipe dream without the active participation of all stakeholders. Regarding the implementation of NEP 2020, the Ministry of Education promises to follow Swamiji's advice to "Arise, Awake, and Stop not till the goal is reached."

14.5 CONCLUSION

The National Education Policy (NEP) 2020, which emphasizes the need for a holistic and multidisciplinary approach to education, is in line with Swami Vivekananda's ideology. He supported values-based education, transdisciplinary learning, and education for social change in addition to the overall development of people. With a focus on minimizing gaps and advancing social justice, the NEP 2020 seeks to establish an educational system that is open, equitable, and accessible to all.

References

1. Merina Islam (January 2013) Philosophy of Swami Vivekanandahttps://www.researchgate.net/publication/272477405_Philosophy_of_Swami_Vivekananda

2. Sutradhar D (September 2022) Educational philosophy of Swami Vivekanandahttps://yoursmartclass.com/educational-philosophy-of-swami-vivekananda/

3. Wand of Knowledge Team (n.d.) Swami Vivekananda's philosophy of education| meaning and principleshttps://wandofknowledge.com/swami-vivekanandas-philosophy-of-education-meaning-principles/

4. Bhat S.A (October 2021) An evaluative study educational philosophy of Swami Vivekanandahttps://www.researchgate.net/publication/356787060_An_Evaluative_Study_of_Educational_Philosophy_of_Swami_Vivekananda

5. Sirswal D.R (January 2013) Philosophy of Swami Vivekanandahttps://www.researchgate.net/publication/272477405_Philosophy_of_Swami_Vivekananda

6. Vedantu (Febuary, 2023) Biography of Swami Vivekanandahttps://www.vedantu.com/biography/swami-vivekananda-biography

7. The Indian Express (January 2020) Explained: how Swami Vivekananda became the messenger of Indian wisdom to the westhttps://indianexpress.com/article/explained/explained-how-

swami-vivekananda-became-the-messenger-of-indian-wisdom-to-the-west-6213107/

8. Times Now (September 2020) Nep 2020 reflects Swami Vivekananda-Vice Presidenthttps://www.timesnownews. com/education/article/nep-2020-reflects-the-ideals-of-swami-vivekananda-vice-president/650601

9. Vivekananda International Foundation (December 2020) Webinar on "Nep-2020 and stem education"https://vifindia. org/event/report/2020/december/08/webinar-on-nep-2020-and-stem-education

10. Godkhindi S (July 2021) National education policy 2020: transforming India's education systemhttps://myvoice.opindia. com/2021/07/national-education-policy-2020-transforming-indias-education-system/

11. Gurwara S (August 2021) Re-imaging and re-defining education: Nep 2020 and the vision of Swami Vivekanandahttps://blog. subharti.org/re-imagining-and-re-defining-education-nep-2020-and-the-vision-of-swami-vivekananda/

12. Pokhriyal R (October 2020) Reflections of ideals of Vivekananda on nephttps://www.linkedin.com/pulse/reflections-ideals-vivekananda-nep-ramesh-pokhriyal-nishank-

13. India Today (August 2020) National education policy 2020: How nep is a step towards freedom in educationhttps://www. indiatoday.in/education-today/featurephilia/story/national-education-policy-2020-how-nep-is-a-step-towards-freedom-in-education-1711354-2020-08-15

14. Philpapers (n.d.) Swami Vivekananda Indian youth and value educationhttps://philpapers.org/archive/SIRSV.pdf

15. Vdikyatra (July 2019) Swami Vivekananda and his philosophy of educationhttps://www.vaidikyatra.org/en/swami-vivekananda-and-his-philosophy-of-education/#

16. The Week (August 2020) New education policy 2020 reflects the vision of Swami Vivekananda Atmapriyanandahttps://www.

theweek.in/wire-updates/national/2020/08/09/ces24-wb-nep-academics.html

17. Sarkar c & Sharma D (February 2019) Swami Vivekananda's spiritual thoughts and current problems of educationhttps://www.researchgate.net/publication/339352409_Swami_Vivekananda%27s_Spiritual_Thought_and_Current_Problem_of_Education

Influence of Tagore's Educational Philosophy and His Experimentations on Education in Framing National Education Policy-2020

Mr. Sanjay Das

Assistant Professor, Ambedkar College, Fatikroy, Unakoti, Tripura

E-mail: sanjay281105@gmail.com

ABSTRACT: *Rabindranath Tagore's ideas and pedagogical philosophy are incomparable and unprecedented. Even in his most famous poems, Rabindranath emphasises the key issues: the independence of thinking and speech; active communication; blending nature and man; and the encouragement of the highest possible level of creative expression. Naturalism, idealism, humanism, and internationalism formed the basis of his educational philosophy. His educational ideas and philosophies are practically implemented by establishing two institutions, Shantiniketan and Visva-Bharati. Rabindranath Tagore's educational philosophy is a foundation for several important National Education Policy 2020 (NEP-2020) areas. This paper discusses the influence of Tagore's educational philosophy and his experimentations on education while framing NEP-2020.*

Keywords: *Rabindranath Tagore, Educational Philosophy, Experimentation, NEP 2020.*

15.0 INTRODUCTION

Rabindranath Tagore (1861-1941) was a renowned poet, philosopher, writer, and educator. He won the Nobel Prize in 1913 for his Literature, Gitanjali (Song Offerings), a free-verse translation of his Bengal poetry based on mediaeval Indian religious melodies. Rabindranath Tagore's ideas and pedagogical philosophy are incomparable and unprecedented. Even in his most famous poems, Rabindranath emphasises three key issues: the independence of thinking and speech; active communication; blending nature and man; and the encouragement of the highest possible level of creative expression. He foresaw a holistic education profoundly grounded in an individual's culture and environment and related to the broader world. He preferred a curriculum that fostered creativity, imagination, and morality above the mechanical, formal system. Naturalism, idealism, humanism, and internationalism formed the basis of his educational philosophy.

Moreover, his education philosophy combined nationalist heritage, Western and Eastern philosophy, science, and a global perspective. Shantiniketan and Visva-Bharati, two institutions he established, are practical expressions of his educational ideas and philosophies. Through NEP-2020, steps have recently been taken to change the education system in India. NEP-2020 is found to be influenced by Tagore's philosophy.

15.1 EDUCATIONAL PHILOSOPHY OF RABINDRANATH TAGORE

Rabindranath Tagore was not a systematic philosopher. Still, his thoughts and worldview informed his writings are distinctive and profound. He fused traditional Indian philosophy with Western thought, creating a spiritual humanism that was uniquely his own. Rabindranath Tagore's philosophy of life is deeply reflected in his philosophy of education. Tagore's philosophy of life is deeply reflected in his philosophy of education. Possessing philosophical thoughts, he is an idealist and naturalist. Some features of Rabindranath's educational philosophy are discussed below:

- **A close relationship between man and nature**: The flaw in Rabindranath's traditional educational system is its isolation from the natural environment. According to him, there is a close relationship between man and nature. Being in the presence of nature is well-organised, and he can realise the absolute truth. So, he established Santiniketan, inspired by the ideals of education of the ancient Indian *Tapovana*. Here the teacher-students live in the shade of nature.

- **Freedom:** Tagore believed human progress required freedom. Education builds character and explores human potential. It is a liberal procedure that allows people to develop fully. Thus, only freedom-based education imparts learning.
- **Self-Realization:** Tagore believed that humanism is spiritualism. Self-realization and spirituality determine personality. Education is about self-realization.
- **Indian Culture:** Rabindranath's educational scheme does not attempt to imitate foreign ones. He believed in Indian tradition and wanted to incorporate the ancient Indian tradition into his educational system. However, he was opposed to conventional reforms and artificial rituals.
- **Synthesis of Eastern and Western Cultures:** Although he believed in Indian traditions and beliefs, he tried to harmonise Western culture and educational planning. Rabindranath did not ignore the scientific knowledge from Western countries in India. In his educational plan, the synthesis of Eastern and Western cultures was pritiorised.
- **Humanity:** Rabindranath's educational philosophy occupies a vital place for humanity. He did not admit artificial in people. On the contrary, he loved everyone, rich and poor. So, unity and equality have been prioritised in his education system.
- **Sense of beauty:** Rabindranath was a worshiper of beauty. Therefore, the joy of feeling the world's beauty is constantly flowing in him, and the main task of education will be to familiarise the child with it.
- **Self-expression:** Children will have the chance to express themselves in the classroom. Rabindranath believed that the educational system should foster the development of students' creative abilities. According to him, not only are children's organs moved into creative activities like painting, art, and sculpting, but his intellect is also sufficiently developed.
- **Overall development of a child:** Rabindranath emphasised the child's overall development. According to him, the main task of

education will be the complete development of the child's body, mind and soul.

15.2 RABINDRANATH TAGORE'S EXPERIMENTATION IN THE INDIAN EDUCATION SYSTEM

Tagore's writings and the educational experiments he conducted at Santiniketan provide the best insight into his contributions to the field of education. This is primarily because Tagore did not produce any pedagogical manifesto. His views on education shifted over time after much trial and error and exposure to various educational systems worldwide. He envisioned a locally grounded and globally aware education built on joyful discovery tailored to each child's unique interests and personality.

In his opinion, classes should be conducted outside beneath the trees so that students can spontaneously understand the mutability of the plant and animal worlds and the cyclical pattern of the seasons. In between lessons, students could run and climb the trees around the classroom, where they sat on hand-woven mats. Students were required to participate in outdoor activities like hiking and birdwatching and were taught about the natural history of the world around them. Tagore adapted the children's school timetables so that they could take into account weather changes and other natural occurrences, and he also made-up seasonal celebrations for them to enjoy.

Tagore's educational philosophy emphasised the cultivation of the senses and the mind via art. He claimed in his writing that a country bereft of music and the fine arts was one whose people could not express themselves. He believes the arts should be included in every classroom, including music, literature, art, dance, and drama. While Tagore was alive, he was one of the first to promote and unite many styles of Indian dance. He was instrumental in reviving traditional dances and introducing new ones from various areas of India, like Manipuri, Kathak, and Kathakali. Also, he was an advocate for contemporary dance. Tagore included his pupils in his writing and composing sessions, believing this would help them learn more effectively.

In the classroom, he advocated raising literature at challenging levels students may not wholly comprehend but would engage them. Students had access to the chamber where he presented his latest works to academics and critics and were invited to share their works on literary nights. Many student-made illustrated periodicals were published while the students were in Shantiniketan. The children were encouraged to paint and sketch anything they wanted on their ideas or those of the various guest artists and authors.

Tagore envisioned Visva-Bharati as a cultural melting pot, a place of learning where people from different backgrounds and perspectives could come together to learn and grow with the ultimate goal of understanding.

Rabindranath Tagore is a living symbol of the cooperation and inspiration he promoted. Tagore argued for a new approach to teaching that would involve a shift in the curriculum. Instead of teaching about national cultures in terms of the wars they've fought and the cultural domination they've imposed, he argued for an approach that examines history and culture through the lens of the progress achieved in reducing social and religious divisions. Tagore made significant contributions to the field of education. He was an early proponent in India of a humane education system that considered the natural world and sought to cultivate whole people. Shantiniketan provided one of the first coeducational programmes in South Asia. Its approach to teaching in the local language, Bengali, established a model for other regional educational institutions.

Visva-Bharati and Sriniketan were ground-breaking institutions that paved the way for new ways of thinking and doing things across various fields, from mass education to pan-Asian and global cultural interchange to innovative forms of higher education. Rabindranath Tagore had an unusual poetic approach to teaching and learning. He wanted to make poetry at Shantiniketan "in a medium other than words," he said. He created a holistic plan and a one-of-a-kind curriculum for teaching about the environment and encouraging artistic expression in an atmosphere conducive to cross-cultural understanding because of his poetic vision.

15.3 INFLUENCE OF RABINDRANATH TAGORE'S IDEA ON NEP-2020

The National Education Policy 2020 (NEP 2020), which the Indian government approved in July 2020, attempts to regain the flavor of Indian traditional custom culture, heritage and ancient and contemporary knowledge system. The goal of NEP-2020 is to foster the growth of well-rounded individuals who can think critically and act ethically; show compassion and empathy towards others; face adversity and emerge stronger; demonstrate scientific curiosity and imaginative flair; and have strong ethical foundations. Our Constitution calls for a fair, inclusive, and plural society, and this programme seeks to produce people who are actively involved in and contributing to that goal. NEP 2020 shares some striking similarities with Tagore's educational concept. NEP 2020 is a comprehensive framework for transforming India's education system, aimed at promoting equity, access, quality, and affordability in education at all levels. Some key similarities between NEP 2020 and Tagore's educational concept are discussed below:

i. Reviving Ancient Indian Culture, Traditions, and Knowledge:

Rabindranath Tagore's educational scheme does not attempt to imitate foreign ones. He believed in Indian tradition and wanted to incorporate the ancient Indian tradition into his educational system. The main aim of education at Santiniketan is to teach the students the ethics and spirituality of ancient India. The ideal reflection of the moral and spiritual education of ancient India's ascetics is evident in Santiniketan's educational system.

NEP-2020 aims to enhance the relatability, relevance, interest, and effectiveness of education for students. NEP 2020 also proposes that the curriculum and pedagogy should be redesigned to incorporate Indian and local context and ethos, including culture, traditions, heritage, customs, language, philosophy, geography, ancient and contemporary knowledge, societal and scientific needs, indigenous and traditional ways of learning, starting from the foundational stage. Whenever feasible, narratives, artistic expressions, recreational activities, athletic pursuits, illustrations, challenges, and other materials will be selected with a solid connection to the Indian and regional geographical context (Govt. of India, 2020).

ii. Experiential learning:

In Shantiniketan, hospitality, self-help and reverence for elders shaped an essential, regular, and austere life. The students were responsible for all school chores except food preparation. The learning was founded on self-experience of the surrounding universe and thorough reflection. His education system calls for students to spend their free time telling stories, gazing at the stars, singing, and putting on plays during the nighttime play periods. Songs and plays were often composed by students themselves. The student was given autonomy for their education. The concepts of education espoused by Tagore are connected to learning through experience.

NEP-2020 recommends that Experiential learning, including hands-on learning, arts-integrated and sports-integrated education, story-telling-based pedagogy, and others, will be used at all levels as standard pedagogy within each topic and to explore subject relationships. By incorporating cultural aspects of the languages being taught (such as films, theatre, storytelling, poetry, and music), and by drawing connections with a wide range of relevant subjects and with students' own experiences, the instruction of all languages will be enriched through innovative and experiential methods, such as gamification and applications. (Govt. of India, 2020, p.16).

iii. Pedagogy of teaching:

Tagore advocated using the 'activity method', 'Education through excursion', 'Debate and discussion', 'Heuristic method', etc. of education. He believed them to be crucial for developing the body and intellect of a child. Tagore firmly believed that the activity method could generate a learning environment centred on the student's needs. He thought field trips and sightseeing tours of historical sites would be a great way to teach students about economics, geography, and other social sciences. Tagore used the heuristic approach as central to his school's curriculum. In this approach, students are encouraged to express their confusion about a specific subject through questions, and teachers are tasked with providing satisfactory answers. Tagore's school organised narrative, discussion, and debate events to help pupils hone their public speaking skills.

NEP-2020 calls for constructivist teaching methods throughout science, mathematics, the social sciences, literature, and Indian cultural history.

iv. Reduction of curriculum and to enhance essential learning and critical thinking:

In Shantiniketan, although required textbooks had to be studied in matriculation courses, stereotypical texts were banned, and students were encouraged to read widely. The learning was founded on self-experience of the surrounding universe and thorough reflection. His education system calls for students to spend their free time telling stories, gazing at the stars, singing, and putting on plays during the nighttime play periods. Songs and plays were often composed by students themselves. Debates were organised to test their critical thinking. Students were inspired to write and publish them in the magazine. There was a strong focus on the pupils' health. Game time and gardening time were both required.

The NEP-2020 calls for rational decision-making and innovation. NEP-2020 recommends to encourage critical thinking with holistic, inquiry-based, discovery-based, discussion-based, and analysis-based learning, each subject's curriculum will be pared down. The required material will include essential concepts, ideas, applications, and problem-solving. For more profound and more immersive learning, classroom sessions will consist of more enjoyable, creative, collaborative, and exploratory activities for students. Questions will be encouraged from students.

v. Respect for diversity and local context:

Tagore established Sriniketan in Visva-Bharati to study the needs of the locality. He believed that a university's work should include collecting accurate knowledge about rural conditions, the customs of rural people regarding various aspects of life (such as agriculture, the economy, and social issues), as well as the difficulties that rural people face in these areas. He hoped the students and research teams would apply their newfound understanding of rural areas' challenges.

The NEP-2020 emphasises respect for diversity and local context in all curricula, pedagogy, and policy while remembering that schooling is a contemporary topic.

vi. Flexibility and Choice:

Tagore thought education should be flexible and tailored to each student's requirements and interests. He supported students' right to self-direction and choice in their education so they may follow their interests and passions.

NEP 2020 also promotes flexibility and choice in education. It proposes adopting a modular approach to learning, allowing students to choose their courses, subjects, and learning pathways. It also encourages using technology-enabled learning and open educational resources to provide greater access to education and enable self-paced and self-directed learning.

vii. Community and Social Responsibility

Tagore thought having a harmonious relationship between the individual and society was essential. He felt that education should help students create a sense of community and social duty to help make the world better.

NEP 2020 also talks about how important it is for schools to teach about society and social duty. It suggests combining community work and hands-on learning so students can get involved in their neighbourhoods and learn to be socially responsible. It also encourages teaching environmental education and sustainable practices in schools to teach students how to be good global citizens.

viii. Inclusivity and Equity

Tagore felt the importance of inclusivity and equity in the field of education. Regardless of one's social, economic, or cultural background, he thought everyone should have access to education.

NEP 2020, on the other hand, encourages equity and inclusiveness in education. It recommends expanding early childhood, primary, secondary, and higher education. It also encourages women, disabled children, and rural and remote places to participate. Further, it suggests using a gender-sensitive and inclusive curriculum to help all children feel appreciated and valued.

ix. Teacher Empowerment and Professional Development

Tagore believed in the importance of teacher empowerment and professional development. He thought that teachers should be given the freedom and autonomy to create a nurturing and supportive learning environment and should be provided with opportunities for continuous learning and growth.

NEP 2020 also promotes teacher empowerment and professional development. It suggests using a competency-based approach to teacher education, giving teachers the instruments to help students learn throughout the curriculum and in many different ways. Additionally, it encourages the use of technology in teacher preparation programmes and ongoing professional development, giving teachers access to the most recent pedagogical theories and instructional strategies.

x. Cultural and Linguistic Diversity

The value of linguistic and cultural variety in education was something Tagore strongly believed in. He believed that education should instil in students a feeling of global citizenship and an appreciation and respect for many cultures and languages.

The significance of cultural and linguistic diversity in education is particularly emphasised by NEP 2020. To help pupils understand and respect the variety of Indian culture and language, it suggests including regional languages and promoting multilingualism. Additionally, it encourages the integration of indigenous knowledge and customs into the curriculum, enabling students to absorb and value the knowledge of India's many distinct cultures.

xi. Vocational Education:

In Visva-Bharati, Tagore started *Shilpa Sadan*, a Shilpa Shikshan Mahavidyalaya. The institute provided industry works such as weaving, woodworking, bookbinding, leather work, etc.

NEP 2020 intends to introduce elementary and secondary school children to various trades and professions, such as pottery, electrical, metallic, woodworking, paper crafting, textile making, sewing, printing, etc.

15.4 CONCLUSION

NEP 2020 is an extensive blueprint for transforming India's education system that aims to promote equity, access, quality, and affordability at all levels of education. Rabindranath Tagore believed that education should develop the whole person, supporting their physical, intellectual, emotional, and spiritual health and helping them discover their talents. He advocated for a complete, sustainable, inclusive society promoting healthy human-society relations. The National Education Policy 2020 shares striking similarities with Tagore's educational concept. Both emphasise the importance of holistic and multidisciplinary education, flexibility and choice, community and social responsibility, inclusivity and equity, teacher empowerment and professional development, cultural and linguistic diversity, etc. By aligning with Tagore's educational concept, NEP 2020 has the potential to transform education in India and create a more harmonious, sustainable, and inclusive society.

Reference

1. Agarwal, J.C. (2010). *Theory and Practice of Education (13th Edition)*. Noida, UP: VIKAS Publishing House Pvt Ltd.
2. Banarjee, A. (2010). *Philosophy and Principles of Education*. Kolkata: B. B. Kundu Grandsons.
3. Banarjee, J.P. (2010). *Education in India - Present: Past: Future*. Kolkata: Central Library.
4. Chakrabarti, M. (1988). *Philosophy of Education of Rabindranath Tagore: A Critical Evolution*. Michigan: Atlantic.

5. Chakraborty, J. C. (2010). *Modern Education: Its Aims and Principles*. Kolkata: K. Chakraborty Publications.

6. Das, Dreamsea. (2014). Educational philosophy of Rabindranath Tagore. *International Journal of Research in Humanities, Arts and Literature, 2*(6), 1-4.

7. Deep, Vishal. (2019). Relevance of Rabindranath's educational philosophy in present perspective. *International Journal of 360^0 Management Review: Education & its Relevant Areas in New Era, 7*, 119-122.

8. Dutta, Krishna & Andrew Robinson (1995). *Rabindranath Tagore: The Myriad-Minded Man*, London: Bloomsbury.

9. Govt. of India (2020). *National Education Policy 2020*. [Pdf file]. https://www.education.gov.in/sites/upload_files/mhrd/files/NEP_Final_English_0.pdf

10. Jalan, Radha Binod. (1976). *TAGORE—HIS EDUCATIONAL THEORY AND PRACTICE AND ITS IMPACT ON INDIAN EDUCATION*. (Doctoral Dissertation). University of Florida, Florida, USA.

11. Jha, Bhawna (2021). Tagore's Philosophy of Education. *International Journal of Humanities, Engineering, Science and Management (IJHESM), II*(I), 32-34.

12. Joshi, Sunitha. (2000). Great Indian Educational Thinkers, Delhi: Scholarly Books.

13. O'Connell, Kathleen (2002). *Rabindranath Tagore: The Poet as Educator*. Calcutta: Visva-Bharati.

14. Salker, K. R. (1990). *Rabindranath Tagore His Impact on Indian Education*. Delhi: Sterling Publishers Private Limited.

15. (https://archive.org/stream/tagorehiseducati00jala/tagorehiseducati00jala_djvu.txt)

16. (https://www.academia.edu/4659110/Rabindranath_Tagore_on_Education)

17. (https://epgp.inflibnet.ac.in/epgpdata/uploads/epgp_content/S000033SO/P000300/M015159/ET/146043432717ET.pdf)

Indian Philosophical Thoughts and the Contribution of Swami Vivekananda to the Field of Education in India

Dr.Bandi Venu

Asst.Profeser (G.F)

University College Education, Kakatiya University

Hanamakonda, Telangana,

Email Id : venubandi05@gmail.com

Phone : 9966943843.

ABSTRACT: *This paper examines Swami Vivekananda's profound influence on Indian philosophy and education, emphasizing the diversity and core themes of Indian philosophical thought. It explores Vivekananda's life and his philosophical ideas, focusing on his advocacy for religious unity, self-realization, and service to humanity. Furthermore, the paper discusses Vivekananda's significant contributions to education, particularly his holistic vision for personal development and the establishment of the Ramakrishna Mission. It highlights how his ideas have impacted educational reforms and the incorporation of yoga and meditation into mainstream education, along with his global influence through his speeches at the World's Parliament of Religions. The enduring relevance of Vivekananda's teachings is exemplified through the ongoing work of the Ramakrishna Mission, emphasizing spirituality and service. In conclusion, the paper underscores how Vivekananda's synthesis of ancient wisdom and contemporary ideals continues to guide India's educational reforms and spiritual aspirations, offering a path towards a spiritually enriched future. It provides references for further in-depth exploration of these topics.*

16.0 INTRODUCTION

Indian philosophy has a rich and diverse history that spans millennia, encompassing a wide range of thoughts, beliefs, and practices. This profound philosophical heritage has deeply influenced various aspects of Indian society, including education. Swami Vivekananda, a prominent

Indian philosopher and spiritual leader of the late 19th and early 20th centuries, played a pivotal role in revitalizing Indian philosophical thought and reshaping the education system in India. In this article, we will explore the fundamental principles of Indian philosophy and delve into Swami Vivekananda's significant contributions to education in India.

16.1 INDIAN PHILOSOPHICAL THOUGHTS

A. Overview of Indian Philosophy:

- Diverse schools of thought: Nyaya, Vaisheshika, Samkhya, Yoga, Mimamsa, Vedanta, and more.
- Central themes: Dharma, karma, moksha, and the pursuit of truth and self-realization.

India, a land of diverse cultures and ancient wisdom, has given birth to some of the world's most profound philosophical traditions. These philosophical doctrines have not only shaped the spiritual and intellectual landscape of the country but have also left an indelible mark on the global philosophical discourse. Among the myriad luminaries who have been inspired by these age-old traditions and, in turn, have reshaped them, stands Swami Vivekananda, a towering figure whose impact on education in India is immeasurable.

Indian Philosophical Traditions:

Indian philosophy is a vast and intricate tapestry woven over millennia, encompassing a rich array of schools of thought. At its core, Indian philosophy seeks to unravel the mysteries of existence, the nature of consciousness, and the ultimate purpose of human life. These traditions can be broadly classified into six major schools:

1. **Vedanta**: Rooted in the ancient Vedas, Vedanta explores the nature of reality and the self. It includes sub-schools like Advaita (non-dualism), Dvaita (dualism), and Vishishtadvaita (qualified non-dualism).

2. **Yoga**: Yoga delves into the practices and disciplines aimed at achieving spiritual realization and union with the divine. Patanjali's Yoga Sutras are a cornerstone of this tradition.

3. **Nyaya**: Nyaya, the school of logic and epistemology, examines the means of acquiring knowledge and the nature of valid reasoning.

4. **Vaisheshika**: This school focuses on metaphysics and the classification of objects based on their inherent characteristics.

5. **Samkhya**: Samkhya philosophy analyzes the dualistic relationship between matter and consciousness, striving for liberation through discernment.

6. **Mimamsa**: Mimamsa concerns itself with the interpretation of Vedic texts and rituals.

These philosophical traditions are not merely ancient relics but continue to inform contemporary thought and belief systems across India.

Swami Vivekananda: A Brief Biography:

In the late 19th century, against the backdrop of colonial rule and social reform movements, Swami Vivekananda emerged as a spiritual luminary and social reformer. Born as Narendranath Datta in 1863 in Calcutta, he was deeply influenced by the teachings of his guru, Sri Ramakrishna Paramahamsa, and was instrumental in introducing Indian spirituality to the West.

Vivekananda's life was characterized by a relentless quest for truth and a burning desire to uplift the masses through education and spiritual awakening. His historic address at the World's Parliament of Religions in Chicago in 1893 catapulted him to international fame and marked the beginning of his mission to spread the message of India's ancient wisdom.

Swami Vivekananda's Impact on Education in India:

Swami Vivekananda's impact on education in India was profound and multifaceted. He recognized that education was the key to social progress and national regeneration, and he believed that it should be rooted in the spiritual and ethical values embedded in India's philosophical traditions.

Vivekananda's educational vision encompassed several key principles, including the promotion of holistic development, character building, and a harmonious blend of modern and traditional knowledge.

In the subsequent sections of this article, we will delve deeper into Vivekananda's interpretation of Indian philosophy and his specific contributions to the field of education in India, exploring how his ideas continue to shape the educational landscape of the country.

B. Influence on Education:

Swami Vivekananda's influence on education in India was transformative, as he advocated for a holistic approach that extended beyond mere academic knowledge. His vision for education encompassed the development of the whole individual, emphasizing character, ethics, critical thinking, and self-inquiry.

1. Emphasis on Holistic Education:

Swami Vivekananda firmly believed that education should not be confined to the accumulation of facts and figures but should nurture the holistic development of an individual. He viewed education as a means to unfold one's full potential, encompassing physical, mental, and spiritual dimensions. This holistic perspective aligned with India's ancient philosophical traditions, which emphasize the harmonious integration of various aspects of life.

Vivekananda's vision of holistic education called for the inclusion of physical fitness, mental clarity, emotional intelligence, and spiritual growth within the educational curriculum. He advocated for the development of a well-rounded individual capable of addressing life's challenges with resilience and wisdom.

2. Integrating Moral and Ethical Values:

One of the most distinctive aspects of Swami Vivekananda's educational philosophy was his insistence on the integration of moral and ethical values into the educational process. He believed that a strong moral foundation was essential for the well-being of individuals and society at large.

Incorporating moral and ethical values into education meant not only imparting theoretical knowledge but also instilling qualities like compassion, truthfulness, honesty, and a sense of social responsibility. Vivekananda emphasized that education should cultivate individuals who are not only knowledgeable but also virtuous, capable of making ethical choices in their personal and professional lives.

3. Encouraging Critical Thinking and Self-Inquiry:

Swami Vivekananda was a staunch advocate of critical thinking and self-inquiry in education. He believed that students should be encouraged to question, analyze, and explore knowledge independently. This approach aimed to foster intellectual curiosity and a spirit of inquiry, enabling individuals to gain a deeper understanding of the subjects they studied.

Vivekananda's emphasis on critical thinking extended to spiritual matters as well. He encouraged individuals to seek answers to profound existential questions through personal introspection and meditation. He believed that self-inquiry was a path to self-realization, a central goal of Indian philosophical traditions.

By promoting critical thinking and self-inquiry, Vivekananda's educational philosophy aimed to produce individuals who were not passive recipients of knowledge but active seekers of truth, capable of adapting to the changing world and contributing to its progress.

In summary, Swami Vivekananda's influence on education in India was characterized by a holistic approach that encompassed physical, mental, and spiritual dimensions. He advocated for the integration of moral and ethical values into education and encouraged critical thinking and self-inquiry. His educational principles continue to inspire educators and institutions in India and beyond, shaping the way education is perceived and delivered in the 21st century.

16.2 SWAMI VIVEKANANDA'S LIFE AND TEACHINGS

A. Early Life and Spiritual Quest:

Swami Vivekananda's remarkable life journey began with a childhood marked by intellectual curiosity and a deep yearning for spiritual truths. Born as Narendranath Datta in 1863 to a well-educated Bengali family in Calcutta, young Naren displayed a precocious intellect and a questioning mind.

1. Childhood Influences and Spiritual Awakening:

Naren's childhood was shaped by a blend of Western rationality and Indian spirituality. His father, Vishwanath Datta, was a lawyer influenced by Western education, while his mother, Bhuvaneshwari Devi, was deeply rooted in Indian religious traditions. This duality of influences had a profound impact on Naren's early worldview.

As a child, Naren was inquisitive and compassionate, often helping the poor and needy in his neighborhood. His mother's stories of saints and his father's rational discussions at home provided him with a well-rounded perspective on life and philosophy.

Naren's spiritual awakening came in his late teens when he was exposed to the works of Western philosophers and confronted questions about the existence of God and the nature of reality. This inner turmoil led him to seek answers from spiritual leaders and scholars of the time.

2. Meeting with Ramakrishna Paramahamsa:

The turning point in Swami Vivekananda's life occurred when he met Sri Ramakrishna Paramahamsa, a revered mystic and spiritual teacher, in 1881. Ramakrishna's simplicity, authenticity, and profound spiritual experiences deeply impressed Naren. He became a regular visitor to Ramakrishna's ashram, and under his guidance, Naren's spiritual quest intensified.

Ramakrishna's teachings emphasized the direct experience of God and the universality of spiritual truths. He encouraged Naren to explore different paths of spirituality, including devotion (Bhakti), knowledge (Jnana), and meditation (Dhyana), to gain a comprehensive understanding of the divine.

Through his association with Ramakrishna, Naren not only found answers to his philosophical inquiries but also underwent a profound transformation. His intellectual rigor and spiritual yearning converged, and he began to see the harmony between the principles of Western rationality and Indian mysticism.

Naren's life and teachings were forever shaped by his interactions with Ramakrishna. It was under Ramakrishna's guidance that Naren embraced monastic life and eventually became Swami Vivekananda, a name that would resonate globally as a champion of Indian philosophy and spirituality.

In the subsequent sections of this article, we will explore how Swami Vivekananda's spiritual insights and his understanding of Indian philosophical traditions influenced his educational vision and the broader impact of his teachings on India and the world.

B. Key Philosophical Ideas:

Swami Vivekananda's teachings are characterized by profound philosophical insights that continue to inspire individuals worldwide. His philosophy is rooted in the rich tapestry of Indian spiritual thought, and he emphasized several key ideas that remain central to his legacy.

1. Oneness of All Religions:

Swami Vivekananda fervently believed in the essential unity and universality of all religious traditions. He often emphasized that all religions are different paths to the same truth. This inclusive perspective, known as religious pluralism, was a fundamental tenet of his philosophy.

Vivekananda's famous speech at the World's Parliament of Religions in Chicago in 1893 encapsulated this idea. He began with the iconic words, "Sisters and brothers of America," breaking barriers of nationality and faith. He went on to explain that, just as different rivers ultimately merge into the same ocean, all religions lead to the realization of the same divine truth. This message of religious tolerance and interfaith harmony resonated deeply with audiences worldwide.

2. The Importance of Self-Realization:

A core teaching of Swami Vivekananda is the concept of self-realization, often referred to as "Atmano mokshartham jagat hitaya cha" (for one's own salvation and for the welfare of the world). He believed that every individual possesses an innate divinity, the Atman (the inner self), and that the ultimate goal of life is to realize this divine nature.

Vivekananda stressed that self-realization is not a mere intellectual pursuit but a direct experience of one's true self. He encouraged individuals to look inward through meditation and introspection to discover their inner divinity. According to him, self-realization leads to profound spiritual awakening and a sense of purpose in life.

3. The Concept of Service (Seva) and Duty (Dharma):

Swami Vivekananda considered selfless service (seva) to be a central aspect of spiritual practice and social responsibility. He believed that genuine spirituality must manifest in action and service to humanity. For him, service was not just a charitable act but a sacred duty (dharma).

Vivekananda's teachings on service emphasized that individuals should work for the betterment of society, especially for the upliftment of the underprivileged. He coined the term "Daridra Narayana," signifying that serving the poor and needy is akin to serving God in human form. His teachings inspired the establishment of the Ramakrishna Mission, an organization dedicated to social service, education, and spiritual growth.

Incorporating these key philosophical ideas into his educational vision, Swami Vivekananda advocated for a well-rounded education that nurtured not only the intellect but also the spirit. He believed that education should instill a sense of unity, self-realization, and a commitment to selfless service, thereby shaping individuals who could contribute positively to society.

In the subsequent sections of this article, we will explore how these philosophical ideas influenced Vivekananda's vision for education in India and the enduring impact of his teachings on the country's educational landscape.

C. Contributions to Education:

Swami Vivekananda's contributions to education in India are multifaceted and enduring. He was not only a spiritual leader but also a visionary educator who believed in the transformative power of education. His efforts to blend spiritual and material knowledge, character development, and moral values into the educational system have left an indelible mark on the country's educational landscape.

1. Founding the Ramakrishna Mission and Belur Math:

One of Swami Vivekananda's most significant contributions to education was the establishment of the Ramakrishna Mission and the iconic Belur Math. The Ramakrishna Mission, founded in 1897, is an organization dedicated to the service of humanity through various educational, cultural, and humanitarian activities. It serves as a spiritual and educational center, with Belur Math as its headquarters, promoting the ideals and teachings of Sri Ramakrishna, Swami Vivekananda, and other spiritual luminaries.

2. Promoting a Balanced Education System:

Swami Vivekananda recognized the importance of a balanced education system that integrated both spiritual and material knowledge. He believed that a truly educated person should possess not only academic prowess but also spiritual insight and ethical values. His vision aimed to produce individuals who were not only intellectually competent but also morally upright and spiritually awakened.

3. Establishing Educational Institutions:

To realize his vision for holistic education, Swami Vivekananda played a pivotal role in establishing educational institutions across India. Ramakrishna Mission Schools and Colleges are among the most prominent of these institutions. These schools and colleges provide quality education while instilling moral values, character development, and a sense of social responsibility in students.

Through these educational institutions, Vivekananda sought to impart the essence of India's ancient wisdom and philosophical traditions to the younger generation. He believed that this knowledge would empower students to lead meaningful lives and contribute positively to society.

4. Advocating Character Development and Moral Values:

Swami Vivekananda was a staunch advocate for character development and the inculcation of moral values in education. He emphasized that education should not only enlighten the intellect but also purify the character. He believed that individuals with strong moral foundations could become effective agents of positive change in society.

Vivekananda's teachings on character development stressed the importance of virtues such as truthfulness, compassion, integrity, and self-discipline. He believed that these virtues were essential for personal growth and for building a just and harmonious society.

In conclusion, Swami Vivekananda's contributions to education in India encompassed the establishment of the Ramakrishna Mission, the promotion of a balanced education system, the founding of educational institutions, and the advocacy of character development and moral values. His vision for education continues to shape the ethos of educational institutions inspired by his teachings, fostering not only academic excellence but also the holistic development of individuals as responsible and ethical members of society.

16.3 SWAMI VIVEKANANDA'S LEGACY IN MODERN INDIA

A. Influence on Educational Reforms:

Swami Vivekananda's profound influence on education in India extends beyond his own educational initiatives. His ideas have significantly shaped educational reforms in the country, contributing to policy changes and the integration of spiritual practices like yoga and meditation into the mainstream education system.

1. Shaping the National Education Policy:

Swami Vivekananda's vision for holistic education and character development has had a lasting impact on India's educational policies. His emphasis on combining spiritual and material knowledge, along with his call for a balanced education system, resonated with educational reformers and policymakers.

Over the years, Vivekananda's ideas have played a role in shaping the National Education Policy of India. Elements of his educational philosophy, such as the promotion of moral values, character development, and the recognition of the importance of experiential learning, have found their way into educational policy discussions.

2. Encouraging the Integration of Yoga and Meditation in Schools:

Swami Vivekananda was a strong proponent of yoga and meditation as tools for holistic development. He believed that these practices not only nurtured physical and mental well-being but also fostered spiritual growth and self-realization. Recognizing their transformative potential, he advocated for the inclusion of yoga and meditation in the curriculum of educational institutions.

In recent years, there has been a growing recognition of the benefits of yoga and meditation in promoting mental health, reducing stress, and enhancing concentration among students. This has led to the integration of yoga and meditation programs into schools and colleges across India. Vivekananda's advocacy for these practices has contributed to their widespread acceptance as valuable components of modern education.

In conclusion, Swami Vivekananda's influence on educational reforms in India extends to the shaping of national education policies and the encouragement of practices like yoga and meditation in schools. His visionary approach to education, rooted in the integration of spiritual and material knowledge, continues to guide the evolution of India's educational system, fostering the holistic development of students and promoting a harmonious society.

B. Promoting Global Awareness of Indian Philosophy:

Swami Vivekananda's impact extended far beyond the borders of India. He played a pivotal role in promoting global awareness of Indian philosophy, spirituality, and cultural heritage. Two significant aspects of his efforts in this regard were his historic speeches at the World's Parliament of Religions in Chicago and his tireless work in spreading messages of tolerance, universal brotherhood, and harmony.

1. Speeches at the World's Parliament of Religions in Chicago:

Swami Vivekananda's historic address at the World's Parliament of Religions in Chicago in 1893 marked a watershed moment in the history of interfaith dialogue and the global recognition of Indian philosophy. His opening words, "Sisters and brothers of America," transcended national and religious boundaries, instantly connecting with the diverse audience.

In his speeches, Vivekananda eloquently introduced the world to the spiritual and philosophical treasures of India. He expounded on the principles of Vedanta, emphasizing the unity of all religions and the universality of spiritual truths. His message of religious tolerance, acceptance, and respect for all faiths resonated deeply with the audience and garnered widespread acclaim.

Vivekananda's Chicago addresses not only garnered attention but also earned him a place of honor as a representative of India's spiritual heritage. They set the stage for his subsequent lectures and interactions, enabling him to spread the message of Indian philosophy to a global audience.

2. Spreading the Message of Tolerance, Universal Brotherhood, and Harmony:

Swami Vivekananda's message extended beyond the confines of religious discourse. He emphasized the principles of tolerance, universal brotherhood, and harmony as essential components of a peaceful and just society. His teachings transcended religious dogma and sought to unite humanity on the basis of shared values and a common spiritual heritage.

Vivekananda's message of tolerance emphasized that differences in religion and culture should not be sources of division or conflict but opportunities for mutual understanding and growth. He encouraged individuals to rise above sectarianism and recognize the unity that underlies all of humanity.

His concept of universal brotherhood underscored the idea that every human being is interconnected and should be treated with love and compassion. This philosophy of inclusivity and empathy has had a profound impact on fostering a sense of unity and solidarity among people from diverse backgrounds.

Vivekananda's teachings on harmony emphasized the need for balance and equilibrium in all aspects of life. He believed that true harmony could only be achieved by recognizing the interconnectedness of all things and striving for a harmonious coexistence with nature and fellow beings.

In conclusion, Swami Vivekananda's speeches at the World's Parliament of Religions in Chicago and his tireless efforts to spread messages of tolerance, universal brotherhood, and harmony played a pivotal role in promoting global awareness of Indian philosophy and values. His teachings continue to inspire individuals worldwide, transcending cultural and religious boundaries to foster a more compassionate and interconnected world.

C. Continuing Impact:

- The ongoing work of the Ramakrishna Mission in education and social service.

The Ramakrishna Mission, founded by Swami Vivekananda in 1897, continues to play a significant role in education and social service in India and around the world. This organization is guided by the principles of service, spirituality, and selfless action, and its ongoing work reflects its commitment to these ideals.

1. Educational Initiatives:

The Ramakrishna Mission operates a vast network of educational institutions, including schools, colleges, and universities. These institutions provide quality education with an emphasis on character development, moral values, and holistic development.

- Ramakrishna Mission Schools: These schools aim to impart education that fosters not only academic excellence but also the development of strong moral and ethical values. They provide students with a well-rounded education that includes physical fitness, cultural activities, and spiritual guidance.
- Ramakrishna Mission Colleges: These colleges offer undergraduate and postgraduate programs in various fields of study. They uphold the values of Swami Vivekananda and provide an environment that encourages critical thinking and personal growth.
- Ramakrishna Mission Universities: The organization has established universities in India that offer a wide range of academic disciplines. These universities continue to uphold the philosophy of holistic education and character development.

2. Social Service Initiatives:

The Ramakrishna Mission is renowned for its extensive social service activities. These initiatives address various social issues and serve the underprivileged and marginalized communities.

- **Medical Services**: The mission operates hospitals and dispensaries that provide medical care to those in need, often in remote and underserved areas. These facilities offer free or affordable healthcare, including surgeries, consultations, and preventive care.
- **Educational Outreach**: In addition to its formal educational institutions, the mission conducts various outreach programs, including vocational training centers, literacy programs, and scholarships for deserving students. These initiatives aim to empower individuals with skills and education.

- **Relief and Rehabilitation**: The Ramakrishna Mission is known for its swift response during natural disasters and emergencies. It provides relief and rehabilitation services to affected communities, including food distribution, shelter, and medical aid.
- **Rural Development**: The organization is actively involved in rural development projects that focus on improving the quality of life in rural areas. These projects include agricultural training, clean water initiatives, and community development programs.
- **Women's Empowerment**: The mission runs programs aimed at empowering women through skill development, education, and awareness campaigns. These initiatives address issues such as gender equality, domestic violence, and women's health.

The Ramakrishna Mission's work in education and social service is a living testament to Swami Vivekananda's vision of selfless service to humanity. It continues to impact the lives of countless individuals, providing them with opportunities for growth, education, and a better quality of life. The organization's commitment to spirituality, service, and the well-being of all remains unwavering as it carries forward the legacy of its founder.

16.4 CONCLUSION

Swami Vivekananda's legacy in the field of education and philosophy remains a beacon of enlightenment for India and the world. His profound insights into Indian philosophy and his relentless commitment to harmonizing spirituality and modern education have had an enduring impact on India's educational landscape.

Vivekananda's teachings continue to inspire generations of students, educators, and seekers of truth. His emphasis on holistic education, character development, and the pursuit of self-realization serves as a timeless guide for those on the path of knowledge and self-improvement.

As India strides forward into the 21st century, the influence of Swami Vivekananda's educational philosophy remains a source of inspiration and direction for the nation's educational reforms and aspirations. His vision of a harmonious society rooted in tolerance, universal brotherhood, and the unity of all religions remains as relevant today as it was during his time.

In essence, Swami Vivekananda's life and teachings epitomize the fusion of ancient wisdom with modern relevance, offering a blueprint for a brighter and more spiritually enriched future for India and the global community.

Reference

1. Chakrabarti, S. (2005). Swami Vivekananda's Educational Philosophy. Journal of Indian Education, 31(1), 31-36.
2. Vivekananda, S. (1896). The Education Ideal. In The Complete Works of Swami Vivekananda (Vol. 2, pp. 147-152). Advaita Ashrama.
3. Bhattacharyya, K. (2010). A Brief History of Indian Philosophy. Sterling Publishers Pvt. Ltd.
4. Ghose, S. N. (1985). Education for Character Development: Swami Vivekananda's Approach. Journal of Moral Education, 14(3), 165-174.
5. Sarkar, S. (2007). Swami Vivekananda's Vision of Education and Its Relevance in the 21st Century. Contemporary Education Dialogue, 4(2), 111-128.
6. Radhakrishnan, S. (1956). Indian Philosophy (Vol. 1). Oxford University Press.

A Comprehensive Study on Sex Education and the NEP 2020

Nyumme Nomuk

Assistant Professor of Education, Saint Claret College, Ziro.

Email: nomukn92@gmail.com.

Contact No. +91 8732039644

ABSTRACT: *Education is the single greatest tool for achieving social justice and equality. The NEP 2020, similarly, envisages equitable and inclusive education and learning for all. It includes every subject under the sun such as mathematics, astronomy, philosophy, yoga, architecture, medicine, literature, sports, and a multitude of others. However, like its predecessors, it remains largely silent on comprehensive sex education. The concept of sex education has been subsumed by the heading of "ethical and moral reasoning". This policy has reinforced the belief of how sex education is not considered a necessity in our society. Overlooking and not addressing this not only shows the parochial mindset of the policymakers but will also end up framing how the current set of students end up perceiving the issue of sexual and reproductive health, rights, and justice. Propagating and promoting existing taboos, the short-sightedness of this policy will result in health risks as well as unsafe choices. The cases of rape, molestation, sexual abuse etc. can be seen in our modern society despite of various awareness programs. Such cases are arising due to the lack of Moral Etiquettes and Sex Education. It's important to provide Sex Education at various level of our Education to avoid such iniquitous incidents. This paper argues for negligence of sex education curricula. Proper execution of sex education curriculum can bring desirable values that would not be those relating to specific sexual behavior but those relating to the general treatment of human beings, suggesting that sex that involves coercion or exploitation as well as sex that causes harm is wrong. The paper also discusses how physical pleasure is not only a biological phenomenon but one that is culturally constructed, the discussion of which would be important to sex education. Finally, teaching about fantasy as well as sexual "deviance" may be the most important aspect of sex education in order to prevent from abuse, not by placing responsibility on girls to avoid victimization but* *by teaching boys how to express themselves sexually in moral i.e., considerate and respectful ways.*

Keywords: *Sex Education, NEP 2020*

17.0 INTRODUCTION

The word *moral* comes from a Latin root (*mos, moris*) and means the code or customs of a people, the social glue that defines how individuals should live together. Education is a moral enterprise in which "we need to re-engage the hearts, minds and hands of our children in forming their own characters, helping them 'to know the good, love the good, and do the good'". Schooling is unavoidably a moral enterprise. Indeed, schools teach morality in a number of ways, both implicit and explicit. Schools have a moral ethos embodied in rules, rewards and punishments, dress codes, honor codes, student government, relationships, styles of teaching, extracurricular emphases, art and in the kinds of respect accorded students and teachers. Schools convey to children what is expected of them, what is normal, what is right and wrong. It is often claimed that values are caught rather than taught; through their ethos, schools socialize children into patterns of moral behavior. Moral education, then, refers to helping children acquire those virtues or moral habits that will help them individually live good lives and at the same time become productive, contributing members of their communities. In this view, moral education should contribute not only to the students as individuals, but also to the social cohesion of a community.

One of the much-debated topics across the world is the importance of sex education in schools. Sex education refers to a broad program designed to impart knowledge/training regarding values, attitudes and practices affecting family relationships. The real purpose behind sex education is the transfiguration of a male child into manhood and of a female child into womanhood. It is the education that provides knowledge on physical, social, moral, behavioral and psychological changes and developments takes place during puberty. It teaches the adolescents about the role of boys and girls in family and society, responsibility and attitude of boys and girls towards each other, etc. within social context. Sex education is never the most pleasant of the conversations for an adult and child to have. Yet, it is an essential one that many feel should happen in a responsible and safe environment. Due to increasing incidences of HIV/AIDS, RTIs/STIs and teenage pregnancies, there is a rising need to impart sex education. Parents and counselors in Delhi argue that banning sex education is not a solution and will prove disadvantageous instead, given the exposure kids have to the internet.

17.1 SIGNIFICANCE OF THE STUDY

Education is an important human activity. It is related to the life and aspiration in the society and it is therefore a powerful instrument of change. It has the capacity to provide its recipient a better and respectable place in the society. Today, people give importance to education for a better and improved future. Sex education is needed for better family life. Today the Indian society is much backward to realize the importance of sex education. A large population of the rural population is illiterate and ignorant. Many adults and adolescents suffer a lot on account of improper or many a time incorrect information received from misleading literature, movies and sexually perverted, ill motivated or inexperienced companions. Such inaccurate, adequate and even distorted information about sex from unwholesome sources (even parents can misguide their children for saving their prestigious position) not only creates unhealthy attitude towards sex and sex problems. Therefore, sex education is important because young children as well as adolescents and adults need to be told about the venereal diseases in a scientific way. They should learn the causes, measure of prevention and treatment of these diseases. It helps the children in getting proper information about their sex related curiosity and problem. There is much importance of sex education as a means of developing healthy attitude among the students. Educating youth about sex is very essential, so that they can protect themselves against such abuse. Rape cases not only take place in big cities of our country but it has spread all over every state small or big which we can see even in small town. This may be due to lack of parent 's guidance, and the exposure of students to dating clubs, and correct exposure to wrong information which are freely available. Providing them with proper sex education can help tackle their problems to quite an extent. It is important that teachers should be trained to teach and spread awareness on sex education. The curriculum should have information on sex education so that correct information is provided in a formal way. Many parents feel uncomfortable about having conversation with their children about sex, but avoiding the subject will not stop their children from having sex or keep them safe. If enough care and guidance is not given to a child, it would have an adverse effect on the family as well as the society. Therefore, Parents and Teachers have to be very tactful so that their students/children do not obtain wrong information as misconceptions. Hence, in view of the above issues, the investigator is interested to conduct a study on integrating Sex Education with Moral Education. It's necessary to integrate both the subject to bring an appropriate curriculum for the children.

17.2 OBJECTIVES

1. To study the inclusion of Comprehensive Sexuality Education under NEP 2020
2. To study the psychosexual development in human being in relation to Sex Education
3. To highlight the importance and challenges in implementing Sex Education

17.3 METHODOLOGY

Conceptual research is conducted by observing and analyzing already present information on a given topic. The secondary data collected from the books, websites, online journals etc.

17.4 DISCUSSION

1. Comprehensive Sexuality Education (CSE):

Comprehensive Sexuality Education (CSE) seeks to equip young people with the knowledge, skills, attitudes and values they need to determine and enjoy their sexuality – physically and emotionally, individually and in relationships. It views 'sexuality' holistically and within the context of emotional and social development. It recognizes that information alone is not enough. Young people need to be given the opportunity to acquire essential life skills and develop positive attitudes and values" (IPPF, 2010).

NEP 2020 and Comprehensive Sexuality Education (CSE):

- The NEP seeks to provide "equitable quality education" to all Socio-Economically Disadvantaged Groups (SEDGs). NEP includes groups such as students with disabilities, girls, and transgender students, among others, as an SEDG. The NEP talks about creating "a safe, inclusive, and effective learning environment" for "all genders" and to ensure that "all teachers are sensitized to these requirements". The NEP recognizes "education as a tool to fight social mores". We believe that CSE's all-inclusive approach recognizes all sexual orientations, gender identities and expressions. This will help students accept students from a SEDGs without judgement thereby making educational spaces more inclusive. As educational spaces become more inclusive, access to education will become easier for those who have historically lacked access to it.

- NEP aims to help students with "Future judgment surrounding consent, harassment, respect for women, safety, family planning, and Sexually Transmitted Disease prevention" (NEP 2020, 6.2). CSE encourages conversations about bodily autonomy, choice and consent from both the perspective of health and society. This will enable students with the information they need to make informed decisions about their bodies and therefore achieve the aims of consent, safety, awareness and access to contraception and STD prevention.

- The NEP recognizes that dropout rates are high for people belonging to SEDGs. It seeks to make research driven policy to increase enrollment and reduce dropout. (NEP 2020, 6.2.1). CSE may reduce dropout rates. A major reason for higher dropout rates among girls is lack of safety in schools, early marriages, onset of menstrual cycle, and traditional gender roles which make girls stay at home for domestic work, sibling care, etc. (Taneja, A. 2021). CSE combats these by providing correct information about menstrual health and hygiene, consent, sexual violence, and recourse in case of the same. This will be a great addition to the battery of policies that exist to ensure girls stay in school.

- The NEP also believes in "recognizing, identifying, and fostering unique capabilities of each student by sensitizing teachers as well as parents to promote each student's holistic development in both academic and non-academic spheres." CSE has proven to be an effective tool for improving academic performance, increasing self-esteem, and fostering healthier interpersonal relationships among students (UNFPA, 2015). Inclusion of CSE in the NEP will help achieve the goal of holistic academic and non-academic development.

- There is no mention of "Sexuality Education" and any near definition of it, the overall belief is that CSE has been included under "ethical and moral reasoning" - with an intent to advance "basic health and safety training, as a service to oneself and to those around us". The CSE not only focuses on basic health and safety training but also on physical, sexual and mental wellbeing. It provides students with relevant information on sexual and reproductive health to make righteously informed decisions about emotional, sexual health and physical well-being, thereby advancing NEP's objective to provide "ethical and moral reasoning".

2. Freud's 5 stages of Psychosexual Development: Freud (Freud, S. 1905) believed that life was built round tension and pleasure. Freud also believed that all tension was due to the build-up of libido (sexual energy) and that all pleasure came from its discharge.

- **Oral Stage (Birth to 1 year)**: In the first stage of psychosexual development, the libido is centered in a baby's mouth. During the oral stages, the baby gets much satisfaction from putting all sorts of things in its mouth to satisfy the libido, and thus its id demands. Which at this stage in life are oral, or mouth orientated, such as sucking, biting, and breastfeeding.

- **Anal Stage (1 to 3 years)**: During the anal stage of psychosexual development, the libido becomes focused on the anus, and the child derives great pleasure from defecating.

- **Phallic Stage (3 to 6 years)**: The phallic stage is the third stage of psychosexual development, spanning the ages of three to six years, wherein the infant's libido (desire) centers upon their genitalia as the erogenous zone. The child becomes aware of anatomical sex differences, which sets in motion the conflict between erotic attraction, resentment, rivalry, jealousy and fear which Freud called the Oedipus complex (in boys) and the Electra complex (in girls).

- **Latency Stage (6 years to puberty)**: The latency stage is the fourth stage of psychosexual development, spanning the period of six years to puberty. During this stage the libido is dormant and no further psychosexual development takes place (latent means hidden).

- **Genital Stage (puberty to adult)**: The genital stage is the last stage of Freud's psychosexual theory of personality development, and begins in puberty. It is a time of adolescent sexual experimentation, the successful resolution of which is settling down in a loving one-to-one relationship with another person in our 20's. Sexual instinct is directed to heterosexual pleasure, rather than self-pleasure like during the phallic stage.

Freud's Five Psychosexual Stages of Development

Birth to 12 mths	1 to 3 yrs	3 to 6 yrs	7 – 11	Puberty onward
Oral Stage Infant's pleasure centers on **mouth** 'suckling'	**Anal Stage** Child's pleasure focuses on **anus** and from elimination Toilet Training. Relationship between parents.	**Phallic Stage** Child's pleasure focuses on **Genitals** Oedipus (boys) Electra (girls) *Penis envy*	**Latency Stage** Child represses sexual interest and develops social and Intellectual skills An interlude	**Genital Stage** A time of sexual reawakening; source of sexual pleasure becomes someone outside of the family continues

Source: Internet

Freud's personality theory - 1923 (Frank, G. 1999) saw the psyche structured into three parts (i.e., tripartite), the id, ego and superego, all developing at different stages in our lives. These are systems, not parts of the brain, or in any way physical. The id is the primitive and instinctual part of the mind that contains sexual and aggressive drives and hidden memories, the super-ego operates as a moral conscience, and the ego is the realistic part that mediates between the desires of the id and the super-ego.

- **Id**: The id operates on the pleasure principle (Freud, S. 1920) which is the idea that every wishful impulse should be satisfied immediately, regardless of the consequences. When the id achieves its demands, we experience pleasure when it is denied we experience 'unpleasure' or tension. The id engages in primary process thinking, which is primitive, illogical, irrational, and fantasy oriented. This form of process thinking has no comprehension of objective reality, and is selfish and wishful in nature.

- **Ego:** The ego operates according to the reality principle, working out realistic ways of satisfying the id's demands, often compromising or postponing satisfaction to avoid negative consequences of society. The ego considers social realities and norms, etiquette and rules in deciding how to behave. The ego has no concept of right or wrong; something is good simply if it achieves its end of satisfying without causing harm to itself or the id.

- **Superego:** The superego's function is to control the id's impulses, especially those which society forbids, such as sex and aggression. It also has the function of persuading the ego to turn to moralistic goals rather than simply realistic ones and to strive for perfection. The superego consists of two systems: The conscience and the ideal self. The conscience can punish the ego through causing feelings of guilt. For example, if the ego gives in to the id's demands, the superego may make the person feel bad through guilt. The ideal self (or ego-ideal) is an imaginary picture of how you ought to be, and represents career aspirations, how to treat other people, and how to behave as a member of society.

3. Sex Education: Education is one of the largest endeavors for the purpose of the development and growth of the individual by bringing in him the desired changes according to his needs and demand of ever-changing society. It is the process of receiving knowledge and making use of that knowledge to the maximum utilization. Education develops personality of an individual in all fields and aspects making him intelligent, learned, bold, and courageous and possessing strong good character, on the other hand it contributes to growth and development of the society. It is only through education that moral ideas and spiritual values, as aspiration of the nation and its cultural heritage is transferred from one generation to another for preservation, purification and sublimation into higher and higher achievements. Education develops the individual like a flower which distributes its fragrance all over the environment. Thus, education is a conducive process which develops child's individually in all aspects – physical, mental, emotional and social. With the growth and development of individual, the society also develops to higher levels of attainments. Thus, education is essential for the growth and development of individual as well as society. While growing, it is important to receive correct information for wholesome development of personality and one of the programs is sex education. It is an educational program to assist young people in their physical, social and emotional development as they prepare for adulthood, marriage, personal-hood and aging. Sex education involves the acknowledgement and understanding of the process of sexual development and interaction that starts at conception and affects the individual for the rest of his/her life. It enables individual to recognize and be comfortable with their sexuality.

- **Sex education in various countries**

  a. **Malaysia:** The Women, Family and Community Development Ministry in Malaysia has called for better sex education. Currently, sex education is integrated into subjects such as Moral and Islamic studies, science and biology. The basis of the sex education revolves around abstinence. It also focuses on the biological aspect of sex, ignoring many other crucial facets like consent, emotional wellbeing and contraception.

  b. **The Netherlands:** The Dutch are famously liberal. The general ethos in The Netherlands is that sexuality is a natural part of human life and should be taught as such. It is compulsory for all children aged four and older to receive age-appropriate sex education. Often, this education emphasizes building respect for; their (own) bodies and sexuality, as well as their peers'. One of their first lessons is on consent. Everything is covered, from contraception to relationships, STIs to pleasure. As a result of their extensive program the country's teenage pregnancy rate is very low.

  c. **Indonesia:** In Indonesia, sex education is considered an "extra-curricular" activity. Worryingly, often parents do not have a comprehensive understanding of the topic so it is down to the government to ensure teachers are well-informed and supplying this knowledge. Many young couples are forced to wed due to accidental pregnancies. Indonesians are usually warned of the dangers of having sex, but not taught why it can be dangerous or how to do it safely.

d. **Belgium**: Belgians are a rather relaxed bunch, like many of their European neighbors. While this is seen as very reasonable by some, others find the Belgian approach to sex education rather disturbing.

e. **China**: Chinese sex education is often very reductive or even completely absent. With the number of abortions and contractions of sexually transmitted diseases (STIs) rising at an alarming rate, something clearly needs to change. Sex education is not compulsory in China which leads to great gaps in children's knowledge as they enter adulthood. Many Chinese universities have installed vending machines selling home testing kits for HIV to students.

f. **India**: Much like China, in India sex education is not compulsory in schools. The statistics are shocking: a disturbing 53 percent of children between the ages of five and 12 have been subjected to sexual abuse. India has the fastest growing population in the world and one of the highest rates of HIV infection. According to The Times of India, more than 50 percent of girls in rural India are unaware of menstruation or what it even means. The culture around sex promotes silence and shame which confuses young people. Often, they are unable to recognize abuse. However, The Guardian has suggested India has the best sex education program in the world. The YP foundation designed and implemented a progressive curriculum for sex education. The program teaches gender equality, sexual diversity and consent among other subjects. It incorporates role play, art and games to engage 12 to 20-year-olds across the 14 classes it runs. While India may run a successful program, it needs to be implemented in all schools to have a positive effect on its young audience.

4. Importance of Sex education

- HIV/AIDS and other STIs: Because HIV/AIDS has been deemed a health crisis in India, prevention techniques have been set as a priority by the government which has been pushing NGOs to implement programming that focuses on training, support, and outreach. HIV/AIDS prevention education in India has been focused on educational materials like newspapers and pamphlets as well as conversations with educated professionals. In a study conducted in Tamil Nadu, 29% of women and 58% of men attending an outpatient clinic were aware of AIDS/STDs, however only 12% of women and 26% of men attending an STD clinic were aware of AIDS. The conclusion from this study was that mass media had been more effective at disseminating information about HIV/AIDS than the radio. However, this study also showed that mothers were not knowledgeable about Mother-to-Infant transmission because the information hadn't filtered down to them. Additionally, a 2008 survey (McManus, A. 2008) conducted among 11 and 12 class girls (aged 14 to 19; mean age was 16.38) in South Delhi found that 71% had no knowledge about the effects of genital herpes. 43% did not know the effects of syphilis and 28% did not know gonorrhea was an STD. 46% thought the all STDs, except AIDS, could be cured. The major sources of information about STDs and safe sex among the girls were their friends (76%), media (72%), books and magazines (65%) or the internet (52%). 48% felt that they could not talk to their parents about sex.

- For Adolescents: There are about 190 million adolescents in India - a demographic in which over 30% of people are illiterate. Disparities in gender at this age can often be explained by relatively poor access to reproductive health care and the fact that girls often have less access to food, which adversely affects their growth patterns. Additionally, adolescent girls often work long hours in the home with no opportunity for employment

(Selvan, K. S. et al. 2019). Adolescents, both males and females, tend to not be informed about sexuality. This is often caused by lack of education in general (but sex education in particular) and conservative attitudes towards sex. Parents are often reluctant to teach accurate and relevant information about sex to adolescents because of the stigma associated with the topic. More than taboo, mothers especially feel like talking about sex is embarrassing and dirty (Tripathi, N. et al. 2013). This same attitude is held by teachers. First, when the National Council of Educational Research and Training initiated sex education, they structured it as a part of existing studies, rather than a separate subject. However, teachers tried to avoid teaching the topic. Second, a school in Gujarat implemented a system where students could anonymously drop letters into a box for trained counselors to read. The nature of these questions tended to split by sex. Girls› questions tended to focus on menstruation, physical appearance, and 'normal' sexual behavior while boys' questions tended to focus on nocturnal emission, masturbation and body size (Abraham et al. 2015). Though these programs exist, they are unable to reach girls who are not in school, a significant section of the population.

- Family planning for adults: India's family planning programs are mainly run by the government in conjunction with NGOs. Because these programs are often quota-based, they take two forms: sterilization programs and contraceptive programs (Gray, A. et al. 2017). Both use an incentive-based approach, where families are often given kitchen items or cash to undergo procedures (Bhatnagar et al.). The efficacy of India's family planning programs is dependent on the paradigm that is being used. Programs like Accredited Social Health Activist (ASHA) encourage women to register pregnancies and visit local health centers, and also encourage family planning through sterilization. ASHA also holds information meetings and raise awareness on such issues as women's health, disease, and social determinants of health, nutrition and sanitation. Additionally, they serve as counselors on adolescent and female sexual and reproductive health (Scott, A. 2006). Past hospital care, ASHA also gives out free birth control pills and condoms which remove the stigma associated with couples buying contraceptives at drug stores (Scott, A. 2006).

5. Challenges faced in implementing Sex Education in India

- There has been significant opposition to sex education, specifically for adolescents. In 2007 (Ismail, S. et al 2015), when sex education curriculum was promoted by India's Ministry of Human Resource Development, controversy developed. Many opponents believed that sex education would corrupt youth and be anathema to traditional Indian values. Additionally, they believed it would lead to promiscuity and irresponsible behavior. Finally, they argued that sex education was a western construct that was being forced upon India. Opponents of sex education for adolescents are swayed if sex education is deemed to be culturally sensitive and in line with Indian values. This can be achieved if the government and NGOs work in tandem to create curriculum that is acceptable to schools and the community. This trend may change as year's progress because adolescents tend to have a more liberal view towards sex than adults.

- The most significant criticisms of India's family planning program are those that advocate that it should be education-based rather than quota-based. They argue that India's program isn't sustainable because it does not stop women from marrying early or from spacing their pregnancies. Second, critics state that India's program does not consider the psyche of women who often undergo irreversible procedures like sterilization because it doesn't provide the infrastructure for regular follow-ups. Finally, critics state that the program is inherently gendered because most sterilization is performed on women even though the procedure is less invasive for men (Vicziany, M. 1982).

- Opposition to HIV/AIDS prevention education in India has been scarce because of the recognition of the importance of stopping this disease. However, there has been a hesitance to acknowledge and interact with men who have sex with men (MSM). This has decreased the efficacy of programming because of the stigma associated with this population.

17.5 CONCLUSION

Adolescence is a transitional period in life when rapid physical growth and development and sexual maturation lead to one's physical capability to reproduce. Based on the definition offered by WHO (World Health Organization), adolescents are "young people between the ages of 10 and 19 years". Since adolescents and young adults are going through the growth stage, their health can be affected either positively or negatively by their interactions with their environment, their friends and peers, their parents and family members, people in the society, policies and social rules. In the course of sexual maturation, adolescents undergo fundamental changes and face with questions and ambiguities, and if they do not receive the right answers, they turn to their peers or media such as satellite TV, Internet and cyberspace. In this way, they often do not find proper answers and may even receive wrong ones, which will be problematic in the future. Therefore, education on the subject of sex and sex ethics is a necessity that must not be overlooked, and not only has to be provided by the parents and the society, but is also a fundamental right of adolescents. Although sex education has improved and different aspects of it have been dealt with, there has been little discussion about the associated ethical issues or the development of moral codes. It is clear that ethical considerations cannot be ignored when nationwide macro-policies and educational programs are involved, especially regarding such a sensitive issue. In this conceptual study, the investigator has tried to clarify the moral considerations are to be taken care of while introducing sex education for the adolescents. The sex education should be implemented under the umbrella of moral education.

As we can see in the moral development theories by Piaget and Lawrence, the individual has the capacity to understand the moral responsibilities at various stages. Some studies prove that moralities are situational. In this case, it is important to create such kind of conducive environment where the young ones can learn and practice age-appropriate sexual behavior with moral consideration. According to Freud's psychosexual theory, he focused on Id, Ego and Superego. Id should be controlled by superego. That superego can be brought if the sex education is provided in proper manner. For that reason, more awareness is needed related to value-based sex education. As our country, India, is famous for its ethical values, it's important to look sex education beyond arousal of sexual intentions among the adolescents. Rather, focus should be given on creating healthy and respectful behavior. Education is always the medium of transforming the society in a humane direction. Well informed youth can bring positive change in our society. Now the world is a global village, and the information can be transmitted very quickly. It is almost impossible to put restrictions on youth or even to small kids not to be familiarized to sexual intentions. Thus, it will be better if such sensitive information can be provided in a positive manner from the educational institutions as well as from parents. To make it success, the educational stakeholders i.e., parents, the governmental bodies, institutions, teachers, students and the society as a whole, should join hand. The NEP 2020 and the importance of sex education can gauge what we have been missing out on and what the youth continues to miss out on. It is baffling how in our so-called "modern" times, society is still stuck in its conservative and traditional set of values, beliefs, and mindset. As a consequence, the seeds we will reap will be those of unawareness, ignorance, and possibly misinformation.

References

1. Kumar, A. (2021). New education policy (NEP) 2020: A roadmap for India 2.0. University of South Florida M3 Center Publishing, 3(2021), 36.

2. Vicziany, M. (1982). Coercion in a soft state: the family-planning program of India: part I: the myth of voluntarism. Pacific Affairs, 55(3), 373-402.

3. Nanda, K., Stuart, G. S., Robinson, J., Gray, A. L., Tepper, N. K., & Gaffield, M. E. (2017). Drug interactions between hormonal contraceptives and antiretrovirals. AIDS (London, England), 31(7), 917.

4. Ismail, S., Shajahan, A., Rao, T. S., & Wylie, K. (2015). Adolescent sex education in India: Current perspectives. Indian journal of psychiatry, 57(4), 333.

5. Scott, A., & Glasier, A. (2006). Evidence based contraceptive choices. Best practice & research clinical obstetrics & Gynaecology, 20(5), 665-680.

6. Abraham, J., & Rahardjo, W. (2015). Psychopathy, sexual values dimensions, and premarital sexual behaviour among urban unmarried adolescents. Procedia-Social and Behavioral Sciences, 165, 2-11.

7. Carson, D. K., Foster, J. M., & Tripathi, N. (2013). Child sexual abuse in India: Current issues and research. Psychological Studies, 58, 318-325.

8. Selvan, K. S. (2019). Media and Information Literacy Training in India: Plenty amidst Scarcity-A Case study in Indian Scenario. International Journal of Research in Social Sciences, 9(7), 101-116.

9. McManus, A., & Dhar, L. (2008). Study of knowledge, perception and attitude of adolescent girls towards STIs/HIV, safer sex and sex education:(A cross sectional survey of urban adolescent school girls in South Delhi, India). BMC women's health, 8, 1-6.

10. Frank, G. (1999). Freud's concept of the superego: Review and assessment. Psychoanalytic psychology, 16(3), 448.

11. WHO, U., & UNFPA, W. B. (2015). Trends in maternal mortality: 1990 to 2015. Geneva: World Health Organization.

12. Taneja, A. (2021). Ambarish Rai: In Memory.

13. Claeys, V. (2010). Brave and angry–The creation and development of the International Planned Parenthood Federation (IPPF). The European Journal of Contraception & Reproductive Health Care, 15(sup2), S67-S76.

A Theoretical Analysis of New Education Policy 2020 of India

Dr. Kunjalata Baro, Assistant Professor, Bhattadev University
Shaikhong Basumatary, Librarian, KV IOC Noonmati, Guwahati
Jumri Riba, Research Scholar, Department of Education Mizoram University

ABSTRACT: *The National Education Policy 2020 (NEP 2020), which was approved by the Union Cabinet of India on 29 July 2020, outlines the vision of India's new education system. The new policy replaces the previous National Policy on Education, 1986. The policy is a comprehensive framework for elementary education to higher education as well as vocational training in both rural and urban India. The vision of the National Education Policy is: "National Education Policy 2020 envisions an education system rooted in Indian ethos that contributes directly to transforming our nation sustainably into an equitable and vibrant knowledge society by providing high-quality education to all." The objectives of the Study were to understand the Historical Evolution of Indian Educational Policies, to highlight the different stages of National Education Policy 2020, to compare the National Education Policy 2020 with previous National Education Policy 1986 and to highlight the challenges related to National Education Policy 2020. This research is a descriptive study. The necessary secondary data was collected from various websites, magazines, journals, other publications, etc.*

18.0 INTRODUCTION

The National Policy on Education (NPE) is a policy formulated by the Government of India to promote education amongst India's people. The policy covers elementary education to colleges in both rural and urban India. The first NPE was promulgated by the Government of India by Prime Minister Indira Gandhi in 1968, the second by Prime Minister Rajiv Gandhi in 1986, and the third by Prime Minister Narendra Modi in 2020.

The National Education Policy 2020 (NEP 2020), which was approved by the Union Cabinet of India on 29 July 2020, outlines the vision of India's new education system. The new policy replaces the previous National Policy on Education, 1986. The policy is a comprehensive framework for elementary education to higher education as well as vocational training in both rural and urban India. The policy aims to transform India's education system by 2021. The language policy in NEP is a broad guideline and advisory in nature; and it is up to the states, institutions, and schools to decide on the implementation. The NEP 2020 enacts numerous changes in India's education policy.

In January 2015, a committee under former Cabinet Secretary T. S. R. Subramanian started the consultation process for the New Education Policy. Based on the committee report, in June 2017, the draft NEP was submitted in 2019 by a panel led by former Indian Space Research Organisation (ISRO) chief Krishnaswamy Kasturirangan. The Draft New Education Policy (DNEP) 2019, was later released by Ministry of Human Resource Development, followed by a number of public consultations. The Draft NEP had 484 pages. The Ministry undertook a rigorous consultation process in formulating the draft policy: "Over two lakh suggestions from 2.5 lakh gram panchayats, 6,600 blocks, 6,000 Urban Local Bodies (ULBs), 676 districts were received." The vision of the National Education Policy is: "National Education Policy 2020 envisions an education system rooted in Indian ethos that contributes directly to transforming our nation sustainably into an equitable and vibrant knowledge society by providing high-quality education to all."

18.1 OBJECTIVES OF THE STUDY

1. To understand the Historical Evolution of Indian Educational Policies.
2. To highlight the different stages of National Education Policy 2020.
3. To compare the National Education Policy 2020 with previous National Education Policy 1986.
4. To highlight the challenges related to National Education Policy 2020.

18.2 RESEARCH METHODOLOGY

This research is a descriptive study. The necessary secondary data was collected from various websites, magazines, journals, other publications, etc.

18.3 INDIAN EDUCATIONAL POLICIES' HISTORICAL EVOLUTION

The government of India experienced various difficulties, including illiteracy, after obtaining independence in 1947. The government of India introduced and sponsored a variety of programmes, policies, and rules to address the issues of illiteracy. Maulana Abul Kalam Azad, India's first education minister, envisioned a consistent educational system through strict central government regulation of the educational system and policies. In order to develop suggestions to modernise India's five educational systems, the Union Government established the University Education Commission in 1948–1949, the Secondary Education Commission in 1952–1953, the Kothari Commission in 1964–1966, and the University Grants Commission in November 1956.

The First National Policy on Education, 1968: this policy Based on the report and recommendations of the Kothari Commission (1964–1966), the then Prime Minister Indira Gandhi's government declared the first NEP in 1968. Equal educational possibilities (for both rural and urban sectors) were recommended as part of the policy's "radical reform" to promote national integration and better cultural and economic growth. The policy encouraged its usage and study to encourage the use of Hindi as a universal language throughout India. The ancient Sanskrit language, which was regarded as an essential component of India's culture and tradition, was urged to be taught as part of this particular programme.

Second National Education Policy: Former Prime Minister Rajiv Gandhi introduced a new National Policy 1986 to advance education at all economic levels in 1986. According to the accepted policy, there is a

"Special Emphasis on the Elimination of Inequalities and to Sequalise the Educational Opportunity", regardless of caste (scheduled caste, scheduled tribes), gender (predominantly for females), and economic background. In order to foster social integration, the programme advocated for the expansion of grants, subsidies, allowances, adult education, and a number of other strategies. This NPE is renowned for its "child-centered approach," particularly in primary education, and as a result, it launched "Operation Blackboard," a very well-liked educational reform.

Revision Second National Education Policy in 1992 and 2005: The NEP was amended in 1992 by former prime minister PV Narasimha Rao. The Common Entrance Examination (CEE) was adopted under this educational philosophy, which is well-known. A revamped "Common Minimum Programme" programme was launched by Manmohan Singh, a former Indian prime minister. A unified entrance exam was envisaged for all admissions to vocational and technical training programmes in India under the NEP, 1986, and the Programme of Action (PoA) 1992.

Third National Policy on Education, 2020: The National Employment Plan (NEP) 2019 Draught was published by the Ministry of Human Resource Development (MHRD) in 2019, and it was followed by several suggestions and consultations from the public and other stakeholders. In order to improve fundamental learning and critical thinking, the Draught NEP discusses lowering curriculum content. Promoting comprehensive experiential, dialogical, and analytical learning is the goal. For the first time, it also discusses a change of the curriculum. The biggest change is from a 10 + 2 + 3 system to a 5 + 3 + 3 + 4 system in the pedagogical structure. An effort is being made to optimise learning depending on children's cognitive development. The government passed a NEP on July 29, 2020, with the goal of introducing various reforms to the current Indian educational system. The NEP 2020 scripts a big improvement in our educational system that is appropriate and liberal.

18.4 DIFFERENT STAGES:

1. Foundation Stage

The Foundational Stage offers a foundational education that is adaptable, multilayered, play-based, activity-based, and discovery-based. This stage is continually developed for the cognitive and emotional stimulation of youngsters using time-tested Indian traditions and cultures.

2. Preparatory Stage

Three years Preparatory stage consists of building on the play-, discovery-, and activity-based learning. Also included in this stage is the gradual introduction of textbook-based formal classroom instruction. The emphasis is on exposing the pupils to many topics and getting them ready to dig further into ideas.

3. Middle school education Stage

The middle school curriculum concentrates on more complex ideas in the humanities, social sciences, maths and science subjects. When studying specialised subjects with subject-matter experts, experiential learning is the best approach. The semester system is introduced to the class, and there are two exams at the class level each year.

4. Secondary education Stage

The secondary school curriculum, cover a variety of courses, including liberal arts education. This stage will be based on the subject-oriented instructional methodology and curriculum with increased breadth, flexibility, critical thinking, and focus on life goals.

5. Under-graduation Education Stage

Undergraduate Education Every topic will have three- or four-year undergraduate degrees with a variety of exit alternatives, such as a certificate after the first year, a diploma after the second year, or a bachelor's degree after the third. The undergraduate degree with research in the last for four years.

6. Post-graduation Education Stage

The Master's degree is available as a one-year degree for students with a four-year bachelor's degree, a two-year degree for students with a three-year bachelor's degree, and an integrated five-year degree with an emphasis on excellent research in the final year. To improve professional competence and prepare students for a research degree, the Master's degree will have a significant research component.

7. Research Stage

The research stage involves conducting outstanding studies leading to a Ph.D. in any core topic, transdisciplinary subject or interdisciplinary subject for a minimum of three to four years for full-time and part-time study, respectively. They should complete 8 credits of courses in teaching, education, and pedagogy relating to their chosen Ph.D. subject during their doctoral programme. The previous MPhil programme has been discontinued.

8. Lifelong learning

In order to prevent people from losing the information, abilities, and experience necessary to lead comfortable lives in society, the NEP 2020 recommends lifelong learning and research. Research and education have been suggested to increase awareness for life happiness at any stage of life.

18.5 COMPARISON OF NATIONAL EDUCATION POLICY 2020 & NATIONAL EDUCATION POLICY 1986

NEP 2020	NEP 1986
1. Objective is to provide Multidisciplinary & interdisciplinary liberal education.	The holistic development of students is the purpose of education.
2. It follows the standard 10+2 educational system.	The suggested common educational framework is 5+3+3+4.

3. There are common subjects and elective subjects in the four-year secondary education stage. Liberal educational policy promotes choice.	Students choose disciplines and specialisations during the first two years of higher education, such as science, business, and arts.
4. A four-year undergraduate study may be completed in only a year with a diploma, two years with an advanced diploma, three years with a pass degree, or four years with a project-based degree.	Programmes for undergraduates last three to four years.
5. Postgraduate education endures one to two years with more focused-on research and specialisation.	A two-year postgraduate programme focuses on specialisation.
6. Multiple entry and exit options are available. Their credits will be transferred through Academic Bank of Credits	This is the main difference between both the policies with credit storing for higher studies
7. Equal preference will be given to Open Distance Mode.	Regular was given more preference
8. The top Indian institutions will open campuses abroad, and the top 100 international universities may come to India to open campuses.	No foreign universities are allowed to function directly in India
9. With the exception of medical and legal, HECI (Higher Education Commission of India) is the controlling authority.	Controlling Authority- UGC, AICTE(Technical), ICAR (Agriculture), BCI (Legal), CCIM (Medical), ICAI, ICSI, CBSE, NCERT, etc.

divided into four sections: the National Higher Education Regulatory Council (NHERC), the General Education Council (GEC), the Higher Education Grants Council (HEGC), and the National Accreditation Council (NAC), which oversees accreditation.	
10. The coursework for the Ph.D. programme consists of basic subject-related study specialisation and research concentration, as well as components of teaching and curriculum creation.	The coursework of Ph.D. programme comprises of research methodology and core subject related study

18.6 CHALLENGES RELATED TO EDUCATIONAL POLICY OF 2020

Regional languages: The introduction of mother tongues for each topic in academic institutions is a difficulty due to the poor teacher to student ratio in India, which is a factor in the New Education Policy 2020. Finding qualified teachers can be difficult at times, and the introduction of the NEP 2020, which includes study materials in mother tongues, presents a new obstacle. In accordance with the National Education Policy 2020, children attending private schools will begin learning English far earlier than those attending public schools.

Cooperation - Education of states is a concurrent subject. This is why most states have their school boards. Therefore, the State Governments have to come forward for the actual implementation of this decision. Additionally, the states may object to the introduction of a National Higher Education Regulatory Campus as the principal governing body.

Expensive Education - The new educational policy opens the door for enrollment at universities abroad. According to some scholars, the Indian educational system will undoubtedly incur high costs for admission to overseas universities. For lower class pupils, pursuing further education can be difficult as a result.

The challenge of teaching in the mother tongue: It will be difficult to teach the essential courses in the mother tongue because India has 22 official languages and many dialects. First, the course material will need to be translated into various languages, and then qualified instructors will be needed to put this into practise.

Widening the gap between learners: The introduction of English after the fifth standard in government schools will widen the gap with private schools that have been offering education in English since the beginning, as the mother tongue will continue to be the preferred medium of instruction until class 5.

Challenge of the digital divide: In rural areas where not everyone can afford smartphones, India's digital divide is much more severe. The issue has been made worse by the inadequate IT infrastructure of government-run schools, which may cause problems with implementation when education is digitised.

18.7 CONCLUSION

It can be concluded that this study revealed the Indian Educational Policies' Historical Evolution from university education commission to new educational policy 2020. This study also highlighted different stages - Foundation Stage, Preparatory Stage, Middle school education Stage, Secondary education Stage, Under-graduation Education Stage, Post-graduation Education Stage, Research Stage, Lifelong learning which are recommended in new educational policy 2020 and make comparison between New Education Policy 2020 and National Policy of Education 1986. The study mentioned various challenges relating to new education policy 2020.

References

1. Aithal, P. S.; Aithal, Shubhrajyotsna (2019). "Analysis of Higher Education in Indian National Education Policy Proposal 2019 and Its Implementation Challenges". *International Journal of Applied Engineering and Management Letters.* 3 (2): 1–35. SSRN 3417517.

2. B. Venkateshwarlu, "A Critical Study of NEP 2020: Issues, Approaches, Challenges, Opportunities and Criticism", International Journal of Multidisciplinary Educational Research, 2(5), 2277-7881.

3. Deep Kumar, "A Critical Analysis and a Glimpse of New Education Policy -2020", *International Journal of Scientific & Engineering Research*, 11(10), 2020, 2229-5518.

4. Gopalan K.R., "Public Opinion on The New Education Policy 2020", *Journal for Educators, Teachers and Trainers,* 13 (1), 1989–9572.

5. Kalyani Pawan. (2020). An Empirical Study on NEP 2020 with Special Reference to the Future of Indian Education System and Its effects on the Stakeholders. *Journal of Management Engineering and Information Technology,* 7 (5), 2394 – 8124.

6. Rahul Pratap Singh Kaurav, Prof. K.G. Suresh, Dr. Sumit Narula, Ruturaj Baber "New Education Policy: Qualitative (Contents) Analysis and Twitter Mining (Sentiment Analysis)", *Journal of Content, Community & Communication*, Vol. 12 Year 6, December – 2020, ISSN: 2395-7514.

7. Rupesh G. Sawant, Dr. Umesh B. Sankpal, "National Education Policy 2020 and Higher Education: A Brief Review", *IJCRT,* 9, 2320-2882.

8. Shubhada M R, Niranth M R (2021), "New Education Policy 2020: A Comparative Analysis with Existing National Policy of Education 1986", *IJRAR*, Volume 8, Issue 2, 2349-5138.

Science, Indian Philosophy and NEP 2020

*Vasty Lalthanpuii, **Lalbiakdiki Hnamte

(* Research Scholar, ** Professor, Department of Education, Mizoram University)

ABSTRACT: *In this paper, the profound convergence of science, Indian philosophy, and the 2020 National Education Policy (NEP) in India is examined, shedding light on the significant contributions of ancient Indian philosophers to fields such as mathematics, medicine, and philosophy. The interplay between science and spirituality is underscored as essential for holistic societal development. NEP 2020, a pivotal educational reform, emphasizes the breakdown of traditional subject boundaries, advocating for a holistic, multidisciplinary approach to learning. Rooted in India's history, NEP recognizes that all forms of knowledge, whether scientific, vocational, or artistic, should be considered 'arts,' fostering an integrated educational framework. The paper highlights the favorable outcomes of merging humanities and arts with STEM disciplines, including enhanced creativity, critical thinking, and social awareness. The authors contend that the NEP's holistic, multidisciplinary education model is paramount for India's educational evolution in the 21st century and the fourth industrial revolution, calling for a collective effort across diverse fields to embrace interdisciplinary learning and harmonize the wisdom of the past with contemporary science and technology.*

19.0 INTRODUCTION

Indian history has been blessed with stories and sagas of legends, sages, seers and scholars from all fields. It is often argued that Science and Technology in India have had a long history and owe its birth during ancient and medieval periods. From the birth of 'zero, to the decimal system, to astronomy, analysis of Ayurveda medicine and the first knowledge of surgery to the illustrative sculptures and architectures, all these are the contributions of ancient Indian philosophers who have dedicated their lives in the field of Science for India.

During the Age of Science and Reason (1000 B.C to the 4th C A.D) contributions in astronomy, mathematics, logic, medicine and linguistics were done by different philosophers. The philosophers of the Sankhya school, the Nyaya-Vaisesika schools and early Jain and Buddhist scholars made substantial contributions to the growth of science and learning in India. Advances in the applied sciences like metallurgy, textile production, scientific method, and dyeing were also made during these periods. With the help of Upanishads philosophers like Pythagoras and Herodotus become aware of geometry. Scientific exchanges between Greece and India were mutually beneficial and helped in the development of the sciences in both nations.

Baudhayana in 800 B.C calculated the value of pi and discovered what is now known as the Pythagoras' theorem. Brahmagupta lived in seventh century Ujjain and wrote several books on mathematics and astronomy. India was considered to be the source of the number system, but now it is called as the Arabic numerals because the Arabs took it everywhere. During the Vedic Period, the science of Ayurveda - (the ancient Indian system of healing) blossomed. Medical practitioners took up the dissection of corpses, practiced surgery, developed popular nutritional guides, and wrote out codes for medical procedures and patient care and diagnosis.

Indian philosophy includes the systems of thought and reflection that were developed by the civilizations of the Indian subcontinent. Indian thought has been concerned with various philosophical problems, significant among which are the nature of the world (cosmology), the nature of reality (metaphysics), logic, the nature of knowledge (epistemology), ethics, and the philosophy of religion.

The present age is dominated by science. What is being experimented and proved by science is readily being accepted by the civilizations. Science makes contributions in the field of research by attempting to investigate in the contributions of Scriptures. With the help of ancient science, we are able to travel long distances using planes, trains, and motors. For travelling across the seas and shipping large goods, large ships and cargos have been built. Even for communication, satellite-based phones, mobiles, video conferencing have been invented and are possible. From these we can see that it appears that nowadays there is no need for a Guru for learning since one can learn directly from computers and with the help of internet. But it is with the help of different philosophies of Indian philosophers these different inventions become possible. Their visions and spiritual thinking helps science to be in the right track and makes it less harmful. This is because science can contribute immensely in the field of destruction.

Without science, Dharma (right behavior and social order) is incomplete and without Dharma so is Science. Spiritual power alone can neutralize the forces of evil. India has repeatedly made it clear that nuclear weapons are made solely for her own protection and not for destroying any other nation. If the spirit of this message is clearly understood by the whole world, then no one need have any kind of fear and today's powerful science also need not cause any apprehension.

19.1 INDIAN PHILOSOPHERS IN THE FIELD OF SCIENCE

Ayurveda:

Ayurveda (Sanskrit for "knowledge of life") is a comprehensive system of traditional health care that emphasizes the relationship among body, mind, and spirit. Originating in India roughly 3,000 years ago, Ayurveda seeks to restore an individual's innate harmony. Primary Ayurvedic treatments include diet, exercise, meditation, herbs, massage, exposure to sunlight, and controlled breathing. It is a functional system of health care, more akin to traditional Chinese medicine than to conventional Western medicine.

According to the principles of Ayurveda, the five basic elements (ether, air, fire, water, and earth) combine with each other and manifest themselves in the human body as three humors or doshas, the essential energetic essence of a person, known as vata, pitta, and kapha. The doshas govern all biological, psychological, and pathophysiological functions in the body, mind, and consciousness. It is an imbalance of these doshas that leads to illness, and Ayurveda seeks to bring the doshas back into harmony.

C. V. Raman

Shree Chandrasekhara Venkata Raman was an Indian physicist known for his work in the field of light scattering. His main philosophy was education. He believes that education is the only key that can change the mentality of human beings and brings peace to society.

By the name of Dr. C.V Raman on 5th September on the occasion of his birthday Teacher's Day has been celebrated every year. Hence early life and education is the main philosophy of Dr. C.V Raman's life.

Sushruta

The Pioneer for Surgery, Sushruta considered surgery as "the highest division of the healing arts and least liable to fallacy". In his well-known work, "Sushrutb Samhita", he mentions about 121 surgical instruments and 760 medicinal herbs. He wrote the book as an instruction manual for physicians to treat their patients holistically. He gave importance to holistic development of both the medical practitioner and the patients. He believe that disease is caused by imbalance in the body, and it was the physician's duty to help others maintain balance or to restore it if it had been lost.

As per NEP 2020 recommendation, the categorization of subjects will no longer be entertained. The policy envisaged a large holistic and multidisciplinary learning from universities. Ancient Indian literary works described a good education as knowledge of the 64 Kalaas or arts; and among these 64 'arts' were not only subjects, such as singing and painting, but also 'scientific 'fields, such as chemistry and mathematics, 'vocational' fields such as carpentry and clothes-making, 'professional 'fields, such as medicine and engineering, as well as 'soft skills' such as communication, discussion, and debate.

The very idea that all branches of creative human endeavour, including mathematics, science, vocational subjects, professional subjects, and soft skills should be considered 'arts', has distinctly Indian origins.

Assessments of educational approaches in undergraduate education that integrate the humanities and arts with Science, Technology, Engineering and Mathematics (STEM) have consistently showed positive learning outcomes, including increased creativity and innovation, critical thinking and higher-order thinking capacities, problem-solving abilities, teamwork, communication skills, more in-depth learning and mastery of curricula across fields, increases in social and moral awareness, etc., besides general engagement and enjoyment of learning. Research is also improved and enhanced through a holistic and multidisciplinary education approach.

A holistic and multidisciplinary education would aim to develop all capacities of human beings -intellectual, aesthetic, social, physical, emotional, and moral in an integrated manner. This holistic education shall be, in the long term, the approach of all undergraduate programmes, including those in professional, technical, and vocational disciplines.

A holistic and multidisciplinary education, as described so beautifully in India's past, which has been embedded in the new education policy (NEP 2020) is indeed what is needed for the education of India to lead the country into the 21st century and the fourth industrial revolution. Students of arts and humanities will aim to learn more science and all will make an effort to incorporate more vocational subjects and soft skills.

19.2 CONCLUSION: In conclusion, this paper has explored the intricate interplay between science, Indian philosophy, and India's transformative National Education Policy (NEP) of 2020. It has underscored the essential fusion of scientific knowledge and spiritual wisdom for holistic societal development. The NEP's visionary approach, advocating the dissolution of traditional subject boundaries in favor of a holistic, multidisciplinary education, reflects India's rich historical traditions. Embracing all forms of knowledge as 'arts,' this integrated approach fosters creativity, critical thinking, and social awareness, underlining the benefits of combining the humanities and arts with STEM fields. We propose that the NEP's multidisciplinary education model is essential for India's journey into the 21st century and the challenges of the fourth industrial revolution. It requires a collective effort to blend ancient wisdom with modern science and technology, preparing future generations to address the complexities of our ever-changing world, ensuring India produces enlightened, creative, and well-rounded individuals who can lead and shape a brighter future.

References

1. *C.V. Raman the Raman Effect - Landmark - American Chemical Society.* (n.d.). American Chemical Society. https://www.acs.org/education/whatischemistry/landmarks/ramaneffect.html

2. *DEVELOPMENT OF SCIENCE IN ANCIENT AND MEDIEVAL INDIA | VMC Blogs - Vidyamandir Classes.* (2020, December 9). https://blog.vidyamandir.com/development-of-science-in-ancient-and-medieval-india/

3. India Today. (2019, July 1). *Know all about Sushruta, the first ever plastic surgeon who was Indian.* https://www.indiatoday.in/education-today/gk-current-affairs/story/sushruta-works-indian-physician-medicine-plastic-surgery-rhinoplasty-nose-job-1559599-2019-07-01

4. *Math, Science, and Technology in India.* (n.d.). Asia Society. https://asiasociety.org/education/math-science-and-technology-india

5. Ministry of Human Resource Development. (2020). National Education Policy 2020. In *Ministry of Education*. Retrieved April 9, 2023, from https://www.education.gov.in/sites/upload_files/mhrd/files/NEP_Final_English_0.pdf

6. *Philosophy of Ayurveda | 2005-03-01 | AHC Media: Continuing Medical.* (n.d.). Relias Media | Online Continuing Medical Education | Relias Media - Continuing Medical Education Publishing. https://www.reliasmedia.com/articles/85340-philosophy-of-ayurveda

7. *Philosophy of Indian Science and Texts - Hindupedia, the Hindu Encyclopedia.* (n.d.). https://www.hindupedia.com/en/Philosophy_of_Indian_Science_and_Texts

8. *Science and Indian Philosophy.* (2006b, June 3). Economic and Political Weekly. https://www.epw.in/journal/2006/22/book-reviews/science-and-indian-philosophy.html

National Education Policy 2020: Challenges and Solutions in School Education in India

Dr. Gangasani Naveen, Teacher Educator, Govt College of Teacher Education (Tribal Welfare),
ITDA Bhadrachalam. E-Mail id: ngangasani@gmail.com.
Dr. D. Hassan, Assistant Professor, Department of Education, Andhra Kesari University
Ongole Campus, Ongole. E-mail.id:- hassan_d@rediffmail.com.

ABSTRACT: *The National Education Policy 2020 (NEP 2020) was recently introduced in India to reform the education system and bring about an inclusive, multidisciplinary, and holistic approach to learning a comprehensive policy document; the NEP 2020 addresses all facets of education, covering early childhood education and care schooling, and higher education. Despite its promising goals, the implementation of the NEP 2020 in school education is facing various challenges, such as a shortage of trained teachers, inadequate infrastructure, lack of funds, and resistance to change. This research paper aims to study the challenges and potential solutions in implementing the NEP 2020 in school education in India. Through a literature review, the paper highlights the importance of effective stakeholder engagement, adequate funding, and capacity building for teachers, among others. The study concludes that the successful implementation of the NEP 2020 in school education in India will require sustained effort and collaboration from all stakeholders, including the government, educators, and the community.*

Keywords: *National Education Policy 2020, National Education Policy 2020 with regards to school education, and Suggestions for successful implementation of NEP 2020*

20.0 INTRODUCTION

The National Education Policy 2020 (NEP 2020) was developed to reform the Indian educational system by fostering equitable access to education, inclusivity, and the development of skills and creativity. In the context of school education, the NEP 2020 proposes several key reforms that have the potential to significantly impact the Indian education system.

One of the major reforms proposed in the NEP 2020 is the restructuring of the school education system into a 5+3+3+4 design, with five years of foundational education, followed by three years of preparatory, three years of middle school, and four years of secondary education. This new structure aims to provide a more flexible and inclusive education system that caters to the diverse learning needs of student.

The NEP 2020 also proposes the promotion of multilingualism in schools, with the aim of promoting language diversity and enabling students to become proficient in multiple languages. This will help students to communicate effectively in a globally connected world and foster a better understanding of different cultures and perspectives. Another key reform proposed in the NEP 2020 is the integration of technology in education. The policy aims to leverage technology to improve access to quality education, particularly for students in rural and remote areas. Additionally, the use of technology in education can help to improve the quality of education by enabling teachers to deliver interactive and engaging lessons, and by providing students with access to a wealth of educational resources.

The NEP 2020 also proposes significant reforms in teacher education and professional development programs, to improve the quality of teachers and ensure that they are equipped to deliver quality education. The policy proposes the establishment of a National Professional Standards for Teachers (NPST) and the creation of a National Council for Teacher Education (NCTE) to oversee the implementation of these reforms. In conclusion, the NEP 2020 has the potential to significantly impact school education in India by promoting access to quality education, equity and inclusiveness, and skills development and innovation.

However, the successful implementation of the NEP 2020 will require significant effort and resources, and the active participation of the government, educational institutions, and stakeholders.

20.1 OBJECTIVES OF THE STUDY

The following are the specific objectives of the study:

1. To understand the key provisions of the National Education Policy 2020 and its significance for school education in India.
2. To analyze the challenges faced in the implementation of NEP 2020 in schools and evaluate their impact on the quality of education.
3. To identify the strengths and weaknesses of the current school education system in India and assess its readiness to implement the policy.
4. To explore the solutions and best practices for overcoming the challenges in the implementation of NEP 2020 in school education.
5. To provide insights and recommendations for policymakers, educators, and other stakeholders to ensure the successful implementation of NEP 2020 in school education.

20.2 METHODOLOGY

A qualitative methodology, specifically document analysis, was used to study the implementation of the National Education Policy 2020 in school education in India. In this research official documents such as government reports, policy papers, and other relevant materials provide information on the implementation of the policy in schools.

20.3 THE NATIONAL EDUCATION POLICY 2020 MAKES THE FOLLOWING RECOMMENDATIONS FOR SCHOOL EDUCATION IN INDIA:

The National Education Policy (NEP) 2020 has proposed several major recommendations for school education in India, including the 5+3+3+4 model:

- **5 years of foundational stage:** This stage aims to provide universal access to quality early childhood care and education (ECCE) to children from 3-8 years. It focuses on the holistic development of children through play and activity-based learning.

- **3 years of preparatory stage:** In this stage, children will be introduced to language and mathematics along with life skills, physical education, and arts.
- **3 years of primary stage:** This stage will focus on providing a strong foundation in language, mathematics, and science, and preparing students for higher-level learning.
- **4 years of secondary stage:** This stage will emphasize multidisciplinary and vocational education, enabling students to explore their interests and talents. The secondary stage will also provide opportunities for students to take up board exams in grades 10 and 12.

In addition to this, the NEP 2020 recommends the following changes in school education:

- **Curricular Reforms:** NEP 2020 emphasizes a flexible and interdisciplinary curriculum that focuses on critical thinking, creativity, and problem-solving skills.
- **Language Policy:** NEP 2020 advocates for a three-language formula, where students can choose to learn regional languages, classical languages, or foreign languages in addition to English and Hindi.
- **Assessment Reforms:** The policy introduces a comprehensive and continuous assessment system that focuses on learning outcomes and includes both formative and summative assessments.
- **Technology-Enabled Learning:** NEP 2020 recognizes the role of technology in enhancing the quality of education and encourages the integration of technology in the classroom.
- **Focus on Holistic Development:** The policy emphasizes the holistic development of students, which includes the physical, social, emotional, and ethical dimensions of education.

- **Teacher Empowerment:** NEP 2020 focuses on the professional development of teachers, including in- service training, induction programs, and performance-based evaluations.
- **Universal Access:** NEP 2020 aims to provide universal access to school education, with a special focus on disadvantaged communities, such as girls, Scheduled Castes, and Scheduled Tribes.

These are some of the major changes in school education according to NEP 2020. The policy aims to transform the Indian education system into one that is student-centric, culturally sensitive, and globally competitive

20.4 CHALLENGES IN THE IMPLEMENTATION OF NEP 2020 IN SCHOOL EDUCATION:

1. **Lack of infrastructure:** Many schools in India lack basic infrastructure, such as proper buildings, adequate classrooms, libraries, laboratories, and sports facilities.
2. **Resistance to change:** The new policy emphasizes a multidisciplinary approach to education and a shift away from rote learning. This shift is often met with resistance from teachers, students, and parents who are used to traditional methods of teaching and learning.
3. **Funding issues:** Implementing the new policy will require significant investment, which is a major challenge given the limited resources available for education.
4. **Curriculum development**: Developing a new and comprehensive curriculum to support the multidisciplinary approach outlined in the new policy is a major challenge.
5. **Lack of teacher training:** Teachers need to be trained in the new methods of teaching and learning outlined in the new policy. However, there is a shortage of training programs and resources to support teacher training.
6. **Inadequate assessment systems:** The current assessment system in schools is often criticized for being too focused on rote learning

and not adequately reflecting the diverse abilities and needs of students. The new policy calls for a more comprehensive and student-centered assessment system, which will require significant investment and infrastructure

7. **Limited involvement of stakeholders:** The policy calls for the active involvement of students, teachers, parents, and the community in the education process. However, there may be limited engagement and participation of these stakeholders in the implementation process.

8. **Financial constraints:** The implementation of the policy may require a substantial increase in financial resources, which may be a challenge in a budget-constrained environment.

9. **Inequitable access to quality education:** The policy aims to provide equitable access to quality education, but socio-economic and geographical disparities may pose challenges in achieving this goal.

10. **Lack of proper monitoring and evaluation:** The policy calls for regular monitoring and evaluation of its implementation, but there may be limited capacity and resources for this purpose.

11. **Political interference:** Political factors frequently influence education policy, which might affect how the National Education Policy 2020 is carried out.

20.5 SUGGESTIONS FOR SUCCESSFUL IMPLEMENTATION OF NEP 2020 IN SCHOOL EDUCATION:

The successful implementation of the NEP 2020 in schools is crucial for improving the quality of education in the country. To achieve this, several key measures must be taken into consideration. Firstly, the training and development of teachers is of utmost importance. They must be provided with the latest training in pedagogy, technology, and teaching approaches to ensure that they are equipped to implement NEP 2020 efficiently. Workshops and ongoing professional development initiatives can help with this. Secondly, the physical and technological infrastructure of schools must be improved, which includes classrooms, libraries, sports facilities, and computer systems with internet connectivity.

The NEP 2020 recommends a flexible and multidisciplinary curriculum that integrates technology and the latest knowledge from various fields. This requires a revamp of the existing curriculums in schools and ensuring that they align with the latest advancements. The traditional rote-based assessment methods must also be replaced with more holistic and learner-centred assessments that promote critical thinking, problem-solving, and creativity. This requires a major overhaul of the assessment system and the development of new assessment tools and techniques.

The successful implementation of NEP 2020 requires collaboration between various stakeholders, including the government, schools, teachers, parents, and students. This can be achieved through regular meetings and consultations to understand the needs and concerns of each group and find mutually beneficial solutions. Regular monitoring and evaluation of the implementation process will also help ensure that the policy is on track and identify areas that need improvement. This can be done through regular assessments and surveys, as well as through external evaluations by experts in the field.

Sufficient funding is also necessary for the implementation of NEP 2020 in schools. The government can provide funds for the development of infrastructure, teacher training, and implementation of new teaching methodologies. The government can also encourage private-public partnerships between schools and private organizations to provide additional resources, support, and expertise to schools. Additionally, the government can encourage innovation and experimentation in teaching methods and provide support and resources to schools that wish to do so.

Thus, by implementing these measures, the government can support the successful implementation of NEP 2020 in schools and ensure that the policy leads to improved outcomes for students.

20.6 CONCLUSION

In conclusion, the National Education Policy 2020 (NEP 2020) is a comprehensive and visionary policy aimed at transforming the Indian education system and making it globally competitive. However, its successful implementation in the school education sector in India is a challenging task that requires a coordinated and collaborative effort from various stakeholders, including the government, schools, teachers, students, and communities. The study of the challenges and solutions in implementing NEP 2020 in school education highlights the need for adequate funding, infrastructure development, teacher training, curriculum reform, and the effective use of technology. The government can play a crucial role in providing the necessary resources and support to schools and teachers, while schools and teachers can take a proactive approach to embrace and implement the policy recommendations effectively. The implementation of NEP 2020 in school education has the potential to bring about significant positive changes in the quality of education, teacher professionalism, student learning outcomes, and the overall development of the country.

References

1. National Educational Policy 2020 (2020 July 29) Ministry of Education Government of India. https:// www.education.goc.in/ sites/upload files/mhrd/files/National Education Policy 2020. pdf

2. Suresh, J., & Saha, S. (2021). An analysis of the national education policy 2020. Journal of Education and Practice, 12(6), 1-6.

3. Manikutty, S., & Jayakumari, R. (2021). National Education Policy 2020: A review. International Journal of Multidisciplinary Research and Development, 8(4), 87-92.

4. Bhatia, S., & Mishra, D. (2022). Implementation of the National Education Policy 2020: A critical review. Journal of Educational Research and Review, 4(1), 1-5.

5. Khan, M. A., & Shaikh, N. (2022). School education in India: Reforms and challenges under National Education Policy 2020.

International Journal of Social Sciences and Education Research, 2(2), 69-74

6. Naidu, P. (2021). National Education Policy 2020: An assessment of its implications for school education in India. International Journal of Research in Education and Science, 1(3), 217-223.

Educational Philosophy of Rabindranath Tagore in Resemblance With NEP 2020

T.C Rakil Rahmachhuani*, Lalrochami Ralte & L.K Lalbiakfeli*****
*Research Scholar, Department of Education, Mizoram University,
Mizoram- 796004
**Research Scholar, Department of Education, Mizoram University,
Mizoram- 796004
***Research Scholar, Department of Education, Mizoram University,
Mizoram- 796004
Email: rakitochawng@gmail.com, scarletchami@gmail.com,
biakfeli96@gmail.com

ABSTRACT: *The National Education Policy (NEP) 2020 has set forth a vision for India's education system, aiming to transform it into a holistic and multidisciplinary one. To understand the impact of Rabindranath Tagore's works in this context, we need to delve into his philosophy of education and the principles he stood for. Tagore believed in an education that nurtured creativity, critical thinking, and a deep understanding of humanity. His contributions to literature, music, and art continue to inspire and shape minds across generations. In this article, we explore how Tagore's ideas align with the NEP 2020 and how his works can enrich the educational landscape of India.*

21.0 INTRODUCTION

Rabindranath Tagore, renowned poet, philosopher, and Nobel laureate, was a strong supporter of an education system that encouraged students to think for themselves and to develop their natural gifts. His writings expressed his concept of education as a method to promote holistic development, in which intellectual, emotional, and spiritual progress coexisted. As the NEP 2020 makes efforts to restructure India's education system, it is critical to examine Tagore's ideas and works in developing this new paradigm.

Rabindranath Tagore's Philosophy of Education:

Rabindranath Tagore's educational philosophy has had a considerable impact on many facets of education in India, and some of its tenets are consistent with the National Education Policy (NEP) 2020. The NEP 2020 is a modern framework for education policy, yet it incorporates several principles of education that are consistent with Tagore's outlook.

Tagore's philosophy of education was based on the concept that education should adapt to the individual's intrinsic potential and stimulate creativity. He emphasized the importance of shifting away from rote learning and instead focusing on developing critical thinking skills. Tagore supported an open and immersive way of learning at his school, Santiniketan, which encouraged pupils to study numerous subjects through interdisciplinary techniques. The NEP 2020, with its emphasis on experiential learning, flexibility, and transdisciplinary study, echoes Tagore's vision and offers an opportunity to incorporate his values into the mainstream curriculum.

21.1 HERE ARE SOME KEY ASPECTS OF TAGORE'S EDUCATIONAL PHILOSOPHY AND THEIR RELEVANCE TO THE NEP 2020

1. Holistic Education: Holistic education, which takes into account a person's physical, intellectual, emotional, and spiritual growth, is emphasized in Tagore's philosophy. By emphasizing the cognitive, social, emotional, and ethical facets of education, the NEP 2020 highlights the significance of holistic development.

2. Multidisciplinary learning: In accordance with Tagore's educational philosophy, pupils were exposed to a wide range of subjects and academic disciplines, encouraging a multidisciplinary approach to learning.

   The NEP 2020 supports a multidisciplinary approach that gives students the freedom to select courses from different fields of study in order to promote a more interdisciplinary understanding of knowledge.

3. Regional and Cultural Focus: Tagore placed a strong emphasis on the use of the home tongue in education and supported the preservation and promotion of regional languages, customs, and traditions.

   In order to preserve cultural and linguistic diversity, the NEP 2020 also emphasizes the value of regional languages and the use of the mother tongue as a medium of instruction in the early years of schooling.

4. Critical thinking and creativity: In order to foster imagination and invention, Tagore believed that education should prioritize creativity and critical thinking. In keeping with Tagore's emphasis on nurturing these talents, the NEP 2020 seeks to encourage pupils' critical thinking, creativity, and problem-solving abilities.

5. Flexibility and autonomy: According to Tagore's educational philosophy, learning should be flexible, allowing students to customize their educational paths according to their interests and skills. In keeping with Tagore's principles, the NEP 2020 offers students flexibility and choice by letting them choose classes and career tracks that are suited to their unique objectives.

21.2 IMPACT OF TAGORE'S WORKS ON LITERATURE AND LANGUAGE EDUCATION

The literary works of Tagore, including his poetry, short tales, novels, and dramas, have had a significant impact on Indian literature and language instruction. His writings tackle universal topics that cut beyond ethnic borders in addition to showcasing the beauty of the Bengali language. Students' creativity and imagination can be fostered while also developing a greater understanding and appreciation for Indian literature by incorporating Tagore's works into language teaching. Students can develop their language abilities, critical thinking abilities, and ethical awareness by studying his writings.

Since Tagore's writings have been translated into so many different languages, a larger audience can now read his poetry and prose. This has helped people comprehend and appreciate Indian literature across cultures. When Shantiniketan was established, Tagore's educational philosophy, which was represented in it, placed a heavy emphasis on holistic education, the fusion of the arts and music, and a close relationship with nature. These ideas support the aims of a comprehensive education that are frequently stressed in contemporary educational programs like the NEP 2020.

Language education policy in India has been inspired by Tagore's emphasis on the use of the mother tongue and regional languages in education. The NEP 2020 emphasizes the need for multilingual education based on mother tongues in the early years of schooling.

21.2 EXPLORING TAGORE'S ART AND MUSIC IN THE CURRICULUM

Tagore made numerous and diverse contributions to music and the arts. People of different ages continue to feel emotions and find inspiration in his compositions, known as Rabindra Sangeet. The NEP 2020 supports the inclusion of music and the arts in the curriculum and acknowledges the value of art integration in education. Students can appreciate Tagore's art while also developing their own creative potential by introducing them to his music and paintings. Students can cultivate an aesthetic sense, self-expression, and emotional intelligence through music and the arts.

Tagore's art and music are frequently integrated into the curriculum, promoting creativity and cultural heritage. The Shantiniketan model, founded by Tagore, is renowned for its unique approach to integrating arts and music into education. Students in India are introduced to Tagore's songs and poems at an early age, including the national anthems of India and Bangladesh. Schools and colleges organize cultural events and festivals where students perform Tagore's songs and dances, showcasing their artistic talents. Tagore's philosophy encourages an interdisciplinary approach, integrating arts, literature, and music with other subjects to foster a holistic understanding of knowledge. This aligns with the NEP 2020's focus on maintaining cultural diversity and heritage in education. Tagore believed in the power of creative expression through art and music, encouraging students to express themselves and foster creativity and imagination.

21.3 TAGORE'S PHILOSOPHY OF ENVIRONMENTAL EDUCATION

Tagore's writings demonstrate his love of nature and his profound grasp of the environment. The NEP 2020's focus on environmental education resonates with his view that humans and nature are interrelated. Students are encouraged by Tagore's teachings to adopt a sustainable perspective, cherish biodiversity, and feel accountable for the environment. Students can learn to be stewards of the planet and contribute to a cleaner future by infusing their ecological expertise into the curriculum.

Rabindranath Tagore's environmental philosophy emphasizes a holistic understanding of nature, fostering a sense of interconnectedness with the natural world. His approach often Involves learning in natural settings, promoting creativity and conservation. Tagore's writings also emphasize the importance of preserving the environment for future generations. His philosophy goes beyond scientific understanding, incorporating cultural and ethical dimensions to encourage responsible stewardship.

Tagore's philosophy encourages an interdisciplinary approach, integrating environmental education with other subjects like literature, arts, and ethics. To incorporate Tagore's philosophy into the National Education Policy 2020, considerations include curriculum development, teacher training, nature-based learning, cultural and ethical dimensions, sustainability education, and interdisciplinary integration.

To determine the specific ways in which Tagore's philosophy is incorporated into the NEP 2020 or any subsequent updates, it is essential to refer to policy documents, guidelines, and educational materials provided by relevant educational authorities in India. Educational practices and policies can evolve, and specific details may vary among different regions and institutions.

21.4 CONCLUSION

In light of the NEP 2020, Rabindranath Tagore's writings are extremely pertinent. His educational philosophies, which place a strong focus on creativity and connection to the environment, fit very well with the policy's guiding principles. India's educational system can make great progress toward holistic development and raising well-rounded persons by incorporating Tagore's works into the curriculum. We discover that Tagore's ideals continue to inspire and direct us in our goal of an inclusive and transformational educational system as we examine the influence of his works in the context of the NEP 2020.

References

1. Bhadana, S., & Naaz, I. BHARAT MANTHAN. https://www.researchgate.net/profile/Ishrat-Naaz-2/publication/369920181_TECHNO-PEDAGOGICAL_SKILLS_IN_THE_21_ST_CENTURY_AND_THEIR_RELEVANCE_TO_NEP_2020_FOR_ACHIEVING_THE_VISION_OF_G20/links/6434434720f25554da21f966/TECHNO-PEDAGOGICAL-SKILLS-IN-THE-21-ST-CENTURY-AND-THEIR-RELEVANCE-TO-NEP-2020-FOR-ACHIEVING-THE-VISION-OF-G20.pdf

2. Dey, S., & Srivastava, A. (2022). Reimagining Technical and Vocational Education and Training in India: Prospects and Challenges. *University News*, *60*(20), 3-8. https://www.researchgate.net/profile/Suprabha-Dey/publication/371984145_Re-imagining_Technical_and_Vocational_Education_and_Training_in_India_Prospects_and_Challenges/links/64a11a5295bbbe0c6e06f603/Re-imagining-Technical-and-Vocational-Education-and-Training-in-India-Prospects-and-Challenges.pdf

3. DHAGE, P. R., RIZVI, N., KALNAWAT, A., & SHARMA, P. (2023). TRACING THE ROOTS OF NATIONAL EDUCATION POLICY 2020 AND THE INDIAN CONSTITUTIONAL DIMENSIONS PERTAINING TO IT. *Russian Law Journal, 11*(1S). https://russianlawjournal.org/index.php/journal/article/view/369

4. Endow, T., & Mehta, B. S. (2022). Rethinking Education and Livelihoods in India. *Journal of Human Values, 28*(1), 29-43. https://journals.sagepub.com/doi/full/10.1177/09716858211058777

5. Gopal, R. (2022). Learning in the Arts and Aesthetic Development. *Learning without Burden: Where are We a Quarter Century after the Yash Pal Committee Report.* https://books.google.co.in/books?hl=en&lr=&id=EKN1EAAAQBAJ&oi=fnd&pg=PT172&dq=RABINDRANATH+TAGORE+IN+RESEMBLANCE+WITH+NEP+2020&ots=uBrFvRTh1F&sig=1ePQOdDOEh1IiEryFz72YryKm1M&redir_esc=y#v=onepage&q&f=false

6. Jha, P., & Parvati, P. (2020). National education policy, 2020. *Governance at Banks, 55*(34), 14. https://www.epw.in/online_issues/22_EPW_Vol_LV_No_34.pdf#page=14

7. Jebasingh, D. R., & Sridhar, L. S. (2023). EDUCATION FOR SUSTAINABLE DEVELOPMENT: AN ANALYSIS OF TRANSFORMING EDUCATION FOR SUSTAINABLE FUTURES. *NCSDSGE–2023*, 1. https://www.researchgate.net/profile/Prabu-Vengatesh-T/publication/371856223_ROLE_OF_TECHNOLOGY_IN_SKILL_DEVELOPMENT/links/64992125b9ed6874a5db63ec/ROLE-OF-TECHNOLOGY-IN-SKILL-DEVELOPMENT.pdf#page=16

8. Kharate, P. T. Challenges and Opportunities in Higher Education in India: A Perspective. *Higher Education in India: Retrospect and Prospect,* 46. https://www.joshibedekar.org/monograph/Monograph%20-%20Higher%20Education%20in%20India14.08.2020.....pdf#page=54

9. Laskar, J. H., Khatun, R., & Sarkar, M. C. (2023). *EDUCATION IN RESURGENT INDIA*. Ashok Yakkaldevi. https://books.google.co.in/books?hl=en&lr=&id=yam6EAAAQBAJ&oi=fnd&pg=PA80&dq=RABINDRANATH+TAGORE+IN+RESEMBLANCE+WITH+NEP+2020&ots=UKuRiN6Xx2&sig=SfV-eMmdlXmaIpv3mAWnJWuNdn0&redir_esc=y#v=onepage&q&f=false

10. LALIMA, D., & RANI, R. MUSIC INTEGRATION: INNOVATIVE TEACHING-LEARNING CLASSROOM. https://swarsindhu.pratibha-spandan.org/wp-content/uploads/v10i02a07.pdf

11. Pandey, A. K., & Sharma, A. K. National Education Policy 2020: Transformation of Education System. https://www.researchgate.net/profile/Mohit-Dixit/publication/371986129_Education_as_the_Sustainable_Development_Goal_SDG_NEP_2020/links/64a18bd195bbbe0c6e0835c3/Education-as-the-Sustainable-Development-Goal-SDG-NEP-2020.pdf

12. R. Ravi., (2021) RABINDRANATH TAGORE https://internationaljournalofresearch.com/2021/07/18/rabindranath-tagore/

13. Raj Bhavan, A. (2022). Assam Governor Prof. Mukhi visits Rabindranath Tagore University Asks the university fraternity to reorient itself for successful roll out of NEP 2020. http://rbassam.digitallibrary.co.in/bitstream/123456789/168/1/Governor%27s%20visit%20to%20Hojai.pdf

14. Raju, B. (2022). Comment on New School Education Structure envisaged in NEP 2020. *Journal of Research in Humanities and Social Science*, *10*(11), 294-298. https://www.researchgate.net/profile/Raju-Bondu/publication/370550220_Comment_on_New_School_Education_Structure_envisaged_in_NEP_2020/links/645526924af78873525e9f15/Comment-on-New-School-Education-Structure-envisaged-in-NEP-2020.pdf

15. Sharma, J. K. (2021). National Education Policy 2020: Language Perspective. *language*, *8*(1). https://d1wqtxts1xzle7.cloudfront.

net/89880882/2562-libre.pdf?1660831389=&response-content-disposition=inline%3B+filename%3DNational_Education_Policy_2020_Language.pdf&Expires=1695729164&Signature=O8MWD-N995rKdcDB0zgR7kM0JfpHVeZ94MUgguNMST9Jtq-haNanJuYp6ajVuzzeuRMD8D0p9E6lnEoxAiTQ6i1SNzxYdVObTmEiPMC3la3AM6XKBxBxc8t9ub6gAb7mGyL~M6FFM2tCfMFbwPkV2QzCPgcfCpf1ozcT9MRzHHiRarOqYghgfvPVQRbACsNnBUhvGF53hWU976axz-qRbZfgaYxaxO~j7itxe-nZnIA1O90-zF4msO1egD-LfVus5p9R72Mp9nhw5H2sTKKQksFRCLE7CVFNKPdzj4DnGboiPN8TSgJBiQGcVFXbI5nW7y-MSbHzFoB5dhFlbIUZjA__&Key-Pair-Id=APKAJLOHF5GGSLRBV4ZA

16. Sharma, S. K. (2023). Indian English Literature: Issues and Dimensions. *Akshara*, 137. https://www.researchgate.net/profile/Vijay-Roy/publication/373444487_Akshara_Vol_15_2023_Complete_File/links/64ecb2a3434d3f628c547ed7/Akshara-Vol-15-2023-Complete-File.pdf#page=148

National Education Policy 2020: A Paradigm Shift in Indian Education System

Dr. Lalmuanzuali [1], Dr. Prateek Chaurasia [2] & Lalremsangi [3]

[1] Associate Professor, Department of Education, Mizoram University

[2 & 3] Assistant Professor, Department of Education, Mizoram University

ABSTRACT: *The National Education Policy (NEP) 2020 signifies a significant paradigm shift within the Indian education system. The comprehensive approach to education proposed by NEP 2020 aims to provide students with a well-rounded education that prepares them for life and work in the 21st century. National Education Policy in itself is a comprehensive and complete document on the basis of which school education, higher education, and promotion of Indian knowledge, language, culture and art are included. The National Education Policy emphasizes equal education for all, from which it would not be inappropriate to say that the National Education Policy 2020 will focus on Indian education and the overall development of students to achieve higher goals and social welfare. The present article will discuss the major aspects of NEP-2020 and the shift that it has promised to bring to the educational system of India.*

Keywords: *NEP-2020, Paradigm and Education*

22.0 INTRODUCTION

The National Education Policy 2020 is a policy that has shown the promise to provide strong support to the Indian education system in a comprehensive manner. The National Education Policy seems to be the largest discussion-based documentary on higher education and school education of any country. This policy has been developed by the comprehensive multi-stage discussion done over the different layers of society.

This policy has laid special emphasis on the ***Indian knowledge system, language culture and values,*** and along with this a major thrust has been given on the *"LokVidhyas"* to enhance this local knowledge among our young generation. The policy also promises to states that HEIs will transform themselves to provide quality education and thereby will get the accreditation. The accreditation of the institute will enable them to receive autonomy, which will again result in quality improvement in education and research. They will get higher level of accreditation, which will result in higher level of autonomy. The HEIs may traverse a path of quality, accreditation and autonomy and may become multidisciplinary university. In the present article, basics of NEP-2020 and its major recommendation towards the Indian education system is discussed in a concise way.

Some of the key features of NEP 2020 that represent a paradigm shift in Indian education include:

1. **Holistic and multidisciplinary education:** NEP 2020 promotes a holistic and multidisciplinary approach to education, which integrates the arts, humanities, sciences, and technology, and encourages interdisciplinary studies.

2. **Flexible and adaptable curriculum:** NEP 2020 recommends a flexible and adaptable curriculum, which allows for a variety of academic and non-academic subjects, and enables students to pursue their interests and passions.

3. **Emphasis on 21st century skills:** NEP 2020 recognizes the importance of equipping students with 21st century skills, such as critical thinking, creativity, collaboration, and communication.

4. **Expansion of educational opportunities**: NEP 2020 proposes a major expansion of educational opportunities in India, including the creation of new institutions, and the upgrading of existing institutions.

5. **Improved teacher training and support**: NEP 2020 recognizes the need to improve teacher training and support, including providing ongoing professional development opportunities and access to quality educational resources.

6. **Technology-enabled learning:** NEP 2020 proposes the integration of technology in education, to enhance teaching and

learning, and to provide students with access to digital resources and learning materials.

These measures represent a major departure from the traditional Indian education system, and represent a new vision for education in India, one that is more inclusive, flexible, and adaptable, and that prepares students for the challenges and opportunities of the 21st century.

22.1 NEP-2020 & EARLY CHILDHOOD EDUCATION

The National Education Policy (NEP) 2020 aims to improve early childhood education in India by implementing several key measures. Some of the ways in which NEP 2020 proposes to enhance early childhood education include:

- **Integration of pre-school education with the formal education system:** NEP 2020 recommends the integration of pre-school education with the formal education system, making it an integral part of the overall education system.
- **Expansion of the Anganwadi system:** The Anganwadi system, which provides pre-school education, health, and nutrition services, will be expanded and strengthened to provide quality early childhood care and education.
- **Increased investment in early childhood education:** NEP 2020 recognizes the need to invest more resources in early childhood education, including the creation of well-equipped and staffed Anganwadi centers and the training of Anganwadi workers.
- **Focus on play-based learning:** NEP 2020 proposes a shift towards play-based learning in early childhood education, which has been shown to be effective in promoting cognitive, emotional, and social development.
- **Inclusion of all children:** NEP 2020 stresses the importance of inclusive early childhood education, ensuring that all children, including those from marginalized and disadvantaged

communities, have access to quality early childhood care and education.

These measures are aimed at providing children with a strong foundation for their future learning and development, and ensuring that every child in India has access to quality early childhood education.

22.2 NEP-2020 & PRIMARY EDUCATION

The National Education Policy (NEP) 2020 aims to improve primary education in India by implementing several key measures. Some of the ways in which NEP 2020 proposes to enhance primary education include:

- **Mother tongue or regional language as medium of instruction:** NEP 2020 recommends that the mother tongue or regional language be the medium of instruction in primary education, as research has shown that children learn best in their home language.
- **Reduced burden of rote learning**: NEP 2020 aims to reduce the burden of rote learning in primary education and promote a more child-centered and joyful approach to learning.
- **Multi-disciplinary approach:** NEP 2020 proposes a multi-disciplinary approach to primary education, integrating subjects such as arts, sports, and sciences, and encouraging hands-on and experiential learning.
- **Focus on 21st century skills:** NEP 2020 stresses the importance of equipping primary school students with 21st century skills, such as critical thinking, creativity, collaboration, and communication.
- **Improved teacher training and support:** NEP 2020 recognizes the need to improve teacher training and support, including providing ongoing professional development opportunities and access to quality educational resources.
- **Technology-enabled learning:** NEP 2020 proposes the integration of technology in primary education, to enhance teaching and learning, and to provide students with access to digital resources and learning materials.

These measures are aimed at ensuring that every child in India has access to quality primary education and is equipped with the knowledge, skills, and attitudes needed to succeed in the 21st century.

22.3 NEP-2020 & SECONDARY EDUCATION

The National Education Policy (NEP) 2020 aims to improve secondary education in India by implementing several key measures. Some of how NEP 2020 proposes to enhance secondary education include:

1. Flexible and holistic curriculum: NEP 2020 recommends a flexible and holistic curriculum for secondary education, which allows for a variety of academic and non-academic subjects, and enables students to pursue their interests and passions.

2. Vocational education: NEP 2020 stresses the importance of vocational education and skill development at the secondary level, to provide students with practical training and hands-on experience in a range of trades and industries.

3. Assessment reform: NEP 2020 proposes a major reform of the assessment system in secondary education, to reduce the emphasis on rote learning and high-stakes exams, and to promote more holistic and formative assessments.

4. Focus on 21st century skills: NEP 2020 stresses the importance of equipping secondary school students with 21st century skills, such as critical thinking, creativity, collaboration, and communication.

5. Improved teacher training and support: NEP 2020 recognizes the need to improve teacher training and support, including providing ongoing professional development opportunities and access to quality educational resources.

6. Technology-enabled learning: NEP 2020 proposes the integration of technology in secondary education, to enhance teaching and learning, and to provide students with access to digital resources and learning materials.

These measures are aimed at ensuring that every student in India has access to quality secondary education, and is equipped with the knowledge, skills, and attitudes needed to succeed in the 21st century.

22.4 NEP-2020 & HIGHER EDUCATION

The National Education Policy (NEP) 2020 aims to improve higher education in India by implementing several key measures. Some of the ways in which NEP 2020 proposes to enhance higher education include:

1. Holistic and multidisciplinary education: NEP 2020 recommends a holistic and multidisciplinary approach to higher education, which integrates the arts, humanities, sciences, and technology, and encourages interdisciplinary studies.

2. Improved teacher training and support: NEP 2020 recognizes the need to improve teacher training and support, including providing ongoing professional development opportunities and access to quality educational resources.

3. Greater focus on research and innovation: NEP 2020 stresses the importance of promoting research and innovation in higher education, and encourages institutions to engage in cutting-edge research and development.

4. Expansion of higher education: NEP 2020 proposes a major expansion of higher education in India, including the creation of new institutions, and the upgrading of existing institutions.

5. Improved accessibility and inclusiveness: NEP 2020 recognizes the need to improve accessibility and inclusiveness in higher education, and encourages institutions to provide support and opportunities for students from underrepresented and marginalized communities.

6. Technology-enabled learning: NEP 2020 proposes the integration of technology in higher education, to enhance teaching and learning, and to provide students with access to digital resources and learning materials.

22.5 NEP-2020 & TEACHER EDUCATION

The National Education Policy (NEP) 2020 places a strong emphasis on improving teacher education in India. Some of the ways in which NEP 2020 proposes to enhance teacher education include:

- **Improved teacher training:** NEP 2020 recognizes the need to improve teacher training, and proposes a major overhaul of teacher education programs, to ensure that teachers are equipped with the knowledge, skills, and attitudes needed to effectively support student learning.

- **Emphasis on professional development:** NEP 2020 stresses the importance of ongoing professional development for teachers, and proposes the creation of a comprehensive system of support and resources for teachers to enhance their skills and knowledge.

- **Greater focus on pedagogy:** NEP 2020 recognizes the importance of effective pedagogy in teacher education, and proposes the integration of pedagogy courses into teacher training programs, to ensure that teachers have a deep understanding of how students learn.

- **Integrating technology in teacher education:** NEP 2020 proposes the integration of technology in teacher education, to enhance teaching and learning, and to provide teachers with access to digital resources and learning materials.

- **Collaboration with higher education institutions:** NEP 2020 recognizes the importance of collaboration between teacher education institutions and higher education institutions, and proposes the creation of partnerships to support the development and sharing of best practices in teacher education.

- **Incentives for quality teaching:** NEP 2020 proposes the creation of incentives for quality teaching, such as recognition, promotions, and career advancement opportunities, to encourage teachers to continuously improve their skills and knowledge.

22.6 DISCUSSION

The policy has focused over the various key issues and challenges of the present society and societal needs, for the promotion of every class of the society. The policy seems to be a promising policy in order to make the fundamental changes in order to promote education with the intent of education for all. It seems to be fully inclusive and participatory as well as child-centred in terms of teaching- learning and assessment. The policy gives importance to the citizen teacher and stakeholder of the education. This policy and its recommendation can definitely lead India to grow more and more and become one of the leading countries in terms of digital Education Technology. The policy provides strong support in order to enhance the research (both at the global and local levels). These all measures discussed in the National Education Policy 2020 are aimed at ensuring that every teacher in India has access to quality teacher education, and is equipped with the knowledge, skills, and attitudes needed to effectively support student learning.

22.7 CONCLUSION

The National Education Policy (NEP)-2020 has given many special provisions for higher education, which include teacher-teachers, inclusivity in higher educational institutions, multi-disciplinary education, etc. If we say in conclusion, it would not be wrong at all to say that the National Education Policy seems to be an inclusive policy that shows immense promise to develop a society in a more comprehensive and inclusive way. The foresightedness of the National Education Policy can be seen from the fact that the National Education Policy- 2020 has not only lay focused on the basic education personality building of a child but also on the global development of the society and matching the needs of the society globally. It has also accepted the change and has also basically emphasized on the inclusion of technologies like Artificial Intelligence in education bridging the digital divide etc. National Education Policy 2020 has reflected its philosophy of think globally and acting locally. In a nutshell, it can be concluded that NEP 2020 has promoted the basics of the Indian knowledge system so that our youth can be equipped with the art, culture, and heritage of our own society, and at the same time it has shown the faith of growing technology of the world and has advocated the promotion of them in an appropriate means.

Reference

1. MHRD. (2020, August). National Education Policy 2020. Retrieved August 17, 2020, from https://www.mhrd.gov.in/

2. Gupta, B. L., & Choubey, A. K. (2021). Higher education institutions–some guidelines for obtaining and sustaining autonomy in the context of NEP 2020. *International Journal of All Research Education and Scientific Methods (IJARESM)*, 9(1).

3. Chaurasia, P. (2020). National Education Policy (NEP) 2020: A Boon to Online and Digital Education. *Mizoram Educational Journal*, 6 (2).

Contribution of An Indian Philosopher (Swami Vivekananda) in NEP 2020

Monisha Ado, M.Ed.

monishaado@gmail.com

Department of Education

ABSTRACT: *Swami Vivekananda, a profoundly enlightened monk and Vedantist, dedicated his brief life to spreading the teachings of the Vedas while modernizing India without forsaking its cultural heritage. His enduring principles, which emphasize the development of compassionate, rational, and ethically grounded individuals, find resonance in India's new education policy (NEP) of 2020. NEP 2020 seeks to nurture engaged, empathetic, and resilient citizens capable of contributing to an equitable and pluralistic society, aligning with Vivekananda's vision of peaceful growth through academic, social, moral, and spiritual development. With India's youthful population in mind, NEP 2020 aspires to provide inclusive, high-quality education by 2030, echoing the timeless and cross-cultural philosophies of Swami Vivekananda, endorsed even by Prime Minister Narendra Modi as a foundation for the nation's educational rejuvenation.*

23.0 INTRODUCTION

"An investment in knowledge pays the best interest."- Benjamin Franklin. The role of education is to foster and develop knowledge in all fields, making an individual gain the required skills in all the fields. The investment made in education will always pay the best of the result not only to the individual but also to the society and the country. A knowledgeable individual is an asset to the country.

India is often classified as one of the most ancient nations with rich legacies of culture and literary pursuits. According to experts the history of education in India is nearly 5000 years. From the system of Gurukul to Taxila and Nalanda university India has come a long way in its system of education.

The country has seen a frequent change from the history to the present in terms of education. Education is not just learning the subjects like history, economics, mathematics, science, et cetera, but gaining relevant skills.

In ancient India, education was considered a privilege of the elite classes, with only a small portion of the population having access to formal education. In the medieval period, the Mughal and British rulers introduced new forms of education, such as madrasas for Islamic studies and Western-style schools for English language and literature. Right from the beginning of their relationship with India, the British, who had come as traders and had become rulers and administrators, had influenced the economic, political and educational systems of the country. Their impact on India's education scenario cannot be neglected.

The Charter Act of 1813 constitutes a landmark in the educational history of British India. Section 43 of the Charter Act 1813 contained the first legislative admission of the right of education in India in the public revenues. The first Law Member to be appointed was Macaulay who came to India in 1834. This marked a substantial change in the history of educational policy in India. Macaulay's Resolution provided a somewhat clear picture of the British education policy. Macaulay argued that the object of promoting a knowledge of sciences could only be accomplished by the adoption of English as the medium of instruction. Macaulay rejected the claims of Arabic and Sanskrit as against English. The toil for a better education policy continued through the whole British era.

"University Education Commission" was the first education commission established by the Government of India after independence. Dr. Sarvepalli Radhakrishnan headed this commission. So, this commission was also known as the Radhakrishna Commission of University Education. This commission gave importance to university education and differentiated between the school education system and the university education system. According to the recommendation given by this commission, University Grants Commission, the apex body for Higher Education System, was created. Education Commission of 1964 or more popularly known as

Kothari commission was formulated under the able leadership of Dr. Daulat Singh Kothari. This commission was formed to form a general pattern of education in the Indian Education System. This commission's recommendation became the basis for the National Education Policy of 1968. This is one of the Government of India's most significant educational policies, and it was launched by Mrs. Indira Gandhi, who served as prime minister at the time. National Education Policy 1968 was the first education policy that was introduced after independence. Before implementing the policy, various commissions and committees had already given their views on the educational sector. The National Education Policy of 1968 took into account the recommendations made by the education commission. The critical objectives of this policy were to provide Free and compulsory education to fulfil the directive principles of India also To improve the quality of education and provide good salary for the teachers. National education policy of 1986 which has given a solid foundation to the Indian education system was introduced by then Prime Minister Mr. Rajiv Gandhi. This policy was modified in the year 1992. The current system of education is based mostly on this policy i.e., 10+2+3, also the inclusion of quota system for ST, SC and OBC was introduced.

India has seen a tremendous challenge in all the spheres because of COVID 19 pandemic. All individuals' lives were very much disturbed by the pandemic, which challenged all of us to opt for the new normal. In this period of crisis, the Government of India came up with various policies. One among these was the National Education Policy. The draft national education policy was circulated in the year 2019, and it was approved for implemented in the year 2020 by Prime Minister Mr. Narendra Modi. This policy was the fruit of recommendations given by Dr. K. Kasturi Rangan and shows the vision of the present Government. It also lays strong foundation for the introduction of modern and more robust education system. The central vision of the policy is to create a global standard education system in India. The crucial pillars of the policy include Access, Equity, Quality, Affordability and Accountability.

23.1 NATIONAL EDUCATION POLICY-2020

This National Education Policy envisions an education system rooted in Indian ethos that contributes directly to transforming India. The vision of the Policy is to instil among the learners a deep-rooted pride in being Indian, not only in thought, but also in spirit, intellect, and deeds, as well as to develop knowledge, skills, values, and dispositions that support responsible commitment to human rights, sustainable development and living, and global well-being, thereby reflecting a truly global citizen. This is a policy which gives importance for a child to choose his path according to the skills and knowledge and interest of the society. According to this policy, the current 10+2 school system will be replaced with a new 5+3+3+4 educational and curriculum revamping that will serve students ages 3 through 18. Features of this policy include:

- 5+3+3+4 education system is followed.
- At the secondary level of education, the freedom of choice of subjects is given to the students
- Mother tongue or local language will be used to teach the students till 5th standard or preferably till 8th standard
- Multilingualism is given importance.
- Introduction of classical languages
- Teachers will be recruited based on the required qualification.
- Establishment of school complexes
- Higher education institutions should be converted into multi-disciplinary institutions.

The school education system (5+3+3+4): According to the report, school education starts at 3 years and goes up to 18 years.

1. Foundation Stage (Early Childhood Care and Education): Here the child will start its education at the age of 3 years, which includes a total of 5 years of schooling. The child will learn through two methods, i.e., play and learn and activity-based learning. The first three years of study are considered pre-school, and the remaining two years are for 1st grade and 2nd -grade classes. To strengthen this learning facility, Anganwadi will be provided with high infrastructure facilities. Anganwadi teachers will be given the training to promote this stage.

2. Preparatory Stage: In this 3rd grade, 4th Grade and 5th Grade are considered. When the child finishes 3rd grade, he or she should attain foundational literacy and numeracy. This follows the interactive classroom sessions.

3. Middle School Stage: 6th grade, 7th grade, and 8th grade are included in this particular stage. Here, vocational training is introduced for the students to improve their skills in the particular field. Here the introduction of subject teachers will be done.

4. Secondary Stage: 9th grade, 10th grade, and I PU and II PU are included in the same category. However, there are two phases 9th grade and 10th -grade fall in the first phase, and I PU and II PU falls in the second phase.

Features of Higher Education System:

- The newly proposed body called as Higher Education Commission of India will be the regulator of Higher Education.
- The National Accreditation Council (NAC) will be formulated for accreditation of the institutions.
- National Research Foundation (NRF) will be established to fund the research.
- Multi-disciplinary Universities include research-intensive Universities (RU), Teaching-intensive Universities (TU), and Autonomous Degree-Granting Colleges.
- Research-intensive Universities will give higher importance to research activities than teaching. Teaching intensive Universities give importance to teaching. At the same time, research will also be carried out in this type of university. Autonomous Degree-Granting Colleges focus on teaching for undergraduates. It is considered to be a multi-disciplinary institution.
- To increase the Gross Enrolment Ratio in Higher and University Education at least 50% by 2035.

- Four years of Bachelor's degree were exit options are given for the students. • One to two years Master's degree dependent on the Bachelor degree and option to do Ph.D. for four years.
- Choice Based Credit System (CBCS) will be revised by a flexible and an innovative Competency Based Credit System.
- Institutions should have professional career and academic counselling centres with trained counsellors.
- Encouragement for conducting course through Online Distance Learning (ODL) for higher reach and flexibility.
- The quality of Higher Education will be improved to a global quality level so as to attract more international/foreign students towards Indian education.
- National Scholarship Portal will further be strengthened.

Stages of Higher Education System

- **Under graduation either of 3 years or 4 years:** This includes multiple exit options. If the student completes the first year of the undergraduate program, he/ she can get a certificate. If the student completes two years, they can get a diploma certificate and a bachelor's degree after completing 3 years of study. After 4 years Bachelor's degree along with a research degree will be given.
- **Master Programme with different structures**: (a) 2-year program: The second year of this course is dedicated to research for those who have completed the 3- year of Bachelor's degree

  (b) 1-year Programme: This is for those students who have completed 4-year Bachelor's program with research.

  (c) integrated 5-year Bachelor's/Master's program.

- **Research Programme**: To enrol for Ph.D., either 4 years of Bachelor's degree or Master's degree is required.

1986's educational policy was not up to mark for current generation. To provide good quality education for the present generation with employability skills and technological knowledge, the implementation of the New Education Policy of 2020 will be a mark in the history of India.

NEW EDUCATION POLICY 2020 NEP 2020 is considered to be a transformative change in the education field. When any policy is implemented in the country, there will be positives and adverse outcomes for the policies. In the same way, NEP 2020 also has advantages and disadvantages.

NEP 2020 assures that education will be available for everyone. According to the need of an hour, pre-schooling is compulsory because at the age of 3 learning capacity of the child starts. Proposed National Mission on Foundational Literacy and Numeracy will be set up by the Government. National Book Promotion Policy is going to be framed under this policy. Gender Education Fund and Special Education Zone will be created for the sake of disadvantaged regions and gender. Online education is given importance.

Some drawbacks of NEP 2020 may be Increase in the gap between the students who are uncomfortable in speaking the English language as the policy emphasizes on the regional language. Teaching in the local language to make the student understand the concept is a good idea. However, if the student migrates from one state to another, it will be tough for a kid to understand the concept as the kid is not aware of the local language. As the certificates are issued before the completion of the course, there is a tendency for students to quit the course in between.

To implement the policy the challenges in front of the Government are numerous. Coming up with the unique and modern new education policy in the time of pandemic was widely appreciated by many because this policy has so many positive things. There are few things to be considered while implementing the policies.

1. Availability of funding and resources
2. Teaching the students in their local language is a good idea, but content in the local language or mother tongue is a hectic task.

3. Poor students will not get enough opportunities to study in foreign universities due to a lack of funds.

4. It is necessary to fill the vacant posts in the education field while many government schools and colleges are finding a shortage of teachers and lecturers. So, it is better to fill the vacancies.

5. When NEP considers quality education, it is necessary to consider the teaching fraternity where the payment for their service is significantly less. This has to be solved by the Government.

6. When online education is considered in NEP, it has to be noted that the students do not have access to devices and internet connectivity issues are more.

23.2 PHILOSOPHY AND EDUCATIONAL VISION OF SWAMI VIVEKANANDA

"True education is a relentless pursuit of truth and the constant endeavour to improve the human condition."

-Swami Vivekananda

our great-grandparents imagined an educational system that is progressive and rooted in our civilizational values to advance the nation. One such outstanding visionary was Swami Vivekananda. He was far ahead of his time in emphasising the development of educational programmes with a focus on values. Swami Vivekananda was a radical thinker and unconventional educationalist who dared to reject the educational system of his time and proposed to replace it with an all-encompassing, harmonious model centred on students that would lead to a unified society that is just and equitable to all. He had an educational vision that would meet the needs of students on all levels, whether they were academic, social, or emotional. On January 12, 1863, Swami Vivekananda was born in Calcutta to a wealthy Bengali family. In addition to being an educator, Swami Vivekananda was a poet, philosopher, devotee, social worker, and yogi. He continued on in life to become one of the greatest Indians to introduce the Vedic and Yoga philosophies to the West. He was a supporter of the one nation &

multicultural unity. He firmly believed that people could create education. According to Swami Ji, every soul has the capacity to be divine. Vivekananda believed that everyone is born knowing. Knowledge is something that man discovers; it does not come from outside. When Swami Vivekananda says that "education is the manifestation of divine perfection, already in man", he is referring to his general philosophy. He supported the idea of human progress and the idea that all men are brothers in some way. The two fundamental concepts in which he most firmly believed and worked to advance our society were service and renunciation. The more he travelled, the more he realised how impoverished and uneducated the masses were. And how crucial it was to educate both men and women and lift the poor up. He proposed a programme that combined traditional values from our timeless scriptures with contemporary scientific knowledge in order to make India a modern country that would work in tandem with the developed powers of the world. His educational programme is thorough and complete because it aims to help students develop all the necessary skills.to live their lives with vigour and serve the country well. The National Education Policy (NEP) 2020 recommendations echo his outstanding educational philosophy. There are numerous similarities between NEP 2020 and Swamiji's vision for education. When educating young students, Swamiji emphasised the value of mother tongue and advised learning Sanskrit and English to develop a well-rounded personality. While Sanskrit helps in understanding the depths of our vast collection of classics, English is necessary to master Western science and technology. It was implied that social cohesion would become a reality if language was not restricted to a small group of privileged individuals. compulsory for primary school students. With notable initiatives like the establishment of the NRF, NETF, and school curricula that incorporate ML, AI, and other technologies, Swamiji emphasis on science and technology is mentioned in the NEP. The NEP's emphasis on vocational education starting in elementary school resonates with his vision of developing people who would be opportunity providers rather than opportunity seekers. For Atmanirbhar Bharat, this should be a tried-and-true recipe. We should continue learning until the day we die, according to Swamiji, and the real world is the best teacher. His beliefs align with India's interpretation of Vasudev Kutumbakam. The NEP 2020 charter outlines the goal of &outbuildings an education system that is holistic, flexible, multidisciplinary, and responsive to the needs of the 21st century and 2030." Development That Is Sustainable."There was a time when students from all over the world travelled to universities like Nalanda and Taxila to study science and the arts. Quoted not believe that you are weak or small, you can do anything and everything, quote; advised Swamiji. His emphasis on fostering self-confidence and self-esteem was a crucial part of his vision because, in his words, "education is not merely filling the mind with a lot of facts. It must be a meaningful and purposeful exercise. The goal of NEP 2020 is to create whole people in the form of students who possess moral and spiritual values, character, knowledge, skills, creative genius, innovation, and leadership abilities. Swamiji has always supported the growth of both physical and mental toughness 2020 places a strong emphasis on the development of each person creative potential in addition to the life skills that are essential for creating a well-rounded personality, such as leadership, cooperation, communication, and teamwork. It is predicated on the idea that education must foster not only cognitive abilities but also social, ethical, and emotional skills. The new law upholds Swami Vivekananda philosophy.

23.3 EDUCATIONAL PHILOSOPHY OF SWAMI VIVEKANANDA AND ITS IMPLICATION ON THE NEP 2020

1. flexibility, so that learners have the ability to choose their learning trajectories and programmes, and thereby choose their own paths in life according to their talents and interests.
2. multidisciplinary and a holistic education across the sciences, social sciences, arts, humanities, and sports for a multidisciplinary world in order to ensure the unity and integrity of all knowledge.
3. emphasis on conceptual understanding rather than rote learning and learning-for-exams.

4. promoting multilingualism and the power of language in teaching and learning.

5. life skills such as communication, cooperation, teamwork, and resilience.

6. respect for diversity and respect for the local context in all curriculum, pedagogy, and policy, always keeping in mind that education is a concurrent subject.

7. full equity and inclusion as the cornerstone of all educational decisions to ensure that all students are able to thrive in the education system.

8. teachers and faculty as the heart of the learning process – their recruitment, continuous professional development, positive working environments and service conditions.

"Swami Vivekananda always focused on the development of both mental and physical strength. He said one should have muscles of iron and nerves of steel. The government's Fit India Movement and National Education Policy are inspired by his philosophy," PM Modi

23.4 CONCLUSION

"Arise, Awake and Stop not till the goal is reached"

It is taking a lot of effort to complete the Indian government's ambitious plan to reform Indian education. India will have the highest population of young people in the world over the next decade, and NEP-2020 seeks to "ensure inclusive and equitable quality education and promote lifelong learning opportunities for all" by 2030. Tunings may be necessary after implementation depending on how the policy performs in practise. Nearly every suggestion made for NEP 2020 has the ability to succeed and benefit all in the long run. A novel idea is the introduction of vocational programmes, which would also lessen the pressure of board examinations, introduce new topics, break down the wall between streams, and do many other beneficial things.

Students can now select the topic combinations they want to take, which means that they will actually learn what they want to learn. The educational system has changed its emphasis from teaching students, what it wants them to learn to teach them, what they want to learn based on their choices and preferences. The students' innate qualities and talents can be disclosed when deciding on possible fields of study. There are more possibilities for success if a person plots the selection of topics in accordance with their skill set and internal talent.

The last words to sum up are that it is a policy, but in the next few years it will take on its final execution and form. Examine how the NEP 2020 turns out as the plans put into practise on a practical level to see the effects.

References

1. Bharadwaj, N., & Pradeep, M. D. (2023). Educational Thoughts of Swami Vivekananda and its Futuristic Relevance–A Study. *International Journal of Management, Technology and Social Sciences (IJMTS)*, 8(3), 67-82.
2. Murugan, K. R., & Vasimalairaja, M. Moral Values and Relevance of Swami Vivekananda's Thoughts in the Present World.
3. Kumari, S. (2023). National Education Policy and Its Philosophical and Legal Importance. *Issue 2 Indian JL & Legal Rsch.*, 5, 1.
4. De, D., Mitra, S., & Sarkar, C. (2021). Swamiji: Fabulous Facilitator and Ideal Philosopher.
5. Gorain, S. (2021). Vivekananda's Moral and Spiritual Values and Relevance in Current Educational Scenario. *Swamiji: Fabulous Facilitator and Ideal Philosopher*, 94.

Swami Vivekananda's Philosophical Prospective Towards NEP 2020

Anwesa Nath

M.Ed Scholar, Department of Education, Mizoram University

Email id: mzu2108344@mzu.edu.in

Abstract: *In today's globalized and competitive society education is the instrument which has a important role in the growth of a nation and the quality of life for every individual. A diverse and extensive cultural heritage is the best quality of India's nature. To put the educational system in the 19th century in the ideal frame, many remarkable educators arrived with their own theories and educational Philosophies. Swami Vivekananda (12th January 1863 – 4th July 1902) was the greatest illustrious and well-known figure in India as an educationalist and reformer with his theories and educational Philosophy. His views still have an impact on education and every element of life. National Education Policy of India 2020 (NEP 2020) follows the philosophy of Swami Vivekananda for the nation and youth development.*

Keywords: *Man-making, well-rounded development, reconstruction, spiritual development.*

24.0 INTRODUCTION

Swami Vivekananda's Philosophical Prospective Towards NEP 2020. "Education is not the amount of information that is put into your brain and runs riot there, undigested all your life. We must have life-building, man-making, character-making, and assimilation of ideas. We want the education by which character is formed, the strength of mind is increased, the intellect is expanded and by which one can stand on one's own feet"- Swami Vivekananda. According to Swami Vivekananda, "Education is the manifestation of the perfection already in men" . Vivekananda was a prominent figure in Vedantic philosophy, who represented the intellectual communities worldwide with the cultural integrity and traditional pride of

India. He supported the establishment of a national education system to provide all children in the country with a minimum level of knowledge and to impart vital aspects of Indian Culture. He considered that the child's family must educate their child first. Then, his village, society, and nation should be covered. When the child's understanding grows, he will eventually come to see himself as a member of the community and naturally, he will develop a feeling of solidarity toward people. The first Prime Minister of India Jawaharlal Nehru said, "Rooted in the past and full of pride in India's prestige, Vivekananda was yet modern in his approach to life's problems, and was a kind of bridge between the past of India and her present. His mission was the service of mankind through social service, mass education, religious revival, and social awakening through education". (Bhat, S.A. 2021). A great philosopher Swamiji (1863-1902) recognized the urgent necessity to awaken a man to his inner self and called on everyone to "arise, awake, and stop" until the desired outcome was achieved. The study of Swami Vivekananda's educational philosophy results in the change of man through moral and spiritual education. (Bhattacharjee, S.2017). According to Swami Vivekananda, there is an endless struggle among the strong and weak in life. So, the only thing that can prepare fearless people to face difficulties with boldness and confidence in education. Idealism, Naturalism, and Pragmatism are the central principles of Swami Vivekananda's educational philosophy. From his naturalistic viewpoint, he highlighted that only through nature and natural processes the real education is possible. From an idealist perspective, he claims that the goal of education is to help children improve their moral and spiritual traits. He placed a strong emphasis on Western education in technology, business, industry, and science from the perspective of the Pragmatists to create financial prosperity. (Rubi, 2023). Prime Minister of India Shri Narendra Modiji said the New National Education Policy is inspired by Swami Vivekananda's Philosophy as "Swami Vivekananda always focused on the development of both mental and physical strength. He said one should have muscles of iron and nerves of steel". (https://www.hindustantimes. com/2023). Many studies are showing a correlation between NEP 2020 and Swamiji's vision for education. Swamiji emphasized the value of the mother tongue and advised acquiring Sanskrit and English to develop a well-rounded personality in young minds. While Sanskrit helps in understanding the depths of our vast collection of classics, English is important to master Western science and technology. In keeping with the same attitude, NEP aims to make mother-tongue instruction compulsory for pupils at the primary level. Swamiji told, "Do not believe that you are weak or small, you can do anything and everything". This significant goal of Swami Ji, which is stressed in NEP 2020, is to develop students into whole citizens with moral and spiritual values, characters, knowledge skills, creative brilliance, innovation, and leadership qualities that foster a spirit of cooperation among team members. (Gurwara, S., 2021). Swami Vivekananda's vision for the country and the youth is followed by NEP 2020. With this order, the Indian government launched the Ramakrishna Mission's "Jagruti" programme for students in grades I through V to guarantee a child's whole personality development in line with the National Education Policy (NEP) 2020's guiding principles. (Rubi, 2023).

24.1 REVIEW OF RELATED LITERATURE:

1. *Gurwara, S. (2021.):* According to the study, Swamiji's educational philosophy, which is a component of Vedanta, is all about man-making, which is reflected in the very first sentence of NEP 2020, thus "Education is fundamental for achieving full human potential". NEP 2020 places a strong emphasis on the development of each person's creative potential in addition to the life skills that are essential for creating a well-rounded personality, such as leadership, cooperation, communication, and teamwork. It is predicated on the idea that education must empower students' social, ethical, and emotional qualities in addition to their cognitive ones.

2. *Bhattacharjee, S. (2017.).*: The study reveals Swami Vivekananda's ideas for the reconstruction of society in the complex social environment of today, where there is intense competition for material success and a value crisis in the community. This can

be done by incorporating Vivekananda's ideas into the process of human development through education. By letting go of one's ego, this study reveals how to connect with the inner self, which dwells in everything and everywhere and ultimately manifests perfection through education. In the aforementioned work, an effort has been made to examine Swami Vivekananda's approach to education. Swamiji also focused on Women's education because he knows that when a woman is educated, she can solve her problems in life and education will make women fearless and confident throughout her life.

3. *Roy, D.R. (2021.):* The study stated that education is not about collecting information on any topic, it is all about creating people with good characteristics and with different ideologies. According to Swamiji, we can gain knowledge from our minds, not from other outside sources. Self-education is Swamiji's way of education. He said that a child will learn on his own without outside pressure. He emphasized Sanskrit education, modern scientific knowledge and mass education, and religious education which will create spiritual characteristics among all communities.

24.2 OBJECTIVES

1. To emphasize the correlation existence of Swami Vivekananda's Philosophical approach to the Education system of India.
2. To understand the need for Swamiji's Philosophical Idea towards NEP 2020.

24.3 METHODOLOGY

The researcher used the Qualitative method for the study. The study uses all the secondary sources: journals/articles related to Swami Vivekananda's Philosophical Prospectives towards NEP 2020.

The correlation of Swami Vivekananda's Philosophical Vision Towards NEP 2020:

1. The goal of education, according to NEP 2020, will not only be cognitive development but also character development, producing whole, well-rounded individuals who possess the essential 21st-century abilities. In the end, the depth of knowledge will be constant and Education aids in the manifestation of knowledge as the perfection that is already within a person. (https://www.education.gov.in). To achieve all of these significant objectives, the entire curriculum and pedagogy will be reorganized and modified, along with the values and skills that will be reintroduced to the pre-primary through the higher education system. Swami Vivekananda opposes students from remembering material to get good grades since it prevents them from realizing their inner potential for a child's whole development. According to him, "Education is the manifestation of perfection; already existing in man". He emphasized man-making education, character-building, progressive education, and moral education which resonance with the main primary principle of NEP 2020 which is 'Education is fundamental for achieving full human potential'. (Bhat, S.A. 2021).

2. Swamiji said to all the citizens of India that, "we are supposed to learn till our death and the experienced world is the best educator". It means that we can learn from our experiences and this will help in achieving our goals throughout our life. This philosophy of Vivekananda gives importance to NEP 2020's one guideline which is, "creating the education system holistic, flexible, multidisciplinary and aligned to the needs of the 21st century and 2030 Sustainable Development Goal". NEP introduced the lost glory of the education system which is one of the main principles of Swamiji. (Gurwara, S. 2021).

3. The NEP 2020 gives importance to education as it is the main instrument to make India a proud leader worldwide in economic

development. So that India will be Viswa Guru and a global teacher in the world. The new dynamic growth inspires the vision of the Education system of India. Swamiji's Philosophy of education resembles the NEP's vision to make our country famous all over the world. He said, "we have yet to do something to teach the world. This is the very reason that this nation has lived on, despite hundreds of years of persecution, despite nearly a thousand years of foreign rule and foreign oppression. This nation still lives, it still holds to God, to the treasure house of religion and spirituality".(Vedanishthananda, S. 2022).

4. NEP 2020 gives importance to the native indigenous language for the Education system of India. Swamiji's Philosophy accepts this as he said, "the language in which we naturally express ourselves, in which we communicate our anger, grief or love, etc. there cannot be a fitter language than that. We must stick to that idea, that manner of expression, that diction and all". (Vedanishthananda, S. 2022).

24.4 FINDINGS OF THE STUDY

1. Swami ji emphasized man-making, character building, and spiritual and well-rounded development of an individual which resembles Nep 2020.
2. Swamiji focused on experience learning by own which will continue till death is one of the principles of NEP 2020.
3. Swami Vivekananda gives importance to the 'mother tongue' language system for the education of India which is one of the main guidelines of NEP 2020.
4. Swami ji's vision of technological development is inculcated in the NEP 2020.

24.5 CONCLUSION

Swami Vivekananda was one of the most influential educators and spiritual leaders of the modern era. He was a great lover of humanity, extending his unwavering love to everyone regardless of caste, creed, race, area, or religion. He believes that the only way to empower people is through education. Swami ji's Philosophy of education creates more influence in the field of NEP 2020. Swamiji emphasized the value of the mother tongue and advised acquiring Sanskrit and English to develop a well-rounded personality in young minds. While Sanskrit helps in understanding the depths of our vast collection of classics, English is important to master Western science and technology. In keeping with the same attitude, NEP aims to make mother-tongue instruction compulsory for pupils at the primary level. However, Swamiji's ideas on education, which he intended to use to create a powerful nation that will guide the rest of the world toward peace and harmony, are still a long way off. It is high time to give his educational Philosophy some serious thought and to keep in mind his call to action to "Arise, awake, and stop not until the goal is achieved" for everyone.

References

1. Chatterjee, S. & Datta, D. (2007). An Introduction to Indian Philosophy. Rupa Publications India Pvt. Ltd

2. Dashora, N. (1997). Panjalya Yoga Sutra: Yoga Darshan. Randheer Prakashan.

3. GoI (2020). National Educational Policy 2020. Ministry of Human Resource Development.

4. Goyandaka, H. (2021). Vedanta Darshan (Brahmasutra). Geeta Press.

5. Hiriyanna, M. (2013). Essentials of Indian philosophy. Sujeet Publications.

6. Radhakrishnan. S. (2008). Indian Philosophy Vol.1 (2nd Ed.). Oxford University Press.

7. Radhakrishnan. S. (2008). Indian Philosophy Vol.2 (2nd Ed.). Oxford University Press.

8. Sharma, C. (2009). A Critical Survey of Indian Philosophy. Motilal Banarasidas.

9. Sharma, S. & Sharma, B.D. (2020). Nyaya evam Vaisheshik Darshan. Yug Nirman Yojana Vistar Trust.

10. Shastri, U. (2021). Sankhyadarshanam (Vidyodaybhashyam). Vijaykumar Govindram Hasanand.

11. Teerth, V. (2022). Atharvaveda 13th Ed. Manoj Publications

12. Teerth, V. (2022). Rigveda 7th Ed. Manoj Publications.

Contribution of Aastik and Nastik Darshans in Value Inculcation in the Students

Dr. Sweta Dvivedi
Associate Professor
Department of Education
Mizoram University

Ms. Swati Dwivedi
Research Scholar
Department of Education
Mizoram University

ABSTRACT: *At present, among the various challenges of education, a major challenge that is standing before us is indiscipline and lack of values among the students. Society, which is built on values and rests on values, will be directionless and unhesitatingly collapse in the case of valueless impending citizens. In such a situation, for the persistence of society, education and schools should play their role in value inculcation and fostering. If we look at the policies and commissions formed to bring change and development in education in India, each one has discussed the value-education at different levels of education. In NEP 2020 also special emphasis has been laid on inculcating values in the students. What role Indian philosophy can play in inculcating and promoting values among students and how various astika (theist) and nastika (atheist) philosophies can contribute to this will be discussed in this paper. Philosophy has an important role in determining the direction of education and society. Therefore, building a harmonized and balanced society must be done by including these Darshans directly or indirectly in education.*

Keywords: *Aastik Darshan, Nastik Darshan, Value Education, Value Inculcation.*

25.0 INTRODUCTION

Indian philosophy is known for its diverse and profound nature, as well as its pursuit of ultimate truth. There are two fundamental categories in this philosophical landscape: Aastik and Nastik darshans. Astik darshans are theistic schools of thought encompassing traditions such as Vedanta, Nyaya, and Yoga. Nastik darshans, on the other hand, encompass atheistic or non-theistic traditions, such as Buddhism, Jainism, and Charvaka. These philosophical traditions have had a significant impact on Indian society, culture, and education for centuries. The discussion of certain eternal values is common to both Aastik and Nastik Darshans.

These eternal values are deeply rooted in Indian philosophical and spiritual traditions and serve as guiding principles for ethical and moral living. They promote a sense of personal and societal responsibility, fostering compassion, harmony, and social justice. These values have universal applicability and continue to inspire individuals and movements around the world to strive for a more just and peaceful society.

First, various Indian Darshans which fall under theistic and atheistic Darshans will be discussed.

25.1 VEDANTA DARSHAN AND INHERENT VALUES

Vedanta Darshan, often referred to as simply Vedanta is a philosophical tradition that has been at the heart of Indian thought for millennia. It explores profound questions about the self (Atman), the ultimate reality (Brahman), and the path to self-realization (moksha). Vedanta Darshan is one of the six orthodox systems of Indian philosophy, rooted in the Vedas and Upanishads. It has been expounded in various texts, including the Brahma Sutras, Bhagavad Gita, and the Upanishads. Vedanta explores the nature of reality, the self, and the ultimate reality.

Vedanta Darshan teaches students the value of self-realization (Atma-Jnana), leading to the recognition of the unity between the individual self (Atman) and the universal consciousness (Brahman). This realization fosters humility, empathy, and a sense of interconnectedness with all beings. Vedanta promotes the idea that attachment to material possessions and transient desires leads to suffering. By emphasizing the value of detachment (Vairagya) and renunciation (Tyaga), students learn to prioritize inner fulfilment over external acquisitions. Vedanta highlights the importance of ethical conduct (Dharma) to attain spiritual progress. It encourages students to cultivate virtues such as truthfulness, compassion, non-violence, and honesty.

The philosophy of Vedanta has played a crucial role in promoting values of non-discrimination and inclusion. The statement *'Ekam Brahm, dvitiya naste neh na naste kinchan'* (Brahmsutra) highlights the significance of removing all forms of discrimination. As per this philosophy, if everyone is Brahma, then there should not exist any space for discrimination of any sort. Vedanta Darshan also contributes to holistic education by integrating philosophical teachings into the curriculum. Lessons on self-awareness, self-actualization, and ethical decision-making empower students to lead balanced and meaningful lives. Vedanta principles, such as self-realization and detachment, help students manage stress, anxiety, and emotional challenges. They provide valuable tools for achieving emotional resilience and inner peace. Educational institutions are incorporating Vedanta-inspired character development programs that emphasize values like compassion, humility, and ethical conduct. These programs nurture responsible citizens and well-rounded individuals.

Vedanta Darshan, with its profound insights into the nature of the self and the ultimate reality, plays a crucial role in inculcating values among students. Its teachings on self-realization, detachment, and ethical conduct provide a strong foundation for character development and holistic education. As education continues to evolve, incorporating Vedanta's timeless wisdom can empower students to navigate the complexities of the modern world while staying grounded in their ethical and moral values.

25.2 MIMANSA DARSHAN AND INHERENT VALUES

Mimansa focuses on the interpretation of the Vedas, particularly the ritualistic portions (karma-kanda). It provides a framework for understanding dharma (duty) and the role of rituals in one's life. Mimansa Darshan has its roots in the Vedas and is traditionally attributed to Sage Jaimini. It complements other philosophical systems by providing a comprehensive understanding of Vedic rituals and their ethical implications.

Mimansa Darshan instils in students a strong sense of duty and responsibility towards their roles and obligations in society. It emphasizes that fulfilling one's dharma is a moral imperative, fostering a commitment to ethical conduct and societal well-being. The meticulous examination of Vedic texts and rituals in Mimansa promotes critical thinking and ethical decision-making. Students learn to discern right from wrong and to make informed choices based on their understanding of dharma. Mimansa Darshan encourages students to respect and participate in traditional rituals and ceremonies, recognizing the cultural and spiritual significance of these practices. This fosters a sense of cultural preservation and reverence for heritage.

Modern educational institutions incorporate Mimansa-inspired ethics and values education into their curriculum. This includes lessons on the importance of duty, ethical decision-making, and the role of rituals in contemporary life. The study of Mimansa principles enhances critical thinking skills and the ability to analyze complex texts and situations. These skills are valuable for students' academic and personal development. Mimansa Darshan encourages interdisciplinary learning, as it touches upon various aspects of life, culture, and spirituality. Educational programs that integrate this philosophy promote well-rounded individuals.

Mimansa Darshan, with its profound insights into the interpretation of Vedic texts and the ethical dimension of rituals and duty, plays a significant role in inculcating values among students. Its teachings on duty, ethical decision-making, and respect for traditions provide a strong foundation for character development and holistic education. As education continues to evolve, incorporating Mimansa's timeless wisdom can empower students to navigate the complexities of the modern world while staying grounded in their ethical and moral values.

25.3 SAMKHYA DARSHAN AND INHERENT VALUES

Indian philosophy is known for its rich diversity and depth, and Sankhya Darshan is a prominent system that contributes significantly to the understanding of human existence and consciousness. Sankhya Darshan, attributed to Sage Kapila, provides a framework for comprehending the dualistic nature of reality and the individual's quest for liberation (moksha). Sankhya Darshan is a classical school of thought that delves into the metaphysical and epistemological aspects of existence. It analyzes the nature of the self (Purusha) and the material world (Prakriti) and seeks to explain the origins of suffering and the path to liberation.

Sankhya Darshan emphasizes the importance of discernment (viveka) in distinguishing between the eternal and the transitory. Students are encouraged to cultivate the ability to discriminate between the unchanging self (purusha) and the ever-changing material world (Prakriti). This discrimination leads to self-realization and the understanding of one's true nature. The concept of non-attachment (vairagya) is central to Sankhya's philosophy. Students are taught the value of detachment from material possessions, desires, and the fruits of their actions. This detachment fosters a sense of contentment, reducing greed and envy and promoting inner peace. Sankhya Darshan provides a foundation for ethical conduct (dharma) by emphasizing the importance of living in harmony with the natural order. It encourages students to act with compassion, honesty, and responsibility, recognizing that ethical behaviour leads to spiritual progress.

Sankhya Darshan contributes to holistic education by incorporating philosophical teachings into the curriculum. This includes lessons on self-awareness, emotional intelligence, and ethical decision-making, which empower students to lead balanced and fulfilling lives. The practice of Sankhya principles, such as self-realization and non-attachment, supports students in managing stress, anxiety, and mental health challenges. It fosters emotional resilience and provides tools for coping with the pressures of modern life. Schools and colleges incorporate Sankhya-inspired character development programs that emphasize values like self-awareness, compassion, and ethical conduct. These programs promote responsible citizenship and the development of well-rounded individuals.

Sankhya Darshan, with its profound insights into the nature of self and reality, plays a significant role in inculcating values among students. Its teachings on discrimination, non-attachment, and ethical conduct provide a valuable foundation for character development and holistic education. As education evolves, incorporating Sankhya Darshan's timeless wisdom can empower students to navigate the complexities of the modern world while staying rooted in their ethical and moral values.

25.4 YOGA DARSHAN AND INHERENT VALUES

Yoga and Samkhya philosophy complement each other. Yoga is an ancient philosophical system that forms the foundation of yoga practice and encompasses a holistic approach to life, ethics, and values. Yoga, often thought of as a physical exercise regimen, is a comprehensive philosophical system with deep roots in Indian tradition. The Yoga Darshan, attributed to the sage Patanjali, is a classical text that provides a profound understanding of human consciousness, ethical conduct, and the path to spiritual realization. Yoga Darshan is part of the broader system of Indian philosophy and is often classified under the Astik (theistic) category. It consists of 196 sutras that provide insights into the nature of the mind, the control of mental processes, and the ultimate goal of human life - liberation (moksha).

Patanjali's Yoga Darshan outlines the eight limbs of yoga, which serve as a practical guide for individuals seeking self-realization. These limbs include Yama (moral restraints), Niyama (observances), Asana (postures), Pranayama (breath control), Pratyahara (withdrawal of the senses), Dharana (concentration), Dhyana (meditation), and Samadhi (union with the divine). Each limb has ethical and moral dimensions that are relevant to students' character development.

The Yama and Niyama limbs of yoga prescribe a code of conduct that includes principles such as non-violence (Ahimsa), truthfulness (Satya), non-stealing (Asteya), moderation (Brahmacharya), and non-possessiveness

(Aparigraha). These ethical guidelines help students cultivate virtues like compassion, honesty, self-control, and contentment. The practice of asanas (physical postures) and pranayama (breath control) not only enhances physical health but also develops discipline and concentration. Students learn the importance of regular practice, patience, and mindfulness, which are essential values for success in any endeavour. Dharana, Dhyana, and Samadhi are the stages of meditation in Yoga Darshan. These practices encourage students to explore their inner selves, develop self-awareness, and cultivate a deeper sense of spirituality. Through meditation, students can gain clarity of thought, emotional stability, and a profound connection with their inner values.

25.5 NYAYA DARSHAN AND INHERENT VALUES

Nyaya focuses on logic, reasoning, and epistemology. It provides a rigorous framework for understanding the nature of knowledge and the principles of critical thinking. This research article explores how Nyaya Darshan plays a crucial role in inculcating values among students and contributes to their holistic development. Nyaya Darshan has its roots in ancient India and is traditionally attributed to Sage Gautama. It has evolved over the centuries and has contributed significantly to the development of logical and philosophical thought in India.

Darshan promotes the development of critical thinking skills among students. It encourages them to analyze, evaluate, and question information critically, fostering a habit of reasoned inquiry. The emphasis on logical reasoning in Nyaya helps students communicate their thoughts and ideas more clearly and precisely. It teaches them to construct well-structured arguments and convey their points effectively. Nyaya Darshan teaches students to value evidence and rationality in decision-making. This promotes an appreciation for objective analysis and reasoned judgment.

Modern educational institutions incorporate Nyaya-inspired critical thinking programs into their curriculum. These programs teach students how to think critically, evaluate information, and make informed decisions.

Nyaya Darshan's focus on logical reasoning and debate skills is integrated into various educational activities and extracurricular programs. These activities help students develop their ability to construct and defend arguments. The logical and analytical skills developed through Nyaya Darshan are invaluable for problem-solving in various fields. They equip students with the tools to approach challenges methodically and find effective solutions.

Nyaya Darshan, with its emphasis on logical reasoning, critical thinking, and evidence-based knowledge, plays a significant role in inculcating values among students. Its teachings on the importance of clarity, precision, and rationality provide a strong foundation for character development and holistic education. As education continues to evolve, incorporating Nyaya's timeless wisdom can empower students to navigate the complexities of the modern world while staying grounded in their ethical and moral values.

25.6 VAISHESIK DARSHAN AND INHERENT VALUES

Vaisheshik Darshan, one of the six classical schools of Indian philosophy, offers profound insights into the nature of reality, atomism, and the quest for knowledge. Vaisheshik Darshan, often referred to as simply Vaisheshik is a classical school of Indian philosophy that provides a comprehensive understanding of the nature of reality, the universe, and the quest for knowledge.

Vaisheshik Darshan has its roots in ancient India and is traditionally attributed to Sage Kanada. It has evolved over centuries and has made significant contributions to metaphysics, epistemology, and ontology. Central to Vaisheshik's philosophy is the concept of atoms (Anu). This school of thought postulates that the universe is composed of eternal and indivisible atoms, which combine to form all material objects. Vaisheshik classifies all aspects of reality into seven categories, including substance (dravya), quality (guna), action (karma), generality (samanya), particularity (vishesha), inherence (samavaya), and negation (abhava). Vaisheshik explores the principles of causation and the interplay of causes and effects in the material world. It delves into the concept of karma and its role in determining the course of events.

Vaisheshik Darshan encourages students to develop a spirit of empirical inquiry and curiosity. It emphasizes the importance of gaining knowledge through observation, analysis, and logical reasoning. The classification of reality into various categories, including generality (samanya) and particularity (vishesha), promotes an appreciation for the unity in diversity. Students learn to recognize the underlying commonalities that connect all beings and objects. Vaisheshik's exploration of causation and the law of karma has ethical implications. Students are taught to take responsibility for their actions and understand the consequences of their deeds, fostering a sense of accountability and ethical conduct.

Vaisheshik, with its emphasis on empirical inquiry, classification of reality, and exploration of causation and ethics, plays a significant role in inculcating values among students. Its teachings on knowledge acquisition, unity in diversity, and ethical accountability provide a strong foundation for character development and holistic education. As education continues to evolve, incorporating Vaisheshik's timeless wisdom can empower students to navigate the complexities of the modern world while staying grounded in their ethical and moral values.

25.7 NASTIK DARSHAN

25.8 JAIN DARSHAN AND INHERENT VALUES

Jainism, one of the oldest philosophical traditions in India, is renowned for its commitment to non-violence (ahimsa), truth (satya), and asceticism. It is older than Vedas because there is a reference to Rishabhdev, the first Tirthankar of the Jain religion in Rigveda and Atharveda (Rigveda Verses 6.16.47, 10.166, Atharvaveda- 9.4.14–15). Jain Darshan, with its emphasis on non-violence, truthfulness, non-possessiveness, and ethical conduct, plays a significant role in inculcating values among students. Its teachings provide a valuable foundation for character development, ethical decision-making, and a compassionate worldview. As education continues to evolve, incorporating Jainism's timeless wisdom can empower students to navigate the complexities of the modern world while staying grounded in their ethical and moral values.

25.9 BUDDHISM AND INHERENT VALUES

Buddhism, a profound and influential philosophical tradition, offers valuable insights into the nature of human existence, ethics, and personal development. Buddhism, founded by Siddhartha Gautama (Buddha) in ancient India, has had a profound impact on the world's philosophical, ethical, and spiritual landscape. Buddhism emerged in India during the 6th century BCE as a response to the existential questions and suffering inherent in human existence. The teachings of the Buddha are recorded in various sutras and are rooted in the Four Noble Truths and the Eightfold Path. These truths are the foundation of Buddhist thought and address the nature of suffering (dukkha), its causes (samudaya), the possibility of cessation (nirodha), and the path to cessation (magga). This path consists of eight interconnected principles that guide ethical conduct, mental discipline, and wisdom. It includes the right view, right intention, right speech, right action, right livelihood, right effort, right mindfulness, and right concentration.

Buddhist philosophy, with its emphasis on compassion, mindfulness, and ethical conduct, plays a significant role in inculcating values among students. Its teachings provide a valuable foundation for character development, emotional well-being, and ethical decision-making. As education continues to evolve, incorporating Buddhist wisdom can empower students to navigate the complexities of the modern world while staying rooted in their ethical and moral values.

Buddhist philosophy emphasizes compassion (karuna) as a fundamental virtue. Students are taught to cultivate empathy, kindness, and concern for the well-being of all sentient beings, promoting a sense of interconnectedness. Mindfulness (sati) is a core practice in Buddhism. Students are encouraged to develop self-awareness, focus, and presence in their daily lives. This leads to better emotional regulation and decision-making. The Five Precepts in Buddhism outline ethical guidelines, including refraining from killing, stealing, sexual misconduct, false speech, and intoxicants. These precepts instill a sense of moral responsibility among students.

25.10 CHARVAKA DARSHAN AND INHERENT VALUES

Charvaka Darshan, also known as Lokayata, represents a heterodox school of Indian philosophy that challenges conventional beliefs and questions traditional values. Rooted in the writings of Charvaka, the school challenges established religious and metaphysical beliefs. Charvaka Darshan emerged in ancient India, characterized by its skepticism toward religious dogma and emphasis on empiricism and materialism. It represents a significant divergence from other classical schools of Indian philosophy.

Charvaka philosophy asserts that only the material world exists and that sensory experiences are the only source of valid knowledge. It denies the existence of gods, afterlife, and metaphysical entities. Charvaka challenges the authority of scriptures and religious rituals, emphasizing skepticism and questioning of established norms and values. While Charvaka does not advocate moral values in the traditional sense, it promotes ethical hedonism by encouraging individuals to seek pleasure and avoid pain.

Charvaka Darshan encourages students to develop critical thinking skills and skepticism. It urges them to question assumptions, challenge beliefs, and engage in rational discourse. Emphasizing sensory experiences as the only source of knowledge, Charvaka fosters empiricism among students. This encourages them to rely on direct observations and evidence-based thinking. Charvaka philosophy values individual autonomy and decision-making. Students are encouraged to make choices that maximize their own well-being based on their experiences and desires.

Charvaka Darshan, with its emphasis on skepticism, empiricism, and materialism, plays a distinctive role in value inculcation among students. While it challenges traditional values and beliefs, it fosters critical thinking, empiricism, and the ability to question established norms. As education continues to evolve, incorporating Charvaka's unorthodox wisdom can empower students to engage critically with diverse perspectives, strengthening their capacity for independent thought and ethical decision-making.

25.11 NEP 2020 AND VALUES

India's National Education Policy (NEP) 2020 represents a monumental shift in the country's approach to education. Among its many facets, the policy places a strong emphasis on value education, recognizing its pivotal role in shaping responsible and ethical citizens. NEP 2020 marks a significant milestone in India's educational landscape. Drafted with the aim of transforming the country's education system, the policy has a strong focus on holistic development, critical thinking, and value-based education. This research article examines the role of value education within NEP 2020, highlighting its importance in nurturing responsible citizens and fostering ethical values. There are some key provisions of NEP 2020 on value education. It emphasizes the integration of values such as truth, non-violence, and integrity into the curriculum from an early age. The multidisciplinary approach has also been encouraged by the policy, which allows students to explore various subjects, including ethics and value education, alongside their primary academic pursuits. This policy envisions the development of ethical leaders through a strong emphasis on critical thinking, decision-making, and ethical reasoning. The policy underscores the importance of inclusivity and respect for diversity, fostering an environment where students from all backgrounds can coexist harmoniously.

25.12 CONCLUSION

Indian philosophy, deeply rooted in its diverse cultural and spiritual heritage, encompasses both Astik and Nastik schools of thought. Indian Astik and Nastik darshans have made significant contributions to value inculcation among students over centuries. These philosophical traditions provide a holistic approach to education, emphasizing not only academic knowledge but also the development of moral and ethical character. While challenges exist in balancing tradition with modernity and ensuring inclusivity, the rich philosophical heritage of India continues to shape the lives and values of its youth. As education evolves, it is essential to draw from these ancient traditions to nurture responsible and compassionate citizens who can contribute positively to society.

India's National Education Policy 2020 represents a visionary approach to education that places value education at its core. By emphasizing foundational values, ethical leadership, inclusivity, and diversity, the policy has the potential to transform not only the education system but also the entire society. However, the successful implementation of value education will require careful planning, teacher training, and continuous assessment. Through its commitment to holistic development and ethical citizenship, NEP 2020 can shape a brighter future for India.

Value inculcation is not an ancillary aspect of education but a core foundation that shapes the future of individuals and society. By recognizing the significance of values and adopting effective methods, educators can instill ethical behavior, promote social cohesion, and contribute to the betterment of society through school education.

References

1. Bhat, S.A., (2021). An Evaluative study of Educational Philosophy of Swami Vivekananda. IJAMSR, ISSN:2581-4281. DOI: https://doi.org/10.3142 6/ijamsr.2021.4.7.4511. Vol 4, Issue 7, 2021.
2. Bhattacharjee, S. (2017). A study of Educational Philosophy of Swami Vivekananda. www.jetir.org (ISSN-2349-5162). Volume 4, Issue 1,2017.
3. Rubi,(2023). Swami Vivekananda's vision and Indian Education system. DOI: https://doi.org/10.22271/allresearch.2023.v9.i2d.1061.
4. (https://www.hindustantimes.com/2023)

5. Gurwara, S., (2021). Re-imagining and Re-defining Education: NEP 2020 and the Vision of Swami Vivekananda. Swami Vivekanand , Subharti University.

6. Roy. D.R. (2021). Vivekananda's Educational Philosophy. www.irjmets.com(ISSN: 2582-5208). Volume:3,Issue 2,2021. Impact Factor- 5.354.

7. Vedanishthananda, S., (2022.). The new national education policy and Swami Vivekananda's educational ideas. www.SAMSKRITI.com.

8. https://www.education.gov.in

Is UDL Catering the Needs of Diverse Learners: A Review

Dr. Sweta Dvivedi, Associate Professor, Department of Education, Mizoram University, Aizawl, Mizoram

Dr. Adya Shakti Rai, Associate Professor, Department of Visual Impairment, Dr. Shakuntala Misra National Rehabilitation University

Ms. J H Vanlalzuali, Research Scholar, Department of Education, Mizoram University, Aizawl, Mizoram

ABSTRACT: *Universal Design for Learning guarantees equal access to education for all students, regardless of any physical or mental differences they may have. In this review paper, the authors delve into the topic of Universal Design for Learning and its effectiveness in educating students with physical or mental disparities. The paper aims to determine whether UDL can be beneficial for all types of learners. The authors selected both empirical and theoretical studies to conduct their research and analyzed a total of nine research papers. The findings of the review conclude that UDL is indeed a successful framework for ensuring that all students, regardless of their differences, can participate in the learning process.*

Keywords: *Universal Design for Learning (UDL), differently abled, normal students, CAST.*

26.0 INTRODUCTION

Universal Design for Learning (UDL) is a framework that aims to minimize the barriers that follow inflexibility. It aims to make learning accessible to all students, regardless of their individual abilities, learning styles, or needs. It is based on the idea that there is no one-size-fits-all approach to teaching and learning (CAST, 2011). Instead, UDL encourages educators to provide multiple means of representation, engagement, and expression to accommodate the diverse needs of learners. The term UDL was taken from Universal Design coined by Ronald Mace in the 1970s for their designs in architecture that are usable by all people as much as possible (CAST, 2015). It is a philosophy, and structure with guiding principles which has to be used in the teaching and learning environment, addressing the needs of diverse students (Cap, 2016). The Universal Design for Learning (UDL) principles are used to create curricula that cater to the diverse needs of learners (CAST, 2011). Unfortunately, poor or inadequate curricula fail to meet the needs of students who are different from the majority, such as gifted and talented students, students with disabilities, or even those without any disabilities (CAST, 2011). UDL takes into consideration the varying needs of learners and adapts the curriculum accordingly (Lohmann et al. 2018). It emphasizes the use of assistive technologies to help learners engage with their studies (McConlogue, 2020). UDL focuses on the curriculum to achieve educational goals and minimize the impact of differences among students (Courey et al., 2012). It is a flexible, scientific framework that aims to reduce barriers and promote inclusivity in education (King-Sears, 2014).

The classroom is often infused with diverse learners such as gifted students, average students, students with disabilities or some type of disorder, and students belonging to different cultures, languages, and societies. Serving them equally in the basic classroom environment was an ancient practice which is not relevant in the present times. In the present times, with the awareness of inclusion, preparing learners to play an active role rather than a passive one has become the major focus of the education system. Institutions that are committed to inclusion must ensure the central idea of inclusion is integrated into regular education classes. However, despite the mental readiness of administrators and the availability of enough infrastructural facilities, teachers are not ready to handle inclusive classes due to special learning requirements and the diverse needs of students (Cook, 2002). Cook et al (2003) suggested that to provide equal opportunities for learning training of teachers is important. Research findings indicate that faculty members often feel unprepared to teach students with special needs (Forlin & Chambers, 2011). As teachers are responsible for providing facilities and support to all types of learners for their learning, they need to prepare themselves to deal with students with diverse needs. Dolan et al. (2005) noted that integrating UDL into lesson plans and assessment systems had a positive impact on learners' performance.

Research studies have shown that students with Learning Disabilities (LD) have the largest sub-group amongst students with disabilities (Wolanin and Steele, 2004). The academic performance of these students is directly linked to the support provided by their teachers (Allsop et al., 2015; Troiano, 2003; Wallace et al., 2000). Teachers are responsible for ensuring that learners with disabilities achieve academic success comparable to that of their classmates (Hunt and Andreasen, 2011). To promote equitable learning opportunities and minimize barriers for students, Universal Design for Learning (UDL) aims to provide access and flexibility to all learners. The Center for Applied Special Technology (CAST) has outlined three principles of UDL which should be incorporated by all the teachers for better learning of students.

Multiple means of 'Engagement': The 'WHY' of the learning.

One of the key principles of UDL involves engaging learners by tapping into their interests, motivations, and challenges (Edyburn, 2001). Different learners may be more engaged by spontaneity and novelty, while others prefer usual and strict routines. Similarly, some may prefer to work alone, while others enjoy working with their peers. Actively involving learners in the learning process can increase their interest and motivation.

Multiple means of 'Representation': The 'WHAT' of the learning.

The main objective of this principle is to present the information in several formats so that all students can understand the content in the best way. Presenting in multiple ways activates the recognition network of the brain (Nave, 2021). Learning, and transfer of learning, occur when contents are represented in multiple ways because they allow students to make connections within, as well as between, concepts.

Multiple means of 'Action and Expression': The 'HOW' of the learning.

This principle allows the learners alternatives for expressing what they have learned (Edyburn,2001). Choices should be given for expressing what is already acquired as the individuals themselves differ greatly (Nave, 2021). When students express what they have learnt in their way, the teachers can diagnose them, and the students can also convey the learnt concepts in their best way.

26.1 PURPOSE OF THE STUDY

UDL seeks to bestow quality education to all types of learners with disabilities or certain disorders. The objective of this review paper is to find out whether UDL really helps in meeting the educational needs of all learners including brilliants, creatives, disabled/ differently abled or students without any disability etc.

26.2 METHODOLOGY

Relevant papers were identified using databases and digital libraries like JSTOR, ERIC, and Google Scholar, along with search engines. Studies related to the topic of Universal Design for Learning, differently abled education, impairments, and inclusive education were selected, both empirical and theoretical. The selected papers were downloaded, and after carefully reading the abstract, methods, population, and conclusion or discussion, they were reviewed.

26.3 RESULTS

After a careful review of all the papers, the findings obtained by the researchers will be presented here sequentially.

In reviewing the studies related to UDL, it was found that they did not concentrate on the education of students without physical or learning disabilities. Therefore, the studies which had UDL as a keyword and that did not include any disability-related terms or words were categorized as studies that focused on normal students. UDL's effectiveness in the teaching-learning process was assessed through papers and articles that regarded the perspective of teachers, students, or both.

Kennette et al. (2019) did research on college students' and faculty members' perceptions regarding UDL through a survey. Students expressed that UDL was helpful in learning and useful in motivating the learners. It was equally helpful for the teachers and the learners because teachers were getting a variety of ways to present the information. Faculty members also reported that they often used UDL principles particularly 'the what of the learning' as they think it has a positive impact on the learning of the pupil. Wells (2022) carried out mixed-method research on the students' perspectives on the use of UDL in distance education. The study was done through emails and the findings showed that UDL has a significant influence on the majority of them. The students mentioned that feedback from the instructor great positive impact on them and they learned the ability to manage their time. Majuddin et al. (2022) studied the perspective of students on the use of numerous instruments for evaluating university learners. The pilot study was done using a tool called PutraPacer and was found that the tool stimulates the educational experience of the learners, backing up differently-abled students. They also mentioned that it is extremely beneficial for them.

Some studies mentioned the type of abnormality they deal in the classrooms. Hartmann and Weismer (2016) using 3 models which include UDL conferred about the advantages of technology for assisting deafblind students. After going through several findings, the researchers concluded that UDL opens ways for such impairments to participate in the general curriculum resulting in improvement of their learning. Cook et al. (2017) commented that with the utilization of UDL, learners with disorders that are linked to their emotions and behaviour can observe themselves. This is important for their recognition and academic achievements. It has been also mentioned in this paper that it will further increase their engagement and adjustment of their behaviour.

Some studies mentioned the type of abnormality the teachers deal in the classrooms. Hartmann and Weismer (2016) using 3 models which include UDL conferred about the advantages of technology for assisting deafblind students. After going through several findings, the researchers concluded that UDL opens ways for such impairments to participate in the general curriculum resulting in improvement of their learning. Cook et al. (2017) commented that with the utilization of UDL, learners with disorders that are linked to their emotions and behaviour can observe themselves. This is important for their recognition and academic achievements. It has been also mentioned in this paper that it will further increase their engagement and adjustment of their behaviour.

There are some studies that mention both normal and disabled learners without emphasizing only one type of learner and learning needs. For example, King-Sears et al. (2015) conducted exploratory research on the use of UDL by high school students, including students without disabilities and those with high-incidence disabilities (HID). They were exposed to pre- and post-tests and found that UDL improved the learning of HIDs more than that of normal students, as reported post-treatment. Similarly, a study conducted by Kennedy et al. (2014) researched secondary students using a model consistent with UDL. The objective of the study was to build the vocabulary of the learners, and the findings showed that both learners with and without learning disabilities improved greatly.

Caverly and Fitzgibbons (2007) noted that technology can be beneficial for students with disabilities who struggle with reading. It can help both typical and diverse learners to better understand the material being taught, leading to greater overall comprehension. In a mixed-method study of middle school students, Hall et al. (2015) investigated whether Universal Design for Learning (UDL) and a curriculum-based assessment had improved the reading skills of students with disabilities. The analysis revealed that all students had improved after the post-test, with particularly notable gains in online comprehension. The researchers also found that students with learning disabilities benefited significantly from the experiment.

26.4 FINDINGS AND CONCLUSION

Several research studies have been conducted to determine the impact of Universal Design for Learning (UDL) from the perspectives of both students and faculties. The findings reveal that UDL is a useful and motivating tool for students. According to the students, their teachers' feedback has a significant impact on their learning. UDL has also proven to be beneficial for students with specific impairments such as deafness, blindness, and emotional and behavioural disorders, allowing them to participate and engage in the learning process. Studies have also shown that UDL improves the learning outcomes and vocabulary of both normal and differently-abled students. Additionally, students with Learning Disabilities (LD) and those who struggle with reading have reported significant improvement. Despite the introduction of UDL several decades ago, its implementation rate is still minimal, resulting in fewer empirical studies.

The review delved into the implementation of Universal Design for Learning (UDL) as a framework or integrated into specific courses as a project to identify gaps and their implications. The findings of this research support the claim made by the Centre for Applied Science Technology (CAST) regarding the efficacy of UDL for various learners, especially those who are vulnerable.

This review paper highlights the opportunities and challenges in validating the framework of Universal Design for Learning (UDL) universally. The paper also suggests that a strong implementation of UDL always results in positive outcomes. Therefore, it is highly recommended to introduce UDL in all educational institutions, irrespective of the types of learners, as it has been found to be helpful in diverse learning environments.

References

1. Allsopp, D. H., Minskoff, E. H., & Bolt, L. (2005). Individualized course-specific strategy instruction for college students with learning disabilities and ADHD: Lessons learned from a model demonstration project. *Learning Disabilities Research*

and Practice, 20(2), 103–118. https://doi.org/10.1111/j.1540-5826.2005.00126.x

2. Beck Wells, M. (2022). Student perspectives on the use of universal design for learning in virtual formats in higher education. *Smart Learning Environments, 9*(1). https://doi.org/10.1186/s40561-022-00218-6

3. Capp, M. J. (2017). The effectiveness of universal learning design: A meta-analysis of literature between 2013 and 2016. *International Journal of Inclusive Education, 21*(8), 791–807. https://doi.org/10.1080/13603116.2017.1325074

4. Caverly, D. C., & Fitzgibbons, D. (2007). Developmental psychologist, fall 2006-Winter 2007. *Journal of Developmental Education, FALL 2007, Vol. 31, No. 1 (FALL 2007), Pp. 38-39, 31,* 38–39. https://doi.org/10.1037/e517222010-001

5. Centre for Universal Design (2015). Retrieved from http://www.ncsu.edu/ncsu/design/cud/about_ud/about_ud.htm.

6. Cook, B. G. (2002). Inclusive attitudes, strengths, and weaknesses of pre-service general educators enrolled in a curriculum infusion teacher preparation program. Teacher Education and SpecialEducation: The Journal of the Teacher Education Division of the Council for Exceptional Children, 25, 262–277

7. Cook, B. G., Landrum, T. J., Tankersley, M., & Kauffman, J. M. (2003). Bringing research to bear on practice: Effecting evidence-based instruction for students with emotional or behavioural disorders. Education and Treatment of Children, 26, 345–361

8. Courey, S. J., Tappe, P., Siker, J., & LePage, P. (2012). Improved lesson planning with universal design for learning (UDL). *Teacher Education and Special Education: The Journal of the Teacher Education Division of the Council for Exceptional Children, 36*(1), 7–27. https://doi.org/10.1177/0888406412446178

9. Dolan, R. P., Hall, T. E., Banerjee, M., Chun, E., & Strangman, N. (2005). Applying principles of universal design to test delivery: The effect of computer-based read-aloud on test performance of high school students with learning disabilities. Journal of

Technology, Learning, and Assessment, 3(7). Available from http://www.jtla.org

10. Forlin, C., & Chambers, D. (2011). Teacher preparation for inclusive education: Increasing knowledge but raising concerns. *Asia-Pacific Journal of Teacher Education, 39*(1), 17–32. https://doi.org/10.1080/1359866X.2010.540850

11. Hall, T. E., Cohen, N., Vue, G., & Ganley, P. (2014). Addressing learning disabilities with UDL and Technology. *Learning Disability Quarterly, 38*(2), 72–83. https://doi.org/10.1177/0731948714544375

12. Hartmann, E., & Weismer, P. (2016). Technology implementation and curriculum engagement for children and youth who are deafblind. *American Annals of the Deaf, 161*(4), 462–473. https://doi.org/10.1353/aad.2016.0038

13. Hunt, J. H., & Andreasen, J. B. (2011, October 1). *Making the most of universal design for learning.* NCTM Publications. Retrieved March 14, 2023, from https://pubs.nctm.org/abstract/journals/mtms/17/3/article-p166.xml

14. Kennette, L. N., & Wilson, N. A. (2019). Universal Design for Learning (UDL). *Journal of Effective Teaching in Higher Education, 2*(1), 1–26. https://doi.org/10.36021/jethe.v2i1.17

15. King-Sears, P. (2014). Introduction to *learning disability quarterly* special series on Universal Design for Learning. *Learning Disability Quarterly, 37*(2), 68–70. https://doi.org/10.1177/0731948714528337

16. McConlogue, T. (2020). In *Assessment and feedback in Higher Education: A guide for teachers.* essay, UCL Press.

17. Md. Khambari, M. N., Majuddin, C., Wong, S. L., Ghazali, N., & Mohd. Norowi, N. (2022). Students' perspectives on the use of differentiated assessment tool: Results from an explanatory sequential mixed-method pilot study. *Contemporary Educational Technology, 14*(2). https://doi.org/10.30935/cedtech/11667

18. *The UDL guidelines.* UDL. (2011). Retrieved March 15, 2023, from http://udlguidelines.cast.org/

19. Troiano, P. F. (2003). College students and learning disability: Elements of self-style. *Journal of College Student Development, 44*(3), 404–419. https://doi.org/10.1353/csd.2003.0033

20. Wallace, D., Abel, R., & Ropers-Huilman, B. (2000). Clearing a path for success: Deconstructing borders through undergraduate mentoring. *The Review of Higher Education, 24*(1), 87–102. https://doi.org/10.1353/rhe.2000.0026

21. Wolanin, T. R. & Steele, P. E., &. (2004, May 31). *Higher education opportunities for students with disabilities: A Primer for policymakers.* Institute for Higher Education Policy. Retrieved March 14, 2023, from https://eric.ed.gov/?id=ED485430

A Review on the Related Study of Higher Education in Mizoram

Wesly Zarzolawmi, Research Scholar Department of Education
Dr. N.Pramod Kumar, Department of Education, Mizoram University.

ABSTRACT: *The review paper discusses the state of higher education in Mizoram, noting its historical context, challenges, and related studies. Despite Mizoram's high literacy rates, the authors highlight the lag in technical and professional education, attributed to young institutions with inadequate infrastructure. The paper underlines the need to strengthen higher education in Mizoram, aligning with the New Education Policy 2020, which aims to overhaul and enhance the quality of higher education across India.*

27.0 INTRODUCTION

The aim of education is to help realize the national goals which bring an all-round progress of the country as well as the essential self-fulfillment of an individual as a human being. Since the purpose of education is to enrich life and to promote economic development and social transformation; a good, efficient and relevant system of education must be forward looking and flexible to go in hand.

The Mizoram state is situated in the foot of North-Eastern India and shared two international borders with Burma in the east and Bangladesh in its west. It is bounded by the three states of India, Tripura in the west and Assam and Manipur states in the north. The population residing in the state of Mizoram comprises of various sub-tribes or clans namely; Lushai, Hmar, Pawi, Paite, Kuki, Mara, Lai etc. Under the British India, it was named as Lushai Hills and became of one of the district of Assam after independent of India. It was made a union territory of India on 21st January 1972 and Mizoram was given the status of state on 20th February 1987.

The development of education was primarily look after with the arrival of the Britishers and paid little attention to the all round development of the people of Mizoram. The first formal education was set up in the year 1894 as primary school. With due course of time, Mizoram opened its first college at Aizawl on 15th August 1958 as a purely private enterprise called as Aijal College later named as Pachhunga Memorial College and was recognized by Gauhati university in 1960. The North-Eastern Hill University upgraded it to a constituent college of the University in 1979, since then known as Pachhunga University College.

Total number of registered institutions

State	Registered institutions
Arunachal Pradesh	62
Assam	676
Manipur	139
Meghalaya	98
Mizoram	54
Nagaland	92
Sikkim	38
Tripura	69
All India	55165

Source: AISHE, 2019-2020

Among the 54 higher educational institutions, there are 3 universities, 35 colleges and 16 stand alone institutions.

Specialisation-wise Number of Universities

Universities	general	technical	Total
	2	1	3

Specialisation-wise Number of Colleges

Colleges	
General	26
Agriculture	1

Teacher education	1
Engineering and Technology	1
Law	1
Medical-Allopathy	1
Nursing	1
Paramedical	1
Social work	1
Veterinary	1
Total	35

Number of Stand Alone Institutions

Stand Alone Institutions	
Polytechnics	2
Teacher Training	9
Nursing	5
Total	16

Number of Private and Government Colleges

Private		Government	Total
Un-aided	Aided	31	35
3	1		

From the above table it is observed that although Mizoram is the second most literate state in India, it has been trailing behind as compared to other North-eastern states in higher education particularly in technical, management and professional streams. The institutions of higher learning in Mizoram are still very young and some of the colleges have been established recently and constructing their building while others have not yet been able to acquire their own land and thus, run in a rented building. Therefore, the vital amenities and infrastructural facilities are lacking. Presently, there are 54 higher institutions in the state of Mizoram.

This paper will try to present a brief summary of the related studies undertaken by individual researchers, organizations and various commissions.

B.B.Kumar (1994) highlighted the growth of higher education in North-east India. The author pointed out factors responsible for the slow growth of higher education prior to 1947 such as most part of the north-east region was hilly, sparsely populated, isolated and devoid of communication. Moreover, Manipur, Tripura and Khasi Hills were princely states without systematic foundation of education. The first college in the north-east was Cotton College (Gauhati) which was established in 1901and the first university that is Gauhati University established in 1948. Inspite of the late start, higher education in north-east India witnessed a rapid growth in post independence era. The author also highlighted some of the major drawbacks of higher education in the north-east region. Some of the aspects are lack of productive ethos, lack of concern for proper resource utilization and mobilization of resources, poor governance, autonomy without accountability, lack of social concern and so on.

S.K.Barpujari(1994) examined the growth and development of higher education in north-east India before independence from 1826-1947. This paper highlighted the history of education started way back in 1825-26 mostly in lower Assam by David Scott, the first agent of East India Company with a mission to spread Christianity and to recruit those educated person to help them in the art of new administration. Eventually with the urge of Francis Jenkins the government of India established schools at different Sadar stations of Assam in 1834. To cater the needs of Upper Assam, a school was opened at Sibsagar in 1841 and within a decade quite a number of schools were established. In the year 1866, Gauhati school led the status of collegiate school with affiliation to the first examination in Arts. The first college in the north-east region known as Cotton College was formally opened on 27th May 1901 as second grade under Calcutta University. With the rapid expansion in the courses of instruction and increase enrolment, there has been a rapid extension of higher education.

Vanlalchhawna (2006) made an attempt to analyzed higher education and its unit cost which involves the estimation of direct institutional and private cost of education with special reference to Mizoram. At the time of data collection (1993-94), there were 29 colleges in Mizoram and all of them were affiliated under NEHU. Out of 29 colleges, 13 were general degree colleges whereas 16 colleges were either recognized or affiliated up to Pre-university level. Therefore, the data was collected from 10 general degree colleges of Mizoram. It was observed that the region witnessed considerable expansion of higher education in the post-independence period and a large proportion of increased in public educational expenditure had been accounted. Among the north-eastern states, Assam has the largest economy as well as well-developed diversified in higher education. The major plan expenditure was accounted by elementary education followed by secondary and higher education.

Finances for education came from private and government sources and the share of government in financing education in the state of Mizoram has increased over the years while on the other hand, students' contribution in the form of fees declined considerably. It was found that an increase in enrolment leads to decline in cost per student in different colleges.

Though the region has made rapid progress in education especially in literacy rates over the years; yet, the physical facilities are desperately inadequate in the educational institutions. High literacy rate is accompanied with high dropout rate that indicate the low level of education of the people of the region.

Pallab Jyotis(2013) examined the problems and future prospects of higher education in north east India. The study highlighted those North Eastern states faced lots of problems in access to higher education and opportunities in relation to higher education. The major thread like lack of financial allocation and poor administration in higher educational institutes in North East region drives the colleges and universities into unsatisfactory condition.

Vanengmawii (2017) conducted a study on Higher Education in Mizoram in the context of Knowledge Society: A Critical Analysis and pointed out that since its inception of higher education, arts stream was the main and only subject offered, science stream at undergraduate level was started only in 1973-74 at Pachhunga University College and commerce stream was opened in 1985 under PUC. Professional education was started in 1975 with the establishment of Teacher Training and Hindi Training College and technical education was started with the establishment of Polytechnic Institution at Lunglei in 1981 while National Institute of Technology was established in the year 2010. The study revealed that under Rashtriya Uchhatar Shiksha Abhiyan (RUSA) funds has been allocated to government colleges for upgradation and renovation of the existing infrastructure and facilities. The programme of postgraduate education was started when North Eastern Hill University offered the programme in 1979. In terms of students' enrolment, arts stream has highest enrolment followed by science and commerce. The findings also revealed that majority of college teachers have only master degree as the highest qualification and very few have done research programme.

Jugindro Singh (2018) conducted a study of higher educational inequality in north-east India: case studies in Manipur to find out the regional inequalities in higher education in the northeast states of India with an attempt to analyzed and highlight the level of literacy, the status of higher educational institutes for quality improvement among the states of the region and disparities of institutional quality enhancement. The study revealed that the disparity of quality and quantity of the students among the north-eastern states are due to the variation in physical, socio-economic and cultural development of different states. The quality of education maintain by the authority as well as infrastructures of the institutions are not up to date to meet the requirement of the students and globalization criteria given by the University Grants Commission.

From the above related study, it can be noted that higher education in India has a long way to go in terms of quality development though it has a quite number of higher institutions, none of the institutes could come up to top world ranking. It is also observed that the status of higher education in the north-east region with special reference to Mizoram is not satisfactory in terms of infrastructure and other related academic facilities. Therefore, it is important to look the issues and to strengthen our higher institution to generate quality education.

27.1 CONCLUSION

To conclude, higher education plays an important role in promoting human and national development so the new educational policy NEP 2020, envisions a complete over-haul and re-energising higher education system to overcome various issues and challenges to deliver quality higher education.

References

1. Kumar,B.B.(1994). Higher Education in North-East India. New Delhi: Omsons Publications

2. Barpujari, S.K. (1994). Growth and Development of Higher Education in North-East India. In Kumar,B.B (Ed.), *Higher Education in North-East India,*(pp.10-17). Omsons Publications

3. Vanlalchhawna. (2006). Higher Education in North-East India. New Delhi: A Mittal Publication.

4. All India Survey on Higher Education, 2015-2016, Government of India, Ministry of Education, Department of Education, New Delhi, 2016.

5. Vanengmawii. (2017). *Higher Education in Mizoram in the context of Knowledge Society: A Critical Analysis.* (Unpublished Thesis). Mizoram University.

6. All India Survey on Higher Education, 2016-2017, Government of India, Ministry of Education, Department of Education, New Delhi, 2017.

7. All India Survey on Higher Education, 2017-2018, Government of India, Ministry of Education, Department of Education, New Delhi, 2018.

8. All India Survey on Higher Education, 2018-2019, Government of India, Ministry of Education, Department of Education, New Delhi, 2019.

9. National Education Policy 2020, Ministry of Human Development, Government of India.

10. All India Survey on Higher Education, 2019-2020, Government of India, Ministry of Education, Department of Education, New Delhi, 2020.

Ideological Transformation of Gurukula Education and NEP 2020: Holistic Outlook

***Anoop Kumar Verma**

Ph.D. Research scholar, School of Education, Pondicherry University, Puducherry

Mobile: 9045206110, email: anoopkpbt@pondiuni.ac.in

****Dr. Bhukya Devender**

Assistant Professor, School of Education, Pondicherry University, Puducherry

Mobile: 9490112582, email: devender@pondiuni.ac.in

Abstract: *NEP 2020 recognizes the importance of vocational education and skill development, ensuring that individuals are equipped with practical knowledge and abilities that can lead to economic growth and enable them to contribute effectively in the workforce. This holistic outlook of the NEP 2020 creates a conducive environment for the revival and transformation of gurukula education. With its emphasis on the development of creative potential, the NEP 2020 aligns with the principles of gurukula education that have long been rooted in nurturing holistic development and a deep understanding of values, ethics, and spirituality. This alignment between the NEP 2020 and gurukula education can lead to a transformative shift in the educational landscape of India. It is important to note that while the NEP 2020 provides a framework for the holistic development of students, the successful implementation of this policy requires a significant structural overhaul in the Indian education system. National Education Policy 2020 and the revival of gurukula education have a shared vision of holistic development and values-based education that can create a transformative educational system in India. This transformative shift requires addressing obstacles such as creating new schools, aligning the curriculum and teaching methods, and engaging all stakeholders.*

Key words: *NEP 2020, Gurukula Education, Holistic outlook, Ideological transformation*

28.1 INTRODUCTION

In ancient times, students lived and learned at their Guru's residence, gaining knowledge that could be applied to solve practical problems. It is essential for a guru-shishya emotional bond to exist before engaging in the teaching-learning process. The guru shared extensive knowledge in subjects like religion, sanskrit, scriptures, medicine, philosophy, literature, warfare, statecraft, astrology, and history. Learners not only read books but also connected their knowledge to nature and life. Instead of memorizing facts and figures for exams, I focused on understanding the concepts. The curriculum encompassed vedas, rules of sacrifice, grammar and derivation, the secrets of nature, logic, science, and occupational skills. In ancient India, the education system uniquely prioritized self-realization over societal interference in curriculum, payment, and instructional hours.

The NEP was approved on July 28th, 2020, after 2.5 lakh stakeholders provided feedback through two national committees during over 50 months of consultations and workshops. It is uncertain how many policy recommendations have been implemented. The New Education Policy 2020 covers elementary to higher education levels in India. This policy will revolutionize the Indian Education System by 2021. A comprehensive review of all aspects of the Indian education system is essential. This study explores the diverse educational spheres outlined in NEP 2020. This study will provide readers with deep insight into various aspects of NEP 2020 for the transformation of the education system in India. NEP2020 ensures Universal Access at all levels of schooling from pre-primary school to Grade 12. NEP 2020 strives to position India as a global knowledge superpower.

Aims of Gurukula education

In the gurukula schooling system of ancient India, students lived near their teacher and experienced intensive, holistic learning. In gurukula education, the goals encompass the stated elements.

1. To promote moral and ethical growth, it's essential to cultivate traits like self-discipline, respect, and integrity.
2. To offer a comprehensive education that merges physical fitness, mental enrichment, and spiritual growth, typically incorporating yoga and meditation techniques.
3. Offer individualized guidance and mentoring based on the close teacher-student relationships.
4. Preserving and transmitting comprehensive knowledge of scriptures, literature, sciences, arts, and skills through generations.
5. Develop strong ethical principles and traditional values through daily interactions with the teacher.
6. Encouraging self-reliance involves developing skills that foster independence and self-sufficiency in various life areas.
7. In the Gurukula, communal harmony and the spirit of sharing are promoted through communal living arrangements.
8. To facilitate the spiritual development and enlightenment of students through comprehension of essential Indian philosophies and teachings.

In the gurukula system, individuals were not only taught academics but also shaped into well-rounded humans capable of flourishing in society and living in harmony.

Aims of NEP 2020

The National Education Policy 2020 in India aims to rejuvenate the entire education system. One of its primary goals encompasses the aforementioned objectives.

1. This education fosters the intellectual, physical, emotional, and ethical growth of students in a comprehensive and interdisciplinary manner.
2. Provide equal access to high-quality education for all students and minimize disparities in educational outcomes.

3. The education system should provide a high-quality, engaging, and diverse learning experience to all students for their future success.

4. Emphasizing vocational education and skill development equips students with the necessary skills for workforce success and economic growth.

5. To provide students with the flexibility to choose subjects from various disciplines, broadening career opportunities and fostering holistic growth.

6. Encouraging critical thinking, creativity, and scientific temper in students is essential for effective learning.

7. Through the National Education Technology Forum, we work to bridge the digital divide and integrate technology into education to improve learning experiences.

8. This text advocates for elevating educators' professionalism and acknowledging teachers' pivotal position in the education system.

9. Encouraging research, innovation and entrepreneurship in educational institutions is essential.

10. Encouraging education in the mother tongue is crucial for safeguarding India's cultural heritage and indigenous knowledge systems.

11. The Indian education system should adopt global standards while preserving Indian values.

NEP 2020 signifies a shift towards an inclusive, learner-centric, lifelong learning-focused, and 21st century-aligned education system.

Women's role in Gurukula Education System

Historically, women's roles in India's gurukula education system was limited. In ancient and medieval India, education primarily catered to men from the upper castes. Women were not completely barred from the educational system or the pursuit of knowledge.

Here are some points concerning the role of women in the gurukula system:

12. **Limited Access**: Women, especially those from non-royalty or upper castes, often had restricted access to the gurukula system, which was largely designed for male students.

13. **Domestic Education**: Women were more likely to be educated at home in areas considered suitable for their roles in society, such as domestic skills, arts, literature, and sometimes religious texts, based on family discretion and status.

14. **Notable Exceptions**: There were exceptions, with some texts and historical accounts indicating that women from royal or learned families, or those of certain philosophical sects, received comprehensive education similar to their male counterparts.

15. **Women as Gurus**: In certain cases, women were acknowledged as teachers or gurus themselves, imparting knowledge and wisdom within their domain. Prominent female philosopher-saints and scholars, like Gargi Vachaknavi and Maitreyi, are notable examples of learned women involved in scholarly debate and teaching.

16. **Spiritual Roles**: Women often held significant roles in the spiritual and religious education within their households and communities, teaching younger family members and transmitting devotional practices and cultural values.

In contemporary gurukulas and educational institutions in India, there's a focused push towards gender equality in education, providing equal access for women and recognizing their potential.

Women's role in National Education Policy 2020

The 2020 National Education Policy in India intends to reshape the educational system with a focus on inclusivity and equity. The NEP acknowledges the significance of equal educational opportunities for all genders, even though it doesn't assign particular roles for women within the policy itself. NEP 2020 aims to ensure equal access to education for both genders and include women through various initiatives.

1. **Gender Inclusion Fund**: NEP 2020 proposes the setting up of a Gender Inclusion Fund to build the nation's capacity to provide

equitable quality education for all girls as well as transgender students.

2. **Increased Participation**: It aims to encourage and increase the participation of girls and women in education through various initiatives, including providing sanitary facilities and promoting a safe and supportive school environment.

3. **Women in Leadership**: There is an implicit acknowledgment of the need for increased representation of women in leadership roles within academic institutions.

4. **Teacher Education**: NEP 2020 emphasizes the recruitment of qualified female teachers and providing them with robust training to inspire and engage students effectively, thereby promoting respect and acceptance of female educators.

5. **Scholarships and Support**: Offering scholarships and financial support to underprivileged and socio-economically disadvantaged girls is a part of NEP 2020's commitment to ensure that they have equal opportunities in accessing education.

6. **STEM Education for Girls**: NEP 2020 encourages the participation of women in Science, Technology, Engineering, and Mathematics fields, aiming to change the socio-cultural factors that have led to their underrepresentation.

7. **Curriculum That Reflects Diversity**: Ensuring that the curriculum is inclusive and reflects the contributions of women in various fields, thus providing female students with role models and broadening their career aspirations.

NEP 2020 aims to eliminate the gender disparity in education and stimulate women's active engagement from primary to higher education.

Nature of education in Gurukula and NEP 2020

The nature of education in Gurukula and under the National Education Policy (NEP) 2020 reflects both similarities and differences, influenced by historical contexts, cultural values, and educational philosophies. Here's a comparison of the nature of education in Gurukula and NEP 2020:

Gurukula Education:

Informal Learning Environment: Gurukula education traditionally takes place in a residential setting, where students live with their guru (teacher) in close proximity. Learning is not confined to classrooms but occurs informally through daily interactions, observation, and hands-on experiences.

Emphasis on Oral Tradition: In Gurukula education, knowledge is transmitted orally from teacher to student, emphasizing memorization, recitation, and oral discussions. Texts are often memorized and interpreted under the guidance of the guru, fostering a deep understanding of the subject matter.

Personalized Instruction: Gurukula education is characterized by personalized instruction tailored to the individual needs, interests, and abilities of each student. The guru serves as a mentor and guide, providing individualized attention and support to help students reach their full potential.

Integration of Life Skills: Gurukula education goes beyond academic learning to encompass the development of life skills, moral values, and character traits. Students learn not only from textbooks but also from observing their guru's behavior and participating in daily chores and rituals.

Connection with Nature and Spirituality: Gurukula education often emphasizes a deep connection with nature and spirituality. Students may engage in activities such as meditation, yoga, and environmental conservation to foster spiritual growth and ecological awareness.

NEP 2020:

Formalized Education System: NEP 2020 operates within a formalized education system with structured curricula, standardized assessments, and institutional frameworks. It aims to provide equitable access to quality education for all children, regardless of background or socio-economic status.

Curricular Reforms: NEP 2020 advocates for curricular reforms to make education more holistic, flexible, and multidisciplinary. It promotes the integration of subjects, competency-based learning, and the inclusion of vocational education to cater to diverse learning needs and interests.

Technology Integration: NEP 2020 emphasizes the use of technology to enhance teaching, learning, and assessment processes. It promotes the integration of digital tools, online resources, and technology-enabled pedagogies to make education more accessible, interactive, and engaging.

Focus on Foundational Skills: NEP 2020 prioritizes foundational literacy and numeracy skills, particularly in the early years of schooling. It recognizes the importance of strong foundational skills as the basis for future academic success and lifelong learning.

Teacher Professional Development: NEP 2020 emphasizes teacher professional development to build a competent and motivated teaching workforce. It promotes continuous training, mentoring, and support mechanisms to empower teachers with the knowledge, skills, and resources they need to facilitate student learning effectively.

Inclusive Education: NEP 2020 emphasizes inclusive education, ensuring that every child, including those with disabilities and special needs, has access to quality education. It advocates for the removal of barriers to learning and the provision of appropriate support services to promote the full participation and inclusion of all learners.

While Gurukula education and NEP 2020 have different approaches and contexts, both share common goals of fostering holistic development, nurturing lifelong learners, and promoting values of integrity, compassion, and social responsibility.

Admission process in Gurukula

The admission process in a Gurukula, which is a traditional Indian educational system, typically involves a few key steps, although these may vary depending on the specific Gurukula and its practices. Here's a general overview:

Initial Inquiry: Parents or students interested in enrolling in a Gurukula usually initiate the process by making an inquiry. This could involve contacting the Gurukula directly, visiting the campus, or attending informational sessions to learn more about the educational philosophy, curriculum, facilities, and admission requirements.

Meetings and Interviews: Prospective students and their parents may be required to attend meetings or interviews with the Guru (teacher) or other designated authorities. These interactions serve as opportunities for the Gurukula to assess the suitability of the student and for the student and parents to ask questions and understand the expectations of the Gurukula.

Assessment of Readiness: Depending on the age and prior educational background of the student, the Gurukula may conduct assessments to evaluate the student's readiness for the Gurukula environment. This could involve tests of academic proficiency, aptitude, character assessment, and sometimes physical fitness.

Acceptance and Enrollment: Upon successful completion of the assessment process and meeting any other requirements set by the Gurukula, the student may receive an offer of admission. If accepted, the student and their parents are typically required to complete enrollment forms, provide necessary documentation, and pay any applicable fees or deposits to secure their place.

Orientation: After enrollment, new students usually undergo an orientation program to familiarize themselves with the Gurukula's rules, routines, expectations, and campus facilities. This may include introductions to faculty and staff, tours of the campus, and information sessions on academic and extracurricular activities.

Commencement of Studies: Once the admission and orientation process is complete, the student officially begins their studies at the Gurukula. Depending on the Gurukula's schedule and practices, this may involve joining ongoing classes or starting at the beginning of a new academic term.

It's important to note that the admission process in Gurukulas can vary widely based on factors such as the specific Gurukula's traditions, location, size, and educational philosophy. Some Gurukulas may have more formalized processes, while others may rely more on informal arrangements and personal connections.

Admission process in NEP 2020

The National Education Policy (NEP) 2020 in India aims to bring about significant reforms in the education system, including changes in the admission process across various levels of education. While NEP 2020 outlines broad principles and recommendations, the specific implementation of admission processes will depend on policies developed by educational institutions and authorities. Here's an overview of how the admission process might be impacted under NEP 2020:

Early Childhood Education (Pre-School):

- NEP 2020 emphasizes the importance of early childhood care and education, including three years of pre-primary education for children aged 3 to 6 years.
- Admission processes for pre-schools may become more structured and standardized, ensuring equitable access to quality early childhood education for all children.

School Education:

- NEP 2020 advocates for a flexible and multidisciplinary approach to curriculum and assessment, with an emphasis on holistic development and foundational literacy and numeracy.
- Admission processes for schools may prioritize holistic assessments of students' abilities, interests, and needs, rather than relying solely on academic performance in entrance exams.

- Schools may adopt inclusive admission policies to ensure access for children from diverse backgrounds, including those with disabilities and special needs.

Higher Education:

- NEP 2020 proposes significant reforms in higher education, including the establishment of a single regulator for higher education (the Higher Education Commission of India).
- Admission processes for colleges and universities may undergo changes to align with the proposed reforms, such as standardized entrance exams (like the Common Entrance Test), common counseling processes, and credit transfer mechanisms.
- NEP 2020 encourages the integration of vocational education and multiple pathways for higher education, allowing students to choose from a wide range of academic and vocational courses based on their interests and aptitudes.
- There may be a greater emphasis on holistic assessments of students' capabilities, including their skills, talents, extracurricular achievements, and life experiences, in addition to academic qualifications.

Online and Open Education:

- NEP 2020 promotes the use of technology to expand access to education, including online and open learning platforms.
- Admission processes for online and open education programs may become more accessible and inclusive, allowing learners to enroll in courses and programs remotely and at their own pace.

Overall, under NEP 2020, the admission process across different levels of education is likely to evolve to become more inclusive, flexible, and aligned with the principles of equity, quality, and lifelong learning. However, the specific implementation of admission policies will vary across educational institutions and may require further guidelines and regulations from relevant authorities.

Educational structure of Gurukula and NEP 2020

The educational structures of Gurukula and the National Education Policy (NEP) 2020 differ significantly due to variations in historical contexts, cultural practices, and educational philosophies. Here's a comparison of the educational structures of Gurukula and NEP 2020:

Gurukula Educational structure:

Informal and Decentralized: Gurukula education is traditionally informal and decentralized, with each Gurukula operating autonomously under the guidance of a guru (teacher). There is no standardized curriculum, and learning occurs through direct interaction between the guru and students.

Residential Model: Gurukulas often follow a residential model, where students live with their guru in a close-knit community. This immersive environment allows for holistic learning, with students engaging in academic study, vocational training, and daily chores as part of their education.

Oral Tradition: Knowledge transmission in Gurukula education is primarily oral, with an emphasis on memorization, recitation, and oral discussions. Students memorize sacred texts, philosophical treatises, and practical skills under the guidance of their guru, fostering a deep understanding of the subject matter.

Customized Curriculum: The curriculum in Gurukula education is highly customized and tailored to the individual needs, interests, and abilities of each student. There is a focus on personalized instruction, with the guru adapting teaching methods and content based on the student's learning pace and preferences.

Integration of Life Skills: Gurukula education goes beyond academic learning to encompass the development of life skills, moral values, and character traits. Students learn through practical experience, participation in community activities, and observing the behavior of their guru.

Educational structure of NEP 2020:

Formalized and Centralized: NEP 2020 operates within a formalized and centralized education system, with standardized curricula, assessments, and institutional frameworks. It aims to provide equitable access to quality education for all children, regardless of background or socio-economic status.

Structured Curriculum: NEP 2020 advocates for a structured curriculum framework with a focus on foundational literacy, numeracy, and holistic development. While allowing for flexibility and choice, the policy emphasizes the importance of a common curriculum to ensure consistency and quality across schools.

Multiple Entry and Exit Points: NEP 2020 introduces multiple entry and exit points in the education system, allowing students to enter and exit at different stages of their academic journey. This includes flexible pathways for vocational education, skill development, and lifelong learning.

Technology Integration: NEP 2020 emphasizes the integration of technology in education to enhance teaching, learning, and assessment processes. It promotes digital literacy, online resources, and technology-enabled pedagogies to make education more accessible, interactive, and engaging.

Teacher Professional Development: NEP 2020 prioritizes teacher professional development to build a competent and motivated teaching workforce. It advocates for continuous training, mentoring, and support mechanisms to empower teachers with the knowledge, skills, and resources they need to facilitate student learning effectively.

Inclusive Education: NEP 2020 emphasizes inclusive education, ensuring that every child, including those with disabilities and special needs, has access to quality education. It calls for the removal of barriers to learning and the provision of appropriate support services to promote the full participation and inclusion of all learners.

While Gurukula education and NEP 2020 have different educational structures, both share common goals of fostering holistic development, nurturing lifelong learners, and promoting values of integrity, compassion, and social responsibility.

28.2 CONCLUSION

The National Education Policy 2020 presents a remarkable opportunity for the transformation of India's educational system, including the revival and reimagnation of gurukula education. By aligning with the aspirational goals of 21st-century education and incorporating India's rich traditions and value systems, the NEP 2020 aims to provide a holistic outlook on education. This holistic outlook includes not only the development of cognitive capacities such as literacy and numeracy but also the nurturing of social, ethical, and emotional capacities. Under this policy, the purpose of education is not just to produce individuals with academic knowledge, but to cultivate good human beings capable of rational thought, compassion and empathy, courage and resilience, scientific temper and creative imagination, with sound ethical moorings and values. Furthermore, This transformation will require effective decision-making procedures, dedicated financial resources, and a streamlined approach to opening new educational institutes. The implementation of NEP 2020 and the revival of gurukula education require a comprehensive approach that addresses the challenges and loopholes in the current education system. This includes addressing the obstacle of creating new schools and institutes, which requires careful planning, resource allocation, and streamlined processes. Additionally, there is a need to ensure that the curriculum and teaching methods align with the principles of holistic education. In order to address these challenges and ensure the successful implementation of NEP 2020 and the revitalization of gurukula education, it is essential to engage all stakeholders, including policymakers, educators, parents, and students themselves. By working together and synergizing efforts, we can create a transformative educational system that fosters the holistic development of individuals, equipping them with the necessary knowledge, skills, and values to thrive in the 21st century while preserving and building upon India's rich traditions and value systems.

Reference

1. Shanwal, V. K. (2023). Development of the Gurukula Education System in India. *Journal of Education and Teacher Training Innovation, 1*(2), 60-67.

2. Pal, P. K. (2022). Education psychology in the Ancient Indian Gurukula System.

3. Geddam, M. S. (2022). IDEOLOGICAL AND PHILOSOPHICAL TRANSFORMATION OF INDIA EDUCATION POLICIES AND NEP 2020.

4. Joshi, D. (2021). Gurukul and modern education system in India: Holistic outlook. Int J Eng Res Manag, 8(2), 6-8.

5. Saxena, A. (2021). The glimpse of NEP 2020. Multidisciplinary research, 2, 1.

6. Govinda, R. (2020). NEP 2020: A critical examination.

7. Smitha, S. (2020). National Education Policy (Nep) 2020-Opportunities and Challenges in Teacher Education. *International Journal of Management (IJM), 11*(11), 1881-1886.

8. Yadav, U. (2018). A comparative study of ancient & present education system. *Education, Sustainability and Society, 1*(1), 1-3.

9. Soni, B. K., & Trivedi, J. C. (2018). A case study on gurukul system of education. Rajagiri Management Journal, 12(2), 39-63.

10. Shanwal, V. K., & Fatmi, S. N. (2015). Oral tradition in education: From gurukul to modern. The Social ION, 4(1and2), 75-82.

NEP 2020 and the Transformation of Educational Environments: Cultivating Diversity and Inclusion in Indian Schools

Dr. Bhukya Devender[1]

[1]Assistant Professor, School of Education, Pondicherry University,
Mobile:9490112582. E-mail: devender@pondiuni.ac.in

Chandan Das[2]

[2]Research scholar, School of Education, Pondicherry University
Mobile:6290579188. E-mail: chandandas.jk@gmail.com

Abstract: *The National Education Policy 2020 marks a significant milestone in the evolution of India's education system, aiming to create an inclusive and equitable landscape that respects and embraces diversity. This paper examines the transformation of educational environments under NEP 2020, with a focus on the policy's initiatives to foster diversity and inclusion in Indian schools. It delves into the policy's vision, specific strategies and recommendations, and the potential challenges and benefits of implementing such a transformative framework.*

Keywords: *NEP 2020, diversity, inclusion, Indian schools, transformative framework.*

29.0 INTRODUCTION

The introduction would set the stage for the discussion on how the National Education Policy 2020 aims to transform the educational landscape in India. Here's a breakdown of the components in this section:

A. Overview of NEP 2020: The paper would begin with a succinct explanation of NEP 2020, touching upon its development, key objectives, and its historical context in the evolution of Indian education policy. The overview would outline the policy's intention to overhaul the current education system and detail the overarching goal of making education more holistic, flexible, student-cantered, and aligned with global educational standards.

B. Importance of diversity and inclusion in education: The introduction would emphasize the critical importance of diversity and inclusion in modern education systems. It would highlight how embracing diversity within the classroom be it cultural, linguistic, socio-economic, or learning ability can enhance the educational experience for all students. Moreover, it would stress that inclusive education is essential for building equitable societies and preparing students to thrive in a diverse and interconnected world.

C. The need for transformation in the Indian educational context: This section would set forth the reasons why transformation is necessary in the Indian context, pointing out existing challenges such as disparities in access to quality education, the need for pedagogical renewal to cater to diverse learning needs, and the urgency to eliminate social and educational inequities. It would articulate how NEP 2020's reforms are envisioned as responses to these challenges, in an effort to create a system that is more reflective of and responsive to the diverse fabric of Indian society.

NEP 2020: An Overview of Key Tenets for Inclusion and Diversity

In this section, the paper would delve deeper into the specific elements of NEP 2020 that directly address inclusion and diversity, elaborating on how they are expected to manifest in educational settings:

A. Multilingualism and the promotion of local languages: NEP 2020 emphasizes the use of mother tongue or local language as the medium of instruction at least until Grade 5, which is aligned with global studies underscoring the benefits of early education in a child's home language. This policy change is intended to be inclusive of India's linguistic diversity and to support a better cognitive connection with the content taught, thus facilitating a more inclusive setting for all students, including those from tribal and rural backgrounds.

B. Holistic and multidisciplinary approaches: Another key tenet of NEP 2020 is the shift towards a holistic education model that blurs the hard boundaries traditionally placed between the sciences and the arts, curricular and extracurricular activities, and vocational and academic streams. The multidisciplinary approach is more inclusive as it recognizes multiple intelligences and learning styles, catering to a broader spectrum of student interests, strengths, and career paths.

C. Equity and accessibility for all student populations: The policy contains several provisions aimed at ensuring equity and accessibility for students from different socio-economic backgrounds, such as scholarships and support for underrepresented groups. It prioritizes not only physical accessibility to schools but also the accessibility of educational materials and instruction, and it seeks to remove barriers for students with disabilities through inclusive classrooms and the integration of appropriate pedagogies.

Revamping Curriculum and Pedagogy

This section would discuss how NEP 2020 proposes to revamp both the curriculum and pedagogical approaches to foster a more inclusive and diverse educational environment:

A. Strategies for integrating diverse cultural knowledge: NEP 2020 encourages the inclusion of local content in the curriculum. This entails incorporating regional culture, history, and knowledge systems into mainstream education to ensure students from all backgrounds see their identities reflected in their learning materials. This approach can boost engagement among students from various cultural backgrounds and contribute to a rich, diverse educational tapestry that respects and celebrates indigenous and local knowledge alongside global perspectives.

B. Curriculum inclusivity and representation: The reformed curriculum under NEP 2020 aims to be more inclusive by representing the diverse voices and experiences of India's population. This could involve updating textbooks to include a wider range of narratives, ensuring that all students feel seen and heard. An inclusive curriculum would challenge stereotypes and encourage respect and understanding among students of different ethnicities, religions, and social backgrounds.

C. Innovative pedagogy sensitive to diversity: Finally, NEP 2020 calls for teaching methods that are tailored to the diverse learning needs of the student body. Educators are encouraged to employ innovative, research-backed pedagogical strategies that support differentiated instruction and personalized learning. Classroom activities would be designed to cater to various learning styles and abilities, ensuring that each student has the opportunity to succeed. The policy also promotes the use of technology to create adaptive learning environments that can meet the needs of a diverse student population.

Institutional Reforms for Inclusive Education

This section would explore the changes NEP 2020 suggests for educational institutions to facilitate and strengthen inclusive education:

A. Teacher training and professional development: NEP 2020 recognizes the pivotal role of teachers in creating an inclusive classroom. The policy proposes rigorous teacher training programs that focus on capacity building to handle classroom diversity. This involves equipping teachers with the skills to implement inclusive pedagogies, address diverse learning needs, and manage a multilingual classroom effectively. Continuous professional development opportunities would be a key part of ensuring that teachers remain sensitive to the socio-cultural dynamics within their classrooms.

B. Administrative changes for accountability: NEP 2020 envisions an education system where institutions are accountable for providing inclusive and high-quality education to all students. Administrative reforms would likely include policy guidelines, oversight mechanisms, and performance metrics specifically designed to ensure that schools meet the inclusivity benchmarks set out in the policy. This might encompass reforms such as decentralized decision-making to better address local needs, greater autonomy for schools in curriculum design, and upgraded school governance structures to include more diverse voices.

C. Infrastructure enhancement for accessibility: To truly foster an inclusive educational environment, NEP 2020 stresses the need for appropriate physical infrastructure. This includes barrier-free access for students with disabilities, well-equipped and safe classrooms conducive to learning, and the availability of technological tools that support diverse learning modalities. Institutions would also need to ensure that sanitary facilities, transportation, and other related services are sensitive to the needs of all students, especially those belonging to marginalized or disadvantaged groups.

Challenges in Implementing NEP 2020

This section would identify the potential hurdles in the practical implementation of NEP 2020's inclusive education reforms:

A. Socio-cultural barriers: The paper would examine the societal and cultural obstacles that may impede the policy's goals, such as ingrained biases and resistance to change. It would analyse how traditional mind-sets and socio-cultural norms can affect the acceptance and effective implementation of inclusive practices, particularly in regions with strong attachment to conventional methods and values. It would also discuss the complexities involved in balancing local cultural practices with modern educational requirements.

B. Resource allocation and logistical concerns: The NEP 2020's ambitious objectives require substantial resource investment and well-thought-out logistics. This section would delve into the challenges of ensuring adequate funding and resources reach the right places, the difficulties of training a large number of teachers on new pedagogies, and the infrastructural upgrades needed to realize the policy's vision. It would interrogate past inefficiencies in resource allocation and suggest ways to avoid repeating these mistakes.

C. Resistance to change and adaptability issues: Resistance to change from stakeholders, including educational institutions, teachers, parents, and even students, could hinder the transformations envisaged by NEP

2020. The paper would explore the psychological and institutional factors contributing to this resistance, the challenge of shifting pedagogical paradigms, and the pace of adaptability required by various entities within the educational system. It might propose strategies for building a culture of innovation and flexibility to accommodate the changes NEP 2020 brings.

This section would offer a critical analysis of the challenges that must be acknowledged and addressed to ensure the successful implementation of NEP 2020 with respect to fostering diversity and inclusion in Indian schools.

Opportunities and Prospects

A. Leveraging technology for inclusive learning: NEP 2020 presents significant opportunities for leveraging technology to enhance inclusive education. The use of digital tools and platforms can provide personalized learning experiences, aid students with disabilities, and bridge gaps for learners in remote areas. The paper would discuss how technology, when strategically integrated, can offer adaptive assessment methods, interactive curriculum, and access to a world of diverse content.

B. Potential for collaboration and community involvement: The policy emphasizes the importance of community engagement in education. This opens avenues for collaboration between educators, parents, and community leaders to support diverse learning environments. The paper would explore how involvement from various stakeholders can enrich learning experiences and ensure the educational needs of all community members are met, thereby cultivating a collective responsibility toward inclusive education.

C. Creating global citizens with a rooted sense of identity: One of the most profound opportunities under NEP 2020 is the potential to educate students who are global citizens with a strong sense of their own identities. By emphasizing diversity and inclusion, the policy supports the cultivation of young individuals who are aware of their cultural roots while being globally competent. The paper would discuss how this dual focus can prepare students to succeed in a globalized world while contributing to societal cohesion and national development.

This section would consider the forward-looking ambitions of NEP 2020, highlighting how its implementation could lead to a transformative era in Indian education with more inclusive, equitable, and diverse classrooms that lay the foundation for a progressive society.

Case Studies and Exemplars

A. Schools embracing NEP 2020's diversity and inclusion principles: This part of the paper would detail practical examples of schools and educational initiatives that have successfully embraced the principles of diversity and inclusion outlined in NEP 2020. It would discuss the methodologies adopted by these institutions, the challenges they faced, and the outcomes of such initiatives. The purpose is to provide tangible evidence of NEP 2020's principles in action and to illustrate best practices that can serve as models for other schools.

B. Comparative analysis with international education policies: The paper might include a comparative analysis of NEP 2020's approach to diversity and inclusion with similar policies in other countries. This analysis would help highlight unique features of NEP 2020, situate it within the global context, and draw lessons from international experiences. It could identify gaps and opportunities in NEP 2020 by examining how other educational systems have addressed challenges related to diversity and inclusion.

C. **Success stories and lessons learned additionally:** This section would analyse anecdotal success stories and more rigorous studies to draw out significant lessons from early adopters of NEP 2020's diversity and inclusion strategies. It would discuss the positive impact on students' engagement, learning outcomes, and community cohesion. Recognizing these success stories can be vital for policy affirmation and provide a roadmap for schools that are in the process of adapting to NEP 2020.

In summarizing these case studies and comparative analyses, the paper would emphasize that although challenges exist, there are clear examples of successful implementation from which to draw inspiration and practical knowledge. This section would showcase the viability of NEP 2020's aspirations and provide an evidence-based argument for the policy's wider adoption.

The Road to Inclusive Excellence

A. Assessing progress: metrics and evaluations: This part of the paper would discuss how progress towards the goals of NEP 2020 can be measured and evaluated. It would underscore the importance of developing robust metrics and assessment tools that can capture the multifaceted nature of inclusive education. These measurements would track not just academic outcomes but also the socio-emotional development of students, the inclusiveness of the learning environment, and the extent to which diversity is genuinely reflected and valued in educational practices.

B. Future direction and policy recommendations: After assessing progress, the paper would provide recommendations for future directions that educational policy could take to build on the achievements of NEP 2020. This could involve identifying areas where further research is needed, outlining next steps for continuous improvement, and suggesting how other policies can align with NEP 2020 to create a cohesive system that supports inclusive excellence.

C. Fostering on-going dialogue between stake holders: Finally, the paper would argue for the importance of maintaining an on-going dialogue among all stakeholders—including educators, students, parents, policymakers, and the community at large—to ensure the dynamism and responsiveness of the education system. It would highlight that the successful implementation of NEP 2020 requires a collective effort where feedback and shared experiences contribute to the policy's evolution.

This section would address the on-going commitment required to achieve and maintain inclusive excellence in education. It would convey that the journey towards fully realizing the goals of NEP 2020 is not a finite one, but rather a continuous process of reflection, engagement, and growth.

29.1 CONCLUSION

The implementation of NEP 2020 heralds a transformative era in the Indian education system, emphasizing inclusivity and diversity as central to the educational experience. The policy holds the potential to revolutionize learning through its embrace of local cultures and languages, its multidisciplinary focus, and its intent to address the unique needs of all learners.

A. **Recapitulation of NEP 2020's transformative potential:** NEP 2020 carries within it the promise of cultivating individuals who are not only academically accomplished but also deeply connected to their cultural roots and global contexts. By reimagining curricula, pedagogies, and learning environments, the policy aims to dismantle the barriers of a one-size-fits-all education, thereby enabling a diverse array of talents and intelligences to flourish.

B. **The critical role of inclusive education in national development:** Inclusion is not just a social imperative but a cornerstone for national development. An education system that values diversity contributes to a harmonious society, fosters mutual respect, and stimulates innovation by leveraging a wide range of perspectives. In preparing students to engage with a diverse world, we prepare them to be the thinkers, leaders, and entrepreneurs of tomorrow.

C. **Call to action for educators, policymakers, and society at large:** To realize the full potential of NEP 2020, a collective effort is required. Educators must continually seek to adapt their teaching to meet the varied needs of their students; policymakers need to ensure that the structures are in place to support these educational reforms, and society, the parents, community leaders, and citizen must advocate for and support an inclusive education system. It is time for all stakeholders to rise to the challenge and play their role in establishing a more equitable, just, and inclusive society.

References

1. NEP 2020 draft : ncert.nic.in/pdf/nep//NEP_2020.pdf
2. Mitchell, D. (2018). *The ecology of inclusive education: strategies to tackle the crisis in educating diverse learners.* Routledge.
3. Gause, C. P. (2011). *Diversity, equity, and inclusive education: A voice from the margins* (Vol. 65). Springer Science & Business Media.
4. Barnes, B. (2011). *Teachers' perceptions and understanding of diversity and inclusive education: A case study* (Doctoral dissertation, Stellenbosch: University of Stellenbosch).
5. Sanchez, P. A., de Haro-Rodriguez, R., & Martinez, R. M. (2019). Barriers to student learning and participation in an inclusive school as perceived by future education professionals. *Journal of New Approaches in Educational Research (NAER Journal)*, 8(1), 18-24.
6. Reddemma, N., & Nehru, R. S. S. Teacher Preparation for Inclusive Education with Reference to NEP 2020: Model for Teacher Education Programs.
7. Varshney, P., & Ahlawat, D. National education policy-2020: Vision of inclusive education for 21st century learners.
8. Malika, G. D. (2030). Understanding the Significance of an Inclusive Education System: Strategies for Developing Qualitative Education. *Multidisciplinary Subjects, 82.*
9. Dhokare, S., & Jadhav, S. (2023). Embracing Diversity: The Multilingual Approach to Education in India's NEP 2020. *Remittances Review, 8*(4).
10. Curran, C. M., & Petersen, A. J. (Eds.). (2017). *Handbook of research on classroom diversity and inclusive education practice.* IGI Global.
11. Loreman, T., Deppeler, J., & Harvey, D. (2005). *Inclusive education: A practical guide to supporting diversity in the classroom.* Psychology Press.

12. Nevin, A., Cohen, J., Salazar, L., & Marshall, D. (2007). Student Teacher Perspectives on Inclusive Education. *Online Submission.*

13. Sanchez-Marti, A., & Ramirez-Iniguez, A. A. (2012). Inclusive education: An examination of school relationships and student interactions. *Intercultural education, 23*(6), 491-500.

14. Setia, S., Leng, P., Muliatie, Y. E., Ekowati, D., & Ratmawati, D. (2021). The principal leadership in developing inclusive education for diverse students. *International Journal of Emerging Issues in Early Childhood Education (IJEIECE), 3*(1), 08-24.

15. Morina, A. (2019). Inclusive education in higher education: challenges and opportunities. *Postsecondary educational opportunities for students with special education needs,* 3-17.

National Educational Policy (NEP) – 2020 Awareness Among Higher Education Students

*T. Lalbiakli, M.A (Education) kuritlangte34@gmail.com
** Remidala Saidulu M.Sc,M.Ed, Teacher (School Assistant)
***Sujatha, (Ph.D) Scholar Department of Education BRAOU, Hyderabad

The New Education Policy (2020) Draft Act was released by the Government of India. The investigator used the survey method for the present study. Sample: thirty-one students of the school of education, B.Ed, M. Ed, and M.A (Education) Mizoram University The total sample was selected through a simple random sampling technique. The tool used to test the National Education Policy 2020. Analysis and discussion B.Ed and M. Ed Student teachers and Student Teacher Educators have the same level of awareness of the national educational policy 2020.

B. Ed Student teachers have a better awareness of National Educational Policy 2020 compared to M. Ed and M.A Education Students. There is a significant mean difference between B. Ed, M. Ed, and M.A Education students on the awareness of the New Education Policy (2020) with respect to the course.

30.0 INTRODUCTION

Opportunities of NEP 2020 New education Policy begins with the unfinished agenda of NEP — 1986. NEP — 1986 was rooted in a very different India. Over the years, remarkable strides have been made in terms of access and equity. Near universal levels of enrolment at primary levels, and subsequent increase in enrolment at higher education levels (GER: 26.3%) have been achieved. However, there has also been a drop in the quality of learning in public school systems, followed by an exodus of elite and middle courses. This also led to the weakening of accountability mechanisms. Despite poor returns on learning, the pay-structures in public systems have seen a gradual increase.

1. Salient Features of NEP, 2020

National Education Policy 2020 has been announced on 29.07.2020. The National Education Policy 2020 proposes various reforms in school education as well as higher education including technical education. A number of action points/activities for implementation in school education as well as higher education are mentioned in the National Education Policy 2020. Details of the salient features of NEP 2020 are as follows

Objective of the studies

1. To study national education policy 2020 awareness among the college students.
2. To study national education policy 2020 awareness between college students of M. Ed, B. Ed and M.A Education
3. To study national education policy 2020 awareness of college students on four major dimensions which is School Education, Teacher Education, Higher Education and Recommendations

Hypothesis of the study

1. There will be no means significance difference on national educational policy 2020 awareness male and female students of college of education.
2. There is no significant difference on national educational policy 2020 awareness among the college students of B. Ed, M. Ed and M.A (Education)

Delimitation of the Study

1. The present study is confined to 131 college students
2. The study is limited to college students of school of education, Mizoram University
3. The investigator has used only survey method.

Review of related literature

Ms. Sujatha Ramesh, Dr. K. Natarajan (2019) they compared the NEP (2019) with the American Education system. The NEP permitted to switchover course like that USA. The flexible approaches are similar to that of the USA.

Kalervo N Gulson, Sam seller (2018), they come to one conclusion that enabling new private and public connections across policy topologies.

Nikil Govind (2019) Aithal P.S, Shybhrajyotsna Aithal (2019) they analysed positive and negative of the proposal and some suggestion to further improvement.

Aggarwal Yash (2019) In his examined the various dimension of access and retention in District Primary Education programs district and specifically focused on the structured trends in the enrolment of DPEP districts and examined the trends in district level performance indicator including retention data was collected from DPEP States using the district information system for education format.

Rai, R.K (2020) Studied about the progress and problems of Secondary Education. The study revealed that though there was some progress and prevailing situation was not satisfactory

Method of the study

The investigator adopted a survey method to collect data from the population for studying the New Education Policy (2020) awareness among college students of school of education Mizoram University.

Population and Sample

The school of Education students who are pursuing their degree in Mizoram University, Aizawl considered as a population for the present study. The investigator has used simple random sampling technique for selecting the sample from the population. The sample consists of 131 college students form following courses B. Ed, M. Ed and M.A(Education).

Tool Used for Data Collection

Personal data sheet: The respondents were asked to fill up a personal data form in order to seek information about them like Gender and Course.

National Educational Policy (2020): The investigator prepared the National Educational Policy (2020) awareness tool. The investigator designated multiple-choice type questionnaire as a tool for gathering data in the present study. The device includes 40 items related to National Educational Policy (2020) awareness.

Method of Data Collection: In any form of research, collection of data is a very important part. If data are not properly and thoroughly it could lead to false results and conclusions. The data of the present study was collected by the researcher by personally visiting the School of Education. The tool mention above was administered personally to the students of the School of Education in Mizoram University.

Statistical Technique used for data analysis: For data analysis simple percentage statistics and ANOVA was used.

Table-1

ANOVA				
Dimensions		Sum of Squares	df	F
School Education	Between Groups	66.518	2	7.380*
	Within Groups	576.841	128	
	Total	643.359	130	
Teacher Education	Between Groups	128.660	2	11.924*
	Within Groups	690.561	128	
	Total	819.221	130	
Higher Education	Between Groups	54.691	2	4.627**
	Within Groups	756.438	128	
	Total	811.130	130	

Reforms	Between Groups	2.889	2	.379
	Within Groups	487.417	128	
	Total	490.305	130	
Over all	Between Groups	569.353	2	4.959**
	Within Groups	7348.647	128	
	Total	7918.000	130	

There is no significant difference on national educational policy 2020 awareness among the college students of B. Ed, M. Ed and M.A (Education)

***significant @0.05 **significant @ 0.01**

From the above table it is observed that in the all dimensions of School Education, Teacher Education, Higher and Education the calculated f-ratios 7.380.11.924, and 4.957 are significant at 0.01 level and 4.627significant at 0.005 level.

Hence the null hypothesis "There is no significance difference regarding National Educational policy 2020 awareness among B.Ed. M. Ed and M.A Education students, with respect to course has been rejected these dimensions School Education, Teacher Education and Higher Education.

From the above table it is observed that in the of reforms the calculated f-ratios 0.379 is not significant at significant at 0.05 level.

Hence In the case dimension of Reforms, the hypothesis "There is no significance difference regarding National Educational policy 2020 awareness among B.Ed. M. Ed and M.A Education students, with respect to dimension of Reforms has been accepted.

Table-2

There will be no means significance difference on national educational policy 2020 awareness male and female students of college of education

Dimensions		N	Mean	Std. Deviation	Std. Error
School Education	B.Ed	36	6.97	1.765	.294
	M.Ed	39	5.51	1.502	.241
	M.A(Education)	56	7.13	2.636	.352
	Total	131	6.60	2.225	.194
Teacher Education	B.Ed	36	7.83	1.558	.260
	M.Ed	39	5.26	1.601	.256
	M.A(Education)	56	6.13	3.040	.406
	Total	131	6.34	2.510	.219
Higher Education	B. Ed	36	8.28	1.446	.241
	M.Ed	39	6.79	1.949	.312
	M.A(Education)	56	6.86	3.130	.418
	Total	131	7.23	2.498	.218
Reforms	B. Ed	36	6.94	.893	.149
	M.Ed	39	6.97	1.646	.264
	M.A(Education)	56	6.66	2.546	.340
	Total	131	6.83	1.942	.170
Over all	B. Ed	36	30.03	4.462	.744
	M.Ed	39	24.54	5.155	.825
	M.A(Education)	56	26.77	10.128	1.353
	Total	131	27.00	7.804	.682

Interpretation: -

The following conclusions have been drawn from the above table here are 131 college students in total. There are 36 B. Ed, 39 M. Ed and fifty-six M.A Education college students of school education, Mizoram University. B. Ed, M. Ed and M. A Education college students' awareness on NEP-20202 with respect to dimension of school education mean values are 6.97,5.51, 7.13 and S. D are 1.765, 1.502, 2.636 and S. Ed .294,

.241 and .352. Teacher Educa mean values are 7.83 5.26, 6.13 and S. D values are 1.558, 1.601, 3.04 and S. Eds are .260, .256 and 406.Higher Education mean values 8.28, 6.79, 6.86. S.D values 1.446, 1.949 3.130. S. Ed values .241, .312 and.418.Refoms mean values 6.94, 6.97, 6.66. S. D values .893, 1.646, 2.546 S. Ed values .149 .264 and .340

Finding:

From the above table it is found that the awareness of school of education students on NEP-2020 dimensions of School Education, Higher Education and Teacher Education there was a significant mean difference among the B.Ed M.Ed and M.A Education students mean value are differ from eatch course and on the other hand there is no significant mean difference on the dimension of reforms.

Discussion:

The above finding reveals that B.Ed students are having better awareness on NEP-2020 when compared with the M.Ed and M.A Education students on the following dimensions School Education, Higher Education and Teacher Education.

Findings of the study

1. The male and female college students of school of education have an average level of national educational policy 2020 awareness.
2. Male and female teacher have same level of awareness of national education policy 2020.
3. B.Ed and M. Ed Student teachers and Student Teacher Educators have same level of awareness of national educational policy 2020.
4. B.Ed Student teachers have bater awareness of National Educational Policy 2020 compared to M.Ed and M.A Education Students.

References

1. Routledge. Corbetta, P (2003). Social Research: Theory, Methods and Techniques. London: SAGE publications.

2. Cohen, L.M & Morrison, K. (2007). Research Methods in Education, USA & Canada:

3. Bryman, A (2008). Social Research Methods. 4th edition. Oxford: Oxford University Press.Camilia, N.C, Ibrahim, S.D &Dalhatu, B.L (2013). Effects of Social Networking Sites Usage on the Studies of Nigerian Students. International Journal of Engineering and Science (IJES)Vol2 Issue7 pp 39-46.

4. Bicen.H, Cavus.N. (2010). The most preferred social network Sites by students. Procedia Social and Behavioral Sciences. Surfed from www.sciencedirect.com Blumler, J. G. & Katz, E. (1974). The uses of mass communications: Current perspectives on gratifications research. CA: SAGE.

5. Adenubi, O.S, Olalekan, Y.S, Afolabi, A.A, Opeoluwa, A.S (2013). Online Social Networking and the Academic Achievement of University Students. The experience of Selected Nigerian Universities. Journal of Information and Knowledge Management Vol3 No5.

6. Aithal, P. S. & Aithal, Shubhrajyotsna (2020). Implementation Strategies of Higher Education Part of National Education Policy 2020 of India towards Achieving its Objectives. International